Curriculum Windows

What Curriculum Theorists of the 1990s Can Teach Us About Schools and Society Today

A Volume in
Curriculum Windows

Series Editor
Thomas S. Poetter
Miami University, Oxford, Ohio

Curriculum Windows

Thomas S. Poetter, Editor

Curriculum Windows:
What Curriculum Theorists of the 1990s
Can Teach Us About Schools and Society Today (2017)
edited by Thomas S. Poetter, Kelly Waldrop, Tasneem Amatullah,
Cleighton Weiland, Jody Googins, and Vanessa Winn

Curriculum Windows: What Curriculum Theorists of the 1980s
Can Teach Us About Schools and Society Today (2016)
edited by Thomas S. Poetter, Kelly Waldrop,
Chloé Bolyard, and Vicka Bell-Robinson

Curriculum Windows: What Curriculum Theorists of the 1970s
Can Teach Us About Schools and Society Today (2015)
edited by Thomas S. Poetter

Curriculum Windows: What Curriculum Theorists of the 1960s
Can Teach Us About Schools and Society Today (2013)
edited by Thomas S. Poetter

Teaching Again:
A Professor's Tale of Returning to a Ninth Grade Classroom (2016)
by Thomas S. Poetter

10 Great Curricula: Lived Conversations of Progressive,
Democratic Curricula in School and Society (2012)
edited by Thomas S. Poetter

Curriculum Windows

What Curriculum Theorists of the 1990s Can Teach Us About Schools and Society Today

edited by

Thomas S. Poetter

Kelly Waldrop

Tasneem Amatullah

Cleighton Weiland

Jody Googins

and

Vanessa Winn
Miami University, Oxford, Ohio

INFORMATION AGE PUBLISHING, INC.
Charlotte, NC • www.infoagepub.com

Library of Congress Cataloging-in-Publication Data

CIP record for this book is available from the Library of Congress
http://www.loc.gov

ISBNs: 978-1-68123-785-5 (Paperback)

978-1-68123-786-2 (Hardcover)

978-1-68123-787-9 (ebook)

Cover art by: Katherine Coy Smith, oil on canvas, *Koch Hall Stairwell.* A note from
the artist: "This window inspired me every time I would walk up the stairwell to my
art classes. I knew that whatever happened in college was just temporary and the
future existed through that window."

Printed in the United States of America

CONTENTS

FOREWORD

William H. Schubert

I begin by commending Tom Poetter, Kelly Waldrop, and their team on another excellent contribution to the curriculum literature through this book. It is important to keep alive perspectives of the past to see how they contribute to an understanding of the present in curriculum theory and practice.

The 1990s were a time of considerable expansion for curriculum studies. The curriculum field continued to explore more ways of knowing or epistemological bases for understanding curriculum. Moreover, there were major efforts to open windows of curriculum that recognized neglected racial and cultural orientations and perspectives.

I was busy in the first half of the 1990s in projects that expanded curriculum by drawing upon the arts, teacher insights, and historical documents. In the first project, George Willis and I increasingly realized that many major curriculum scholars were influenced markedly by the arts and literature; therefore, we invited 35 of them to write autobiographically about the influence of the arts, an artistic genre, or a particular work on their perspective about curriculum and teaching. In doing so, we were able to show the value of the arts and literature regarding curriculum matters and simultaneously illustrate the realization that autobiographical scholarship can advance curriculum studies. The book was titled *Reflections from the Heart of Educational Inquiry: Understanding Curriculum and Teaching through*

Curriculum Windows: What Curriculum Theorists of the 1990s Can Teach Us About Schools and Society Today, pp. ix–xxi
Copyright © 2017 by Information Age Publishing

the Arts (Willis & Schubert, 1991) and included essays by such scholars as Maxine Greene, Harry Broudy, Elliot Eisner, Louis Rubin, Madeleine Grumet, Michael Apple, Ann Lopez Schubert, William Pinar, Max van Manen, Gail McCutcheon, and many more. Emphasis on autobiography, of course, was a major message of the reconceptualization of curriculum theory and practice, and the value of aesthetic forms of inquiry related to educational criticism and connoisseurship derived from Eisner (1979) and colleagues.

The second project on which I embarked was called The Teacher Lore Project. Along with colleague William Ayers, we had encouraged graduate student interests in doing dissertations based on the insights they acquired as teachers or in association with other teachers. This work also related to the emphasis on *currere* in curriculum reconceptualization, as illustrated by Janet Miller's (1990) efforts to help teachers create spaces in which to express their voices on matters of curriculum and teaching. Teacher lore also related to work of Michael Connelly and his students such as Freema Elbaz, D. Jean Clandinin, Ming Fang He, JoAnn Phillion, and others on teachers' personal practical knowledge and their stories, as well as the work of Ivor Goodson on teacher biographies and stories. The students with whom I worked (e.g., Pat Hulsebosch, Virginia Jagla, Mari Koerner, Suzanne Millies, and Tom Thomas) presented with us at conferences; we published articles and chapters together and developed a book called *Teacher Lore: Learning from our Own Experience* (Schubert & Ayers, 1992) in which Janet Miller contributed a chapter (along with ours) that related her work to teacher lore.

In the third project, on curriculum history, five of us compiled a resource of excerpts from influential curriculum literature from 1642 to 1983 (Willis, Schubert, Bullough, Jr., Kridel, & Holton, 1993). Since many curriculum students and scholars did not have access to major libraries, we thought it would be beneficial to provide excerpts of primary source material still relevant to contemporary curriculum dilemmas and debates.

The expansion of curriculum thought in the 1990s also included numbers of books published. According to our attempt to provide a more comprehensive bibliographical history (Schubert, Lopez Schubert, Thomas, and Carol, 2002, p. 531), 1,302 new books appeared in the 1990s, while 2,179 books appeared in the 9 previous decades combined (Schubert & Lopez Schubert, 1980, p. 11). This is a significant expansion!

Such expansion made it difficult, indeed, to for Tom Poetter, Kelly Wardrop, and their team of students and former students to select books for the 1990s Windows book. Nevertheless, they did an excellent job of choosing books that characterize significant dimensions of curriculum studies of the 1990s. By *significant dimensions* I mean points of contribution that uniquely derive from curriculum scholarship of the 90s.

Before commenting on each inclusion in this book, I think that the expansion of the books of the curriculum field in the 90s makes it worthwhile for me to provide overview sources, mostly from the 1990s, so that readers can see the books in context. Although my historical writings (Schubert & Lopez Schubert, 1980; Schubert et al., 2002; and Schubert, 2010) were not written in the 1990s, they provide perspective on them, so I mention and cite them in the References. Several other key overviews published in the 1990s provide insight to the books discussed in this volume. Edmund Short's (1991) *Forms of Curriculum Inquiry* has been a key source on diverse modes of inquiry that emerged in the field during the 1970s and 1980s; he included several forms of philosophical inquiry, historical inquiry, scientific inquiry, ethnographic inquiry, narrative inquiry, aesthetic inquiry, phenomenological inquiry, hermeneutic inquiry, theoretical inquiry, normative inquiry, critical inquiry, evaluative inquiry, integrative inquiry, deliberative inquiry, and action inquiry. Philip W. Jackson's (1992) *Handbook of Research on Curriculum* became the first handbook sponsored by the American Educational Research Association (AERA) on curriculum research. Several handbooks of research on teaching had preceded and served as models for it. Jackson's handbook of 34 chapters and over 1,000 pages stands as a major statement of the state of curriculum research and theory which is organized into four parts: conceptual and methodological perspectives; how curriculum is shaped, for example, history, policy, change, culture, knowledge, ideology, organization, teachers, implementation, and textbooks; curriculum as a shaping force, e.g., student experiences, pedagogy, cognition, morality, differentiation, low income African American children, linguistic minorities, and gender; and a range of subject matter emphases.

Finally, a new form of synoptic text was presented in 1995 by William Pinar, William Reynolds, Patrick Slattery, and Peter Taubman titled *Understanding Curriculum*. The first 239 pages of the Pinar et al. (1995) text consists of an introduction to reconceptualized curriculum theory and a reconceptualized history of the curriculum field. This historical perspective interprets curriculum studies of the 1960s and earlier to be highly tied to demands of the state or other centralized sources such as private wealth or the church. This new curriculum orientation (though still highly diverse) differed from the older emphasis on curriculum development as facilitating state and other centralized purposes. Reconceptualized curriculum thought was portrayed as focusing more fully on *currere* or the living of curriculum that flowed within many social, psychological, and cultural dimensions of life, rather than *curriculum* as content used to shape persons as the state, church, private wealth, or other centralizing forces saw fit. In order to understand curriculum as the personal or public education that occurs in many spheres, not in schools alone, different discourses have emerged. Pinar et al. present the histories and central features of each:

political text, racial text, gender text, phenomenological text, poststructural and postmodern texts, autobiographical/biographical text, aesthetic text, and theological text. They elaborate, as well, on the vast literature that has accumulated under the label of *institutional text*, that is, that which has studied curriculum primarily within the institution of schooling that focuses on curriculum development, teachers or teaching, and students. Pinar et al. also assert that the next move is to understand curriculum as an international or global text. As Reynolds and Webber (2004) have shown, these discourses have brought an evocative expansion of the meanings of curriculum theory.

Most of the books selected for this volume illustrate the diversity of inquiry forms presented by Short (1991), the expansion of research provided by Jackson (1992), and the elaboration of discourses or texts portrayed by Pinar et al. (1995). As attempted in previous forewords to Curriculum Windows volumes, I will continue here to personalize my comments as one who lived through the decade in question.

Although James Banks does not purport to be primarily a curriculum scholar, surely the corpus of his work on multicultural education has powerfully influenced curriculum discourse. This is doubtless why Shaobing Li has selected Banks (1994) *Introduction to Multicultural Education* as a major window to understanding curriculum in the 1990s. In fact, in the same year, William Watkins (my late former student and noted curriculum scholar) published a key article in *Educational Theory* on the importance of seeing curriculum from a standpoint of multicultural education that emphasizes etiology in terms of scholarship on racial history and political economy (Watkins, 1994). Watkins (1993) had already suggested that we derive orientations to curriculum thought from African American intellectual and protest history. Shaobing Li's selection of Banks' book also reminds me of the import of work by Ronald Takaki, such as *A Different Mirror* (Takaki, 1993).

Jennifer Ellerbe's treatment of James Beane's (1997) *Curriculum Integration* brings recollection of conversations I had with Beane relative to his several publications on middle schools, often published by the National Middle School Association. I had always used Beane's (1990/1993) *A Middle School Curriculum* when I taught a middle school curriculum and instruction certification course at the University of Illinois at Chicago. I was impressed with his emphasis on both the personal and social (or democratic) in curriculum and saw within this emphasis similarity to the work of early curriculum scholar, L. Thomas Hopkins, who I came to know during the last decade of his life when he was in his late 80s. I mentioned this to Jim Beane, and he said that he, too, sought out Hopkins as a kind of unofficial mentor. In the 1930s Hopkins (then professor at Teachers College, Columbia) published the first book on curriculum integration

(Hopkins, 1937) and later augmented the emphasis to include both personal integration and social or democratic integration with a book called
Integration: The Democratic Process (Hopkins, 1941). Both the personal and
the democratic were amplified in his *magnum opus* (Hopkins, 1954), which
showed the need to focus on curriculum as the *emerging self* in and out of
school. This appears to me to be a harbinger to curriculum transformed
as *currere*, whether or not it was recognized as such. I commend Jennifer
Ellerbe in her selection, since I think separate subjects are overemphasized
at the expense of an integrative approach to the emerging of the self and
society. Beane (1997) is the best source since Hopkins to tap for this insight
in theory and practice.

I am so glad to see that Cleighton Weiland has written about *The
Manufactured Crisis* by Berliner and Biddle (1995). The fact that the
research done for this book at the Sandia National Laboratory in New
Mexico was suppressed by the Bush administration represents evidence
that curriculum is used too often to support political agendas. The crisis
that Berliner and Biddle clearly showed to be manufactured is still being
manufactured by political pundits and their economic puppeteers who
want to see education privatized. When the Sandia researchers concluded
that U.S. schools were, for the most part, not failing, it was deemed by
political and economic power wielders to be the wrong answer, so results
were not released until the Clinton Administration. By selecting this book,
Weiland provides evidence for the need to have critical inquiry into forces
that want to control education and manipulate curriculum and evaluation
for their own purposes, even when they contradict extant evidence and the
purposes of students, teachers, and the public. I have come to know David
Berliner well through our work in the International Academy of Education,
and I hold his criticism of many educational and curricular policies in high
esteem.

This critical emphasis was furthered by Michelle Fine in her study of
dropouts (Fine, 1991) as one of the best examples of critical ethnography
and interpretation. Thus, I commend Crystal Phillips for selecting and
commenting on its current relevance. The issue of dropouts is at least as
prevalent today as in the early 1990s. Fine's work speaks to the need to
acknowledge and build upon students' capabilities and assets. Indeed,
they have many assets, and conventional curricular policies practices often
translate them into deficits. Many student attributes can and should be
seen as strengths. When students are framed as deficits, it is no wonder
that they drop out. When they are framed as strengths, they can thrive as
emerging selves (to refer back to both Hopkins and Beane) in public spaces
and a society that also is emerging into places where humans can live more
vitally together. I advocate that readers who are moved by *Framing Dropouts*
to search out Fine's other publications and activist work.

Like James Banks, bell hooks might not be considered a curriculum scholar. However, the racial prejudice in such consideration became more vividly recognized in the 1990s. Hence, it is important that Vanessa Winn has chosen to present *Teaching to Transgress* (hooks, 1994) as a curriculum window. In fact, most of the 30-plus books written by bell hooks should be claimed as curriculum books, because they pertain to a larger sphere of curriculum. Although they may not be about curriculum in schools, they are about the many dimensions of culture that shape how we see the world and, thus, how we live it. Her frequent emphasis on "white supremacist capitalist patriarchy" is a massive indictment of much of the curriculum that influences human beings in and out of school. By bringing the work of bell hooks to us as a window to curriculum, Vanessa Winn is calling for us to transgress the overt and covert effects of White supremacy, multiple forms of racism, unleashed capitalism, and patriarchy. In addition to reading *Teaching to Transgress* and other books by bell hooks, I urge those interested in curriculum to watch and listen carefully to some of her engaging presentations, easily available through electronic searches. Her works show the important connections between curriculum studies and cultural studies.

Gloria Ladson-Billings is another African American woman whose work offers much insight to curriculum. She is an educational researcher as evidenced by her major roles in AERA, having served as president and having received numerous AERA awards. Thinking about Gloria reminds me of our times serving together on the AERA Council. In conversations at breaks and dinners we often talked about many different interests. We talked about our families, and we shared interests in sports, even though I grew up in rural Indiana, and she in urban Philadelphia. We talked of basketball and football history (her husband was a pro), music, old television programs of the 50s and 60s, and more. I was impressed with her range of knowledge in many areas of life. To some, our conversations may have seemed like trivia exchanges; however, our conversations pushed boundaries of curriculum to many cultural domains. They spoke to personal and cultural dreams. In 2015, we both presented at the Annual Conference of the American Association for Teaching and Curriculum (AATC), and I was greatly impressed with her extensive work on education and hip hop, clearly a prime dimension of curriculum outside of school. Genesis Ross's decision to emphasize *Dreamkeepers* (Ladson-Billings, 1994) as a curriculum window is to be praised, since I see education as keeping alive the dreams of children, youths, and all of us. We grow because of the multiple and diverse dreams that we have and encounter. I hope that curriculum can increasingly expand to include the sharing of multiple dreams that inspire a better world.

I often wrestle with how to deal with the expansion of curriculum and the need to summarize it or make it synoptic without losing its purport.

I tried to deal with this in writing a synoptic text (Schubert, 1986), and I addressed the problem of balancing the expansive and the synoptic in a lengthy article for the 40th anniversary of the journal called *Curriculum Inquiry* (Schubert, 2010). Authors of synoptic texts who strive to conceptualize and summarize salient dimensions of the curriculum field for leaders of practice or for beginning graduate students of curriculum studies are faced with the dilemma of how to summarize and at the same time portray the immense complexity of the field. An excellent response to this dilemma was provided in *Curriculum: Alternative Approaches*, by Colin Marsh and George Willis (1995), a book that has resulted in several editions. Thus, I am grateful to Kurtz Miller for showing the continued relevance of synoptic texts, which have helped keep alive basic perspectives of the curriculum field since the 1930s. Marsh and Willis present the character of curriculum, its history, alternative approaches, theorizing, development and change, planning and participants, implementation, evaluation and assessment, politics and decision making, along with a glossary and ample references. The message of Miller's selection is that the synoptic must be continually addressed, especially within the accelerated expansion of inquiry, orientations, and publications.

Prior to Cameron McCarthy's (1990) *Race and Curriculum,* I do not think anyone addressed the topic so directly in a book-length treatment since Carter G. Woodson's (1933) *The Mis-education of the Negro.* Moreover, as pervasive as was Woodson's work for scholars, students, and the public, I am astonished at his lack of recognition in the formalized curriculum field into which I was socialized. Therefore, it is enormously appropriate that Loveness Ngorosha has tried to re-center Cameron McCarthy's book in this edition of *Curriculum Windows.* I remember first meeting Cameron at a Bergamo Conference on Curriculum Theory and Practice in Dayton, Ohio, when he had just completed his doctoral studies with Michael Apple and others at the University of Wisconsin–Madison. Since then, Cameron has continued to develop an extensive corpus of work on curriculum, race, and education sketched largely through lenses of communication, literature, postmodern theory, and more. It could be said that the 1990s in curriculum studies brought an emphasis on the interaction and intersection of knowledge, power, culture, politics, identity, class, gender, sexuality, and more. All of this can be found in microcosm throughout the work of Cameron McCarthy.

Ryan Graham's choice of Gail McCutcheon's (1995) *Developing the Curriculum* exemplifies the need, amidst curriculum expansion, to continuously address the daily needs for curriculum development on the part of teachers in schools. The corporate and governmental takeover of curriculum in the past two decades makes it even more relevant to see, as Gail McCutcheon demonstrated in this book, that curriculum development needs to be seen as both a solo task of individual teachers and an ensemble process of deliberation of groups of teachers, students, and others engaged in school classrooms. Her use of the term *deliberation* harkens back to Joseph Schwab's work on practical inquiry (see collection of Schwab's work by Westbury & Wilcof, 1978) as mediated by McCutcheon's doctoral adviser Elliot Eisner, along with Eisner's other students such as Decker Walker and Elizabeth Vallance. Thus, McCutcheon advocated an orientation to educational criticism and connoisseurship that addressed practical problems. Practical inquiry is treated as a kind of action-oriented inquiry that focuses on the situational needs, imagines courses of action, and acts on the best judgment available, rather than accepting a theoretic perspective that assumes one size solutions fit all problems. So, I contend that while McCutcheon's book was highly relevant when it was published, it is even more relevant today, because of the large-scale efforts to take curriculum development out of the hands and lives of teachers, students, and anyone else who is on the ground in (as in *grounded in*) classroom life.

In similar fashion, Judy Googins strives to keep curriculum grounded, by selecting the work of Debbie Meier. Meier's (1995) contributions are a fabulous antidote to decisions that prevent urban youth of color from having meaningful experiences relating to their deepest interests. The inane assumption that impoverished youth of color are incapable of pursuing such education must be overcome. Googins' selection is worthy of praise, since Meier's leadership of the Central Park East schools In New York City is a paragon of progressive practice. In fact, Seymour Fliegel christened the project with the title of another book on the topic: *Miracle in East Harlem* (Fliegel & MacGuire, 1993). The word *their* in Debbie Meier's *The Power of Their Ideas* should be highlighted, for it shows that the guiding ideas of Central Park East evolved from and with the students, parents, and community members, as well as teachers. It flies in the face of and thoroughly contradicts the dominant national and state centered imposition of curriculum. It should be obvious that curriculum that is handed down from on high will never work, except to oppress, discourage, and alienate. Curriculum constructed from the ground up is the only kind that has a chance to illuminate, inspire, and lead to self-educating human beings. As I get older, I am increasingly convinced that those who oppose it are either evil or ignorant. Googins' choice pushes us to consider this kind of curriculum making for our time.

George Posner is one of the first scholars I met at AERA in the curriculum field. We both began our professorial careers in the mid-1970s, and our first collaborative project was to construct a historical view of the curriculum field through a mentor-student connections—a kind of genealogical research that portrays an intellectual sociology of the curriculum field over generations of scholars (see Schubert & Posner, 1980). Posner's background is in science, accompanied by the analytic and empirical thinking that goes with it. The text chosen by Thao Nguyen-Horwitz, *Analyzing the Curriculum* (1992), has progressed through several editions. While Posner draws on many dimensions of curriculum that are treated in synoptic texts or texts on curriculum development, his book uniquely exemplifies how curriculum knowledge can be used to analyze actual curriculum problems. Theory, case studies, philosophy, and history are central themes within the analyses. Also in the 1990s, Posner wrote extensively about course design, providing practical know-how for designing courses (Posner & Rudnitsky, 1994/1997), a book initiated in the 1980s.

Memories of my work with Jim Sears over the years were triggered by Richelle Frabotta's selection of his *Sexuality and the Curriculum* (Sears, 1992). I recall that Sears often courageously took on controversial topics in education, such as gay or lesbian lives, fundamentalist Christianity, race, and multicultural education—all while working as a professor in the U.S. South. These topics of interest were early iterations of expansions that occurred in curriculum of the 1990s through inclusion of oft-considered taboo topics. In the late 1990s, Jim Sears, Dan Marshall, and I began to write a book that we hoped would be a postmodern synoptic text. We wanted to depict curriculum history since 1950, the decade in which histories by Lawrence Cremin (1961), Edward Krug (1966), and Herbert Kliebard (1986) basically concluded. As a result, we published our book, *Turning Points in Curriculum* (Marshall, Sears, & Schubert, 2000) in the first year of the next decade/ century. It, too, reflected Sears' emphasis on controversial topics as standpoints from which to reflect on the continuation of curriculum work, an interest that Sears continues to develop through what might be called a *curriculum* of finding or creating safe homes for LGBTQ individuals, couples, and families.

Pricilla Tamankag's selection of Angela Valenzuela's (1999) *Subtractive Schooling* is a most appropriate choice. The book carefully illustrates how current curricular and pedagogical policies and practices wrought by schools often subtract from the insights and understandings of Latino/a students, their families and communities, and, thus, reduce their sense of positive power to grow and contribute. However, the impact of the book is more extensive, in that it can be interpreted as a warning that educational policies and practices across the board have the sordid potential to subtract from the knowledge, skills, perspectives, and dispositions of all children. Like Valenzuela, educators from Chief Seattle to John Dewey and L. Thomas Hopkins, and from Jane Addams to Carter G. Woodson, Paulo Freire, and Luis Moll advocate that we should build on the cultural and personal knowledge and experience of those persons we purport to educate. If we are uninterested in what they bring to the classroom or if we indicate that it should not have been brought, we do irreparable damage to countless lives.

Tasneem Amatullah has chosen *Understanding by Design* (Wiggins & McTighe, 1998), one of the best-selling books for educational leaders in schools. The book is an elaboration of major principles in the Tyler Rationale, the label often given to *Basic Principles of Curriculum and Instruction* (Tyler, 1949/50) composed as a syllabus at the University of Chicago in the late 1940s, and which was published in response to popular demand by those who taught curriculum courses at other colleges and universities. Sometimes the date is given as 1949, although it is difficult to find a copy with that date on it. In any case, it argues, as do Wiggins and McTighe (1998), that teaching and learning experiences should be explicated and implemented with sound philosophical and cultural or social understanding to fit the needs and interests of students and the society. They should be organized and sequenced according to psychological social research to achieve thoughtfully constructed purposes that grow from student and teacher collaboration that holds all learners to be active, social, and influenced by myriad non-school realms of experience. It holds, too, that evaluation should be established to understand how all dimensions of the purposes are actualized. As much as this seems to be common sense, the restatement and elaboration of Wiggins and McTighe seems necessary today when curriculum is largely developed to fit evaluation by tests controlled by business and governmental interests that support the school (or a privatized version of school) as a societal sorting machine as critiqued by Joel Spring (1989).

After writing Forewords for *Curriculum Windows* of the 1960s, 1970s, 1980s, and now the 1990s, I feel even more glad that Tom Poetter decided to use the term *windows*. While some of the books selected might not be considered formally curriculum books, they all provide views of education that help us understand the curricular phenomena more fully. It is incredibly important to keep alive the legacy of the curriculum field, as these books do. They help us remember the best thought and practice of each decade, while simultaneously expanding curriculum to overcome omissions relative to race, gender, class, culture, and ideology. Clearly, we need to overcome the omissions and prejudices in our field's legacy while still appreciating the contributions that remain relevant. After all, no one knows what will be seen as salient omissions in today's curriculum books from the vantage point of values that guide humans in future decades.

Concluding as I began this Foreword, I again thank the authors and editors of this volume, especially Tom Poetter, who conceived of the Curriculum Windows Project in the first place. The essays and the books selected for discussion point the way to a broader, deeper, and more relevant field by enabling landmarks of curriculum history to coalesce with contemporary perspectives as seeds for cultivating and creating better possibilities for future curricula.

REFERENCES

Banks, J. (1994). *An introduction to multicultural education.* Boston, MA: Pearson.

Beane, J. (1993). *A middle school curriculum: From rhetoric to reality.* Columbus, OH: National Middle School Association. (Original work published 1990)

Beane, J. (1997). *Curriculum integration: Designing a core of democratic education.* New York, NY: Teachers College Press.

Berliner, D. C., & Biddle, B. J. (1995). *The manufactured crisis: Myths, fraud, and the attack on America's public schools.* New York, NY: Longman.

Cremin, L. (1961). *The transformation of the school: Progressivism in American education, 1776–1957.* New York, NY: Knopf.

Eisner, E. W. (1979). *The educational imagination.* New York, NY: Macmillan.

Fine, M. (1991). *Framing dropouts: Notes on the politics of an urban public high school.* Albany, NY: State University of New York Press.

Fliegel, S. & MacGuire, J. (1993). *Miracle in East Harlem: The fight for choice in public education.* New York, NY: Times Books.

hooks, b. (1994). *Teaching to transgress: Education in the practice of freedom.* New York, NY: Routledge.

Hopkins, L. T. (Ed.). (1937). *Integration, its meaning and application.* New York, NY: Appleton-Century.

Hopkins, L. T. (1941). *Interaction: The democratic process.* Boston, MA: D. C. Heath.

Hopkins, L. T. (1954). *The emerging self in school and home.* New York, NY: Harper & Brothers.

Jackson, P. W. (Ed.). (1992). *Handbook of research on curriculum.* New York: Macmillan.

Kliebard, H. M. (1986). *The struggle for the American curriculum: 1893–1958.* New York, NY: Routledge.

Krug, E. A. (1966). *Salient dates in American education, 1635–1964.* New York, NY: Harper & Row.

Ladson-Billings, G. (1994). *The dreamkeepers: Successful teachers of African American children.* San Francisco, CA: Jossey-Bass.

Marsh, C., & Willis. G. (1995). *Curriculum: Alternative approaches.* Columbus, OH: Prentice-Hall.

Marshall, J. D., Sears, J. T., & Schubert, W. H. (2000). *Turning points in curriculum: A contemporary curriculum memoir.* Columbus, OH: Prentice-Hall.

McCarthy, C. (1990). *Race and curriculum: Social inequality and the theories and politics of difference in contemporary research on schooling.* London, England: Falmer.

McCutcheon, G. (1995). *Developing the curriculum: Solo and group deliberation.* New York, NY: Longman.

Meier, D. (1995). *The power of their ideas: Lessons for America from a small school in Harlem.* New York, NY: Beacon Press.

Miller, J. L. (1990). *Creating spaces and finding voices: Teachers collaborating for empowerment.* Albany, NY: State University of New York Press.

Pinar, W. F., Reynolds, W. M., Slattery, P., & Taubman, P. M. (1995). *Understanding curriculum*. New York, NY: Peter Lang.

Posner, G. J. (1992). *Analyzing the curriculum*. New York, NY: McGraw-Hill.

Posner, G. J., & Rudnitsky, A. N. (1997). *Course design: A guide to curriculum development for teachers*. New York, NY: Longman. (Original work published in 1994)

Reynolds, W. M., & Webber, J. A. (2004). *Expanding curriculum theory: Dis/positions and lines of flight*. Mahwah, NJ: Erlbaum Associates.

Schubert, W. H. (1986). *Curriculum: Perspective, paradigm, and possibility*. New York, NY: Macmillan.

Schubert, W. H. (2010). Journeys of expansion and synopsis: Tensions in books that shaped curriculum inquiry. *Curriculum Inquiry 40* (1), 17–94.

Schubert, W. H., & Ayers, W. (Eds.). (1992). *Teacher lore: Learning from our own experience*. White Plains, NY: Longman.

Schubert, W. H., & Lopez Schubert A. L. (1980). *Curriculum books: The first eighty years*. Lanham, MD: University Press of America.

Schubert, W. H., & Posner, G. J. (1980). Origins of the curriculum field based on a study of mentor-student relationships. *The Journal of Curriculum Theorizing, 2*(2), 37–67.

Sears, J. T. (1992). *Sexuality and the curriculum: The politics and practices of sexuality education*. New York, NY: Teachers College Press.

Short, E. C. (Ed.). (1991). *Forms of curriculum inquiry*. Albany, NY: State University of New York Press.

Spring, J. (1989). *The sorting machine, revisited*. New York, NY: Longman.

Takaki, R. (1993). *A different mirror: A history of multicultural America*. Boston, MA: Little Brown.

Tyler, R. W. (1950). *Basic principles of curriculum and instruction*. Chicago, IL: University of Chicago Press. (Original work published 1949)

Valenzuela, A. (1999). *Subtractive schooling: U.S.-Mexican youth and the politics of caring*. Albany, NY: State University of New York Press.

Watkins, W. H. (1993). Black curriculum orientations: A preliminary inquiry. *Harvard Educational Review, 63*(3), 321–338.

Watkins, W. H. (1994). Multicultural education: Toward a historical and political inquiry. *Educational Theory, 44*(1), 99–117.

Westbury, I., & Wilkof, N. (Eds.). (1978). *Science, curriculum, and liberal education: Essays of Joseph Schwab*. Chicago, IL: University of Chicago Press.

Wiggins, G. P., & McTighe, J. (1998). *Understanding by design*. Alexandria, VA: Association for Supervision and Curriculum Development.

Willis, G. H., & Schubert, W. H. (Eds.). (1991). *Reflections from the heart of educational inquiry: Understanding curriculum and teaching through the arts*. Albany, NY: State University of New York Press.

Willis, G. H., Schubert, W. H., Bullough, R., Kridel, C., & Holton, J. (Eds.). (1993). *The American curriculum: A documentary history*. Westport, CT: Greenwood Press.

Woodson, C. G. (1933). *The mis-education of the Negro*. Washington, DC: Associated Publishers.

NOTE ON AUTHOR

William H. Schubert, Professor Emeritus of Curriculum and Instruction at the University of Illinois at Chicago where he taught for 36 years and where he coordinated the PhD Program in Curriculum Studies and chaired Curriculum & Instruction. He was University Scholar and received university awards for teaching and mentoring, as well as the Lifetime Achievement Award in Curriculum Studies from the American Educational Research Association. His recent books include *Love, Justice, and Education: John Dewey and the Utopians* (2009) and *The SAGE Guide to Curriculum in Education* (with Ming Fang He and Brian D. Schultz, 2015), which received an Outstanding Book Award from the Society of Professors of Education in 2016.

PREFACE

LEARNING TO NAVIGATE

The Editing Staff Reflects

Tasneem Amatullah, Jody Googins, Cleighton Weiland, Vanessa Winn, and Kelly Waldrop

Kelly

As we have been working on editing this volume of Curriculum Windows essays, I have begun, for the second time in my life, to engage in the exquisite pain that is teaching a teenager to drive. My middle child will turn 16 this year, and the bulk of her education on safely navigating our streets has landed on my shoulders. Because that work is both challenging and a bit frightening, it is no surprise to me that when I began to think about my experience of immersing myself once again in editing this collection of essays by new scholars and connecting again with the idea of the window as a metaphor for learning and viewing curricula anew, my mind immediately connected the two. My family's car, the vehicle that my daughter is learning to drive, is a large SUV, which has the benefit of being very safe with lots of airbags and the like to protect those inside, but that safety comes with a cost. It has the biggest blind spot of any car I have ever driven. Check

Curriculum Windows: What Curriculum Theorists of the 1990s Can Teach Us About Schools and Society Today, pp. xxiii–xxviii
Copyright © 2017 by Information Age Publishing
All rights of reproduction in any form reserved.

though you might, and crane your neck around though you should, it is still difficult for the driver to be one hundred percent sure she is clear to move, just as it is impossible to be sure that, after reading your own writing for the millionth time, you have clearly and correctly made the point you were going for. Enter the intrepid editing staff.

After years of working with Tom on these projects, I think it is safe to say that, like our authors as they approach the end of their writing process, we are a bit fatigued and have probably developed blind spots of our own. It has been a great help, in these two most recent volumes, to have had student editors join us in working to clarify and polish the chapters as they were readied for publication. As you will see below from their reflections, the project was one they approached with enthusiasm and eagerness, as well as editorial excellence, and I am grateful for their energy, as well as their time.

A common thread through their commentary on the editing process is that of finding their voices as authors and helping others' voices be clearly heard. The foundation of that process is the creation of a feeling of safety. Just as when you are learning to drive, knowing that the person in the passenger seat is an extra set of eyes, checking your blind spots and ensuring that you are not missing anything, having an editor who will help you learn to maneuver through the world safely is a necessary component to finding your voice and expressing your thoughts. It has been a pleasure to have been a part of that experience in working with the Curriculum Windows project.

The origin of that safe space is the support of the faculty and staff in Miami University's Educational Development and Leadership program. We continue to be grateful to them for all they do for us. Blind spots are easier to clear if you have a broad perspective. Dr. Bill Schubert has continued to share the immense depth and breadth of his knowledge of the curriculum field with us, and we could not have asked for a better guide on our journey through curriculum literature. Thank you, Bill, for your invaluable support. Author and business coach Adam Grant argues that the best way to find success is to help others succeed. From that perspective, and from many others, Dr. Tom Poetter has achieved tremendous success. Personally, Tom has encouraged me to engage in my calling of academic editing and has supported me as I have begun building a business enterprise around that work. He has continued to encourage new writers and new editors in learning what it takes to find their voices and speak their truths. Many, many thanks, Tom, for leading us all to the window and encouraging us to describe what we see, and for ensuring us that you will keep an eye on our blind spots so that we can keep an eye on the road ahead.

Vanessa

As a writer, I find the first draft of writing the most difficult. I slog through the first pages over and over again. I create what I call word piles. These are short paragraphs that make the points I plan to arrive at in a paper. I write halting sentences that do not connect with one another. The first draft is always the worst because it is where I find out what I know and what I want to write about. I often panic during these first drafts because they are the time when I either realize that I have an aha-moment or worthwhile analysis, or I flounder with too few sources and no ending in sight. I write and re-write and re-write until I finally arrive at ideas that I can use to structure my arguments. Writing is how I learn, and I enjoy the process because I enjoy the topics that I engage.

But editing was a real treat! The aha-moments and worthwhile analyses were there right at the start. With less anxiety about the finished end, I was able to approach the pieces by working on clarification rather than revelation. As an editor, my role was not to regenerate and recraft meaning, but to enhance the argument of another scholar. It was a unique opportunity to think about how I use the writing process to clarify my own arguments versus reading closely for the arguments of others. It was writing in the most satisfying stage of completion. And I was so glad that I got a chance to work with the incredibly interesting work of my colleagues in such a close way. A piece of writing that engages academic curriculum theory and the lives and work of the writers themselves is an incredible piece of text to take on as an editor.

Cleighton

In 2006, I had just successfully defended my thesis project in school psychology. Armed with skills in data analysis, assessment, intervention programs, and consultation, I set out to grow a career and make a difference in the lives of students and their families. The first few years of my career were energizing and empowering, as I saw schools as malleable, just waiting for fresh ideas to push student achievement forward. The years quickly passed, and I began to see schools become less elastic and more rigid. I found fewer and fewer school teachers and administrators open to new ideas or ready to make changes in pedagogy. As our state testing processes intensified, I wondered if the endless litany of academic initiatives and reforms were truly making a difference. I began to feel that I was missing something both obvious and significant as an educator. There were ideas, histories, theories, and philosophies that seemed to exist right outside the experiences of my school day.

As questions began to surface, I realized that I had a moral obligation to my students, families, and teachers to begin searching for answers.
Somehow, I ended up in Miami University as part of my search. Like most
first year doctoral students, I felt my basic assumptions and understandings regarding the underpinnings of education to be one-dimensional and
vulnerable to critique. At times, it felt like the current of new ideas and concepts served as an undertow that threatened to drag me under and engulf
me. I was continuously confronted with the question: "What do I believe
about education in the public school, and why?" My best effort to date is
the chapter I completed for this current edition of *Curriculum Windows*.
In this chapter, I was tasked with reviewing and elucidating Berliner and
Biddle's (1995) classic work titled, *The Manufactured Crisis: Myths, Fraud, and
the Attack on America's Public Schools*. I found this project to be an immense
challenge to write, as my beliefs about student learning had yet to ripen
or cure. I was writing from a personal foundation that was ever shifting.

In Robert Frost's famous poem *Stopping by Woods on a Snowy Evening*,
he epitomizes my feelings about my evolution as an educator and scholar.
Frost (1923) writes, "But I have promises to keep, / And miles to go before
I sleep, / And miles to go before I sleep." Frost's poem speaks to the promises and responsibilities placed on his shoulders before his life's journey
is complete. I believe Frost's words inform my view of my graduate work.
I finished writing my chapter over a year ago and already find that some
of my ideas about education have since changed. This growth can only
help me in my search for answers, soothe my wonder, and better serve the
schools I work in. Although this particular project is complete, my journey
for answers has just begun ... I have miles and miles to go.

Jody

As a part-time doctoral student and a full-time practitioner, I often find
myself in the minority in my doctoral classes. I am not as immersed in
academia as many of my classmates; I am immersed in practice. I am a
teacher first, a student second. When facing my first attempt at publication
a year or so ago, I struggled with finding the confidence to use my voice,
the voice of a practitioner, over the voice of an academic that, I feel, does
not suit me as well. I vividly recall my interview to be a part of the EDL
program at Miami University, my questions about the "type" of writing
I would be expected to produce. Dr. Poetter reassured me: your writing
will be that comprised of your own voice, your own experiences, your own
direction. It is with his confidence that I was able to write about Deborah
Meier (1995) and draw comparisons to my experiences in schools. It is with

his confidence that I found my own voice and the reassurance that my voice as a practitioner is important enough to be heard.

Shifting from the role of author to editor solidified my confidence in using my own voice, as I was exposed to my classmates boldly using theirs. Being able to read others' chapters critically became essential not only to the book project as a whole, but also to my ability to accept my own chapter and conclusions as valid and important. The journey of one of my classmates, Thao Nguyen-Horowitz, was especially influential to me. Thao was in our doctoral-level class as a master's student, the only master's student enrolled in this particular course. I can remember our first day of class, when Dr. Poetter told us we would be writing a book, our jaws dropped, but Thao was especially taken aback. We all made jokes along the way about each of our abilities to actually write our chapters, even as we worked diligently on them. When I was given the privilege of editing Thao's finished chapter, I was delighted to find that, in my mind, I could very clearly *see* and *hear* Thao saying each word. It was so *her*. And I loved it. And it gave me confidence in my own voice. This was the most essential part of this process for me: Finding my own voice, listening to others' voices, and finding my confidence.

Tasneem

Exploring my own skills and talent has been challenging for me. Having earned a master's of philosophy in textile science from India, I never dreamed of entering a teaching career. It was a decade ago that I decided to switch from homemaker to a working woman. The only statement that echoed my ears was, "Teaching is the best and most rewarding profession for women." I got my resume ready and off to schools in the streets of Dubai. It was day one of my job search, and the last school I visited that day was where I started my teaching career. After teaching for a couple years, my inner self pricked me with several questions that bothered me as a teacher. I addressed those in my chapter "Understanding by Design: From Opacity to Transparency" in this volume. Fast forward, my teaching career demanded specialization in teaching, and here I am in my final destination as a doctoral student at Miami University.

Reading Grant Wiggins and Jay McTighe (1998), *Understanding by Design* (UbD) twice at different points of time provided different perspectives for me. Three semesters of educational leadership doctoral classes and Dr. Poetter's feedback helped me refine my thoughts and step out of the standardized learning and testing regimes epidemic around the globe. Moreover, *ends* preceding the *means* as UbD suggests with a concrete road map is not feasible in a diverse classroom with students of varying abilities.

Eisner (2002) and Pinar, Reynolds, Slattery, and Taubman (2006) gave me a new vision to peep through a new window and transform UbD from opacity to transparency with aesthetic curricula.

I felt honored when Dr. Poetter offered me this opportunity to serve as an editor. We were walking down the stairs, and I could not hold in my excitement. My heart whispered *"Tasneem, being an international student, it's a never-let-go opportunity, grab it!"* And yes, truly it was a great learning experience, getting to know more curriculum scholars of the 90s and my peer doctoral students as budding scholars. I hope that as you read this series of *Curriculum Windows* you enter a world that is filled with lots of hope, challenges, and courage for all stakeholders who invest in education, *Education that can change lives of people!*

REFERENCES

Berliner, D. C., & Biddle, B. J. (1995). *The manufactured crisis: Myths, fraud, and the attack on America's public schools.* Reading, MA: Addison-Wesley.

Eisner, E. (2002). *The educational imagination* (3rd ed.). Upper Saddle River, NJ: Prentice-Hall.

Frost, R. (1923). *New Hampshire.* New York, NY: Henry Holt.

Meier, D. (1995). *The power of their ideas: Lessons for America from a small school in Harlem.* New York, NY: Beacon Press.

Pinar, W. F., Reynolds, W. M., Slattery, P., & Taubman, P. M. (2006). *Understanding curriculum: An introduction to the study of historical and contemporary curriculum discourses.* New York, NY: Peter Lang.

Wiggins, G., & McTighe, J. (1998). *Understanding by design.* Alexandria, VA: Association for Supervision and Curriculum Development.

INTRODUCTION

CURRICULUM WINDOWS OF THE 1990S

Thomas S. Poetter

Note: This introduction, for the fourth volume in a six volume series, is adopted—in some cases nearly word-for-word—from the introduction to the first volume in the series, *Curriculum Windows: What Curriculum Theorists of the 1960s Can Teach Us About Schools and Society Today*, 2013, pp. xxx–xxxiii. I do not use quotation marks to cite the sections that are repeated since they are sometimes several pages long. Sections of that original introduction serve as strong conceptual grounding for the notion of "window" and helped create a window to the project for the class studying curriculum books of the 1990s.

How This Project Came To Be

In the first three volumes of a six volume series titled *Curriculum Windows: What Curriculum Theorists Can Teach Us About Schools and Society Today*, I tell the story of how the Curriculum Windows project came into being. I'll give a shortened version here to get you started as you begin this text on curriculum books of the 1990s. After publishing volumes on curriculum books of the 1960s, 1970s, 1980s, and now the 1990s, upcoming for publication in 2017 and 2018 will be the final volumes in the series focusing on the 2000s and the 1950s.

Curriculum Windows: What Curriculum Theorists of the 1990s Can Teach Us About Schools and Society Today, pp. xxix–xxxviii
Copyright © 2017 by Information Age Publishing
All rights of reproduction in any form reserved.

I "inherited" more than 100 curriculum books from my major professor at Indiana University in the 1990s, Norman V. Overly, several years after his retirement. I received the books in 2005. I put the word "inherited" in quotation marks above because Norm is still living and going strong. In fact, he won the Lifetime Achievement Award from Division B of AERA, Curriculum Studies, in 2014, based on his rich contributions to research in the curriculum field throughout his career, and especially through two very prominent books, *The Unstudied Curriculum* (1970) and *Lifelong Learning: A Human Agenda* (1979), treatments of which bookended the 1970s volume. What Norm wanted was for all of the books he gave to me to be put to good use; I didn't know exactly how I would do that at first, but I decided to store them on a prominent bookcase in my office at Miami University and make them available to students. Students could take them and use them as they willed.

As a result of using Schubert, Lopez, Thomas, and Carroll's (2002) book *Curriculum Books* in a seminar, I began to see how so many of the books in Norm's collection could be sorted by decade, which I began to do. At that moment, a window to the past opened up to me. I immediately thought of the idea of teaching a seminar on curriculum books by decade. Through several wonderful twists of fate in my department, I got the opportunity to teach a core seminar in our curriculum studies in our doctoral program in leadership, culture, and curriculum (LCC), the first one taking place in the spring of 2012. In the course, besides studying prominent curriculum books of a particular decade as well as current ideas, theories, and practices in the field of curriculum studies, I would challenge students to study one book in particular from the decade at hand and write a book length chapter (about 20 pages, double spaced) for the end of course assignment to be included in a book on the subject.

That first seminar in 2012 led to the first volume on the 1960s published in 2013. The second volume deals with books of the 1970s; that book comes from the seminar taught in the spring of 2013. The 1980s book came out of the seminar in 2014. The chapters in this volume come from the seminar on the 1990s taught in the spring of 2015.

From the beginning, I wondered: "How might a review of key books from the curriculum field from a given decade illuminate new possibilities forward for us today? How might the theories, practices, and ideas wrapped up in curriculum texts of that decade still resonate with us, allow us to see backward in time and forward in time, all at the same time? How could these figurative windows of insight, thought, ideas, fantasy, and fancy make us think differently about curriculum, teaching, learning, students, education, leadership, and schools? How could they challenge us? How could they help us see more clearly, even perhaps put us on a path to correct the mistakes and missteps of intervening decades, and today? And, how could I engage doctoral students in curriculum at Miami in a journey like this with me, opening windows to tomorrow by looking back today? How could I get students of curriculum, perhaps on their first formal scholarly journey, to express themselves and new ideas in ways that could be consumed by peers and colleagues in the curriculum field?" (Poetter, 2013, p. xxvii; Poetter, 2010; Poetter, Bird, & Goodney, 2004; Poetter, Wegwert, & Haerr, 2006).

How the Seminar Works

In the first part of the course on the 1990s, students studied several book length works on curriculum theory and history including Schubert et al.'s (2002) *Curriculum Books: The First 100 Years*; Pinar, Reynolds, Slattery, and Taubman's (2002) *Understanding Curriculum*; and the 1970s Curriculum Windows text. And students began to study the book they would write a chapter about from the 1990s. Throughout the first part of the course, about 9 weeks, a student scribe took notes at each seminar, shared them week-by-week, and we encouraged each other to come up with a "window" metaphor through which to frame each book and author.

In the last part of the course, about 6 weeks in length, I encouraged students to think of the chapter writing as a qualitative enterprise, which would involve not only their developing sense of what the book they were studying was about, but more intimately, how the book opened them up personally to new possibilities for seeing their lives and the world. I asked them to connect with the book deeply, by finding a hook in their own lives that would pull them and the reader through a window of insight and experience.

> What I wanted in the end, especially, were chapters that were voiced, mean- ing that the reader of each chapter could sense both the historical impor- tance of the work but also get a sense of the personal stakes at hand through the chapter author's interests, hopes, experiences, and ideas. I wanted stu- dents to write themselves into the book, not out of it. I wanted them to see themselves as conduits for ideas and images and possibilities, that is as "openings," like windows, through which we might see more clearly ahead— or at least somehow differently—the educational possibilities of yesterday, today, and tomorrow (Poetter, 2013, p. xxix)

During the last part of the course, students had individual meetings with me and they met in small groups to share drafts and engage in peer editing. I didn't engage in this process for the first book and regretted it immediately, so peer editing and continuous drafting have become hall- marks of my ongoing pedagogy with this class. These extra group sessions helped students on this project view the experience more like a collective, group process and less like an ominous, individual project hanging over their heads with a finite timeline. What I do try to make clear to each class that takes this challenge from me is that the project won't be finished at the end of the course. In each case, the publication process takes at least a year, often up to 18 months, so that students have the experience of seeing a published piece through several editing processes. And the learning doesn't stop at the end of the course, which transforms the doctoral seminar into something with a life of its own that keeps on giving.

Engaging the "Window" Metaphor

The word "window," early 13th century, comes from the Old Norse "vindauga," or literally "wind eye." It replaced the Old English words "eagpyrl," literally "eye-hole" and "eagduru," literally "eye-door." Originally an unglazed hole in a roof, most Germanic languages adopted the Latin "fenestra" to describe the glass version and later in English used "fenester" as a parallel word until the late 16th century. (Online Etymology Dictionary, 2012)

It's important to recognize that the metaphor of "window" is familiar to us and seems almost natural in terms of its serviceability as a metaphor. Meaning, we have experiences in our own lives of gazing out or into windows (or passing through them), whether they be in homes or cars or elsewhere. Sometimes these are typically present and pleasant memories and actions, tied often to the gift of free time or the opportunity to reflect, dream, ponder, and wonder. Krysmanski (2005) reminds us that metaphor—a figure of speech—grows out of our experiences with objects in the world and explains the unknown through the known. So "windows" had to be *there* before they could be used as metaphors. And literal windows are omnipresent, in our dwellings, works of architecture, the cinema, technology, as well as figuratively through literature, poetry, philosophy, religion, and the technology interfaces of present day computers.

For me, for instance, the literal and figurative notions of "windows" resonate in a very positive way and have had a soothing, almost therapeutic impact on me, and represent, in almost every beat of my heart over 50 years, clarity, beauty, and hope. I remember as a child sitting on the radiator benches just under a picture window in our family's living room facing a busy street. The benches were decorative, with lattice on the sides to let out the heat, but the wooden tops never got too hot to sit on, even in the dead of the frigid northern Ohio winters. I spent considerable time sitting on those benches, that window seat, warming myself, and looking out of the window while taking a break from family action, or from study, or when thinking about next steps for the day or trying to get a grip on life, or dealing with loss, or just taking time to think.

Busy and beautiful, the scene outdoors changed with the seasons, with rainstorms and snow, and sunshine, and familiar faces and characters walking up and down the street. I watched from the inside as my father walked home from church across the street, at which he was the pastor, at about 5 P.M. each night. I waited for him many days. I can recall walking or riding my bike home from school or a ballgame now and then, and seeing my sister waving and smiling out to me, beckoning from inside. So the window worked both ways, calming and inspiring from the inside, and welcoming from the outside. And, I realized, I wasn't the only one who loved that window seat and its life altering powers of view.

I also recall the windows of our very large 1972 Chevy Impala as I looked out of them on long western vacation road trips with my family. Squeezed between my brother and sister in the back seat for thousands of car miles before video games and movies in the car helped the current generation of children pass the time, I soldiered on by taking in the landscape through the side windows. Perhaps that's why I dragged my own sons and wife out West in the car several years ago, in an attempt to show them the beauty of the great western outdoors I appreciated so much as a child myself. I remember saying during patches of boredom for them as the miles rolled by in the car, even beyond the reach of the technology in use, "Just look out the window. There's something new to see every mile."

And on and on it goes, with the stained glass windows of my home church, especially the rose window behind the chancel (my father preached every Sunday of my youth in a large, impressive protestant sanctuary), majestic, beautiful, and luminous, playing an important role as I listened (or not) and meditated as a youth while surrounded by caring and loving adults and other children. Even broken windows of my youth turned out to yield life lessons, and grace, such as the time when I struck a baseball (a terrific line drive as I recall) through the large drive-up bay window of my neighbor friend's insurance business and ran for my life. Of course, since we lived merely steps away and all of us were friends, it didn't take long for his dad to find me and ask me how I intended to pay for it (my first early experience with the application of insurance, how apropos). He also said, "Tommy, it would have been much easier for me if you had just come in for your ball." It's the last time I ever ran from a broken window, both literally and figuratively.

But the metaphor of window, grounded perhaps in the crucible of "real" life experiences outside the sheltered, inviting windows of my own childhood and young adulthood in the 1960s and 1970s and 1980s, isn't always perceived or framed by others, necessarily, in such bucolic ways. In fact, while my experiences enrich me as a person, and make it possible for me to see, imagine, create, and interpret my reality and new realities, sometimes simultaneously, in ways that I think are not oppressive, they may simultaneously cloud my ability to see tragedy, suffering, and pain for others, though I've had my share of such and saw it all unfold on TV and in real life as a child—assassinations, wars, the dead, family deaths, disease, dysfunction, grieving, mental illness, violence, prejudice, racism, extreme social unrest.

What couldn't I see or what did I repress as I gazed out of those windows of my youth? How did my privilege cause blindness? What is it that I see now, or wish I had seen, or think I might have seen with different lenses, born of age, of experience, of context? And how do these images of memory reconstruct my self, my memory, and my current reality? How do I position myself as a child of privilege, who could look out of windows onto a street without fear of being shot at, or who had time to do so without the responsibilities of earning wages for the family or taking care of family members, soaking up the goods of free time and reflection when so many others my age as children and today as children rarely had or have a free moment to wonder? How enriched have I become at the expense of others as I soaked up the cultural capital afforded simply through the opportunity of "looking out of beautiful windows at a beautiful world"?

These are philosophical questions about experience, the kind that might be asked reflectively given time, and the conflation of context, culture, politics, economics, and experience, and the understanding of privilege as they all bear down on our current concepts of reality as we study the curriculum field and practice it, too. Ultimately, as a result of this deeper "seeing," of course, it's possible that the window, psychologically, can act as a metaphor representing, alternately, the reality or feeling of being enclosed, shuttered, sheltered, hidden, in hiding, even imprisoned, whether there are bars across the panes or not (Crenshaw & Green, 2009).

Krysmanski (2005), a contemporary German sociologist, explores the history of the windows metaphor in a short work titled, "Windows: A History of Metaphor," in which he sketches the development of the window metaphor through architecture, fine art, theater/cinema, literature, philosophy, religion, culture, science, and technology. Of particular note in his work are several concepts that may help as you read and interpret the chapters that follow. First is his recognition that the window as metaphor allows humans to use their powers of cognition, perception, intuition, and understanding to connect the seemingly mundane of everyday life with the literal and figurative essence of "light"; this interaction takes us out of our seemingly finite world and helps us connect or not with the infinite, the unknown.

Second is the connection between (a) the literal rise of the window in use in dwellings as a passage for light before the nearly universal access to glass and (b) the subsequent development of early "windows" as "screens."

In the dark ages, glass was only available to the extremely wealthy, who could install the windows in frames of dwellings and look out over feudal landscapes at their "holdings." Before the mass production and affordability of glass, which came much later into the early 20th century, "screens" over windows were held in place by "frames," and oftentimes painted and decorated, becoming works of art themselves even as they performed the function of blocking the elements that the window, as an opening by definition, could not keep out (Krysmanski, 2005). Over time, screens became paintings, works of art in and of themselves, and paintings, for instance, served themselves as metaphorical windows, or screens, representing one reality for a reality in another dimension, simultaneously. Related is the architectural wonder of glass as art, in the case of stained glass windows, for instance, that became part of churches and other institutional structures across continents. Stained glass doesn't so much let light enter or escape as it does reflect or absorb it, making the glass itself more luminous as opposed to lighting another venue. One's eye is drawn to the glass of the window, and its beauty and/or the story it tells, and not to the inside or outside of the dwelling place (Krysmanski, 2005). Stained glass windows don't so much admit or shield light, in so much instead as they absorb and transform it.

All of this connects with a third point, which is that modern day windows —as they take shape and are framed in so many venues, even as complete walls of buildings, as mirrors in interrogation rooms, or as screens where multiple realities meet through digital technology—continue to act as powerful inspiration for metaphor, and representations of human possibility, growth, progress, and even enslavement, while also opening up the potential for postmodern use and interpretation, that is in the sense that positionality, identity, and perhaps even culture and ideology are subject to new frontiers given the transcending energy of emerging interfaces, or screens, or windows, if you will (Krysmanski, 2005). What might our journey to locate ourselves within the complex worlds, interactions, and experiences of curriculum reveal to us as we seek, explore, open our eyes, shine the light, blaze new trails, and recognize windows of opportunity? What might the process of looking back through time at past windows of meaning reveal to us as we deal with today and dream/act for tomorrow? How might the windows we open or develop serve the curriculum field in ways that lie beyond the "screens" that Tyler imagined, for instance, the ones that would serve to filter the value of objectives "objectively" for the classroom? (Tyler, 1970). And how might we acknowledge them, in truth instead, as subjective, value-laden, human, and experiential meanings/ questions derived from normative interests at hand and our own lives, as opposed to some arbitrary, meaningless and indefinable truth that lies outside of us? (Kliebard, 1992).

On the 1990s, and Today

The idea of this project, originally, was to teach three of the seminars on this topic while using the writing project as a centerpiece pedagogy over three consecutive spring semesters, and then to hand the course over to one of my colleagues for them to do something different with it and with students. Unfortunately, when it was time for my longtime colleague Dennis Carlson to teach the course, he became ill, and subsequently, and tragically, passed away in 2015. I agreed to continue teaching the course that spring semester in 2015 and through the spring of 2016, a semester in which I had two sections of the course, probably for the first and last time: one a course with PhD students, and one with EdD students. In honor of Dennis, the book on the 2000s will feature his 2002 curriculum book *Leaving Safe Harbors: Toward a New Progressivism in American Education and Public Life*.

But when this all started coming together, I had every intention of ending this project with the 1980s book. I felt this way, very strongly, for several reasons. First, as stated above, this isn't *my* class. I don't *own* it—it's a core class in our doctoral program. In fact, Denise Taliaferro Baszile, my great colleague in Curriculum Studies at Miami University, will be teaching the PhD cohort this class in the spring of 2017. So I wouldn't have even been teaching the 1990s class, let alone the classes on the 1950s and 2000s to be featured in books to come, if it weren't for the loss of Dennis Carlson since I had already experienced a substantive 3-year run with the course.

Second, to be honest, I didn't really have all that many books from the 1990s in the first place. I read many of them, but I didn't have them at hand and Norm's library wasn't chalk full of them, either. And last, frankly, I could barely stand the 1990s when they happened; I certainly didn't have it in mind that it would be interesting or fun or illuminating or even defensible to revisit them with a complicated, depthful, time-consuming project like examining 15 or so books from that decade.

Let me explain. I never hated the 1990s; they just slipped by me.

I became a college professor in the early 1990s. I left a short teaching career where I had immense freedom in my syllabus and pedagogy to truly teach and then I entered the professoriate, focusing mainly on teacher education courses and issues, as well as working with graduate students studying curriculum as a field. I must say, during those early years in higher education as I cut my teeth, the work was fun, untainted, not regulated by anyone except the students and the board of regents (loosely) and my own professional judgment.

Unwittingly, while between jobs I agreed to help a colleague out by agreeing to score tests for a new national subject area test being piloted by one of the major subject area organizations through a national testing organization on behalf of corporate and state interests. I really didn't know what was going on; at the time I thought I was just reading tests for a friend and making a small stipend. But what I was participating in was a pilot iteration of the first national tests, and of course, the trickle down to scripted curriculum and pedagogy and massive testing for all that would follow in the coming decade. This would change the public face and the practice of education and schooling forever. I was there at the beginning, ripping out the foundations of the system, such as it was with all of its flaws and inconsistencies, with my small evaluative acts. Of course, I know that some other well-trained dupe would have been there if I weren't there. I didn't cause No Child Left Behind (NCLB). But my proximity to it and my relative culpability still sting.

While I taught and learned and became more political, I realized that those first formal movements to standardize "everything" in our education system would portend so many more slights and degradations to come. However, teachers I taught in class and I remained unfazed by most of this through the early 2000s. But after NCLB in 2001, almost every teacher and school person and student I came into contact with had been socialized out of learning for its own sake and the value of a true, liberal arts education for all, and simply pursued the test score or secrets to raising them in their students as the coin of the realm. As I taught and worked, then, I relied on older texts from previous decades to make a case. Even helpful work like Berliner and Biddle's was too new, and while I knew about it, I didn't use it in my classes.

So by 2012 when I started this project, I didn't have a very fond view of 1990s scholarship in the curriculum field because I lived through the decade and found those years to be the haunting grounds of severe, drastic, previously unimaginable, and mostly damaging changes to education and schooling, from pre-K–16. This was also the time in my life when I spent my hours away from work changing diapers and raising two young children. And while doing that, I tried to build my own scholarly career, which of course requires reading, but I spent most of my time writing, trying to participate in the circle of life in my field in terms of the production of knowledge and to make tenure and promotion in my own higher education universe. Those things turned out well, but I didn't read everything written in the 1990s that I should have read. I was too busy for it, sadly. Sometimes you just can't see things happening right under your nose.

So I masked my relative ignorance, thinking that the 1950s and even the 2000s, post-NCLB, to be vastly more interesting and helpful than the 1990s. I was wrong. Almost all of the books chronicled here are masterpieces, not only of the era but also for the field. Except for the circumstances of losing Dr. Carlson, I'm glad I got to work with this class and to produce this book with them. The 1990s, in so many ways, proved to be remarkable. I hope you'll find enjoyment and insight in the chapters to come, as I and the students have.

REFERENCES

Carlson, D. (2002). *Leaving safe harbors: Toward a new progressivism in American education and public life*. New York, NY: Routledge.

Crenshaw, D., & Green, E. (2009). The symbolism of windows and doors in play therapy. *Play Therapy*, retrieved from www.a4pt.org

Kliebard, H. (1992). The Tyler rationale: In H. M. Kliebard's (Ed.), *Forging the American curriculum: Essays in curriculum theory and history* (pp. 153–167). New York, NY: Routledge.

Krysmanski, H. J. (2005). Windows: Exploring the history of metaphor. Retrieved from http://www.uni-muenster.de/EuropeanPopularScience/win-sample/win-authors.htm

Pinar, W., Reynolds, W., Slattery, P., & Taubman, P. (2002). *Understanding curriculum: An introduction to the study of historical and contemporary curriculum discourses*. New York, NY: Peter Lang.

Poetter, T. S. (Ed.). (2013). *Curriculum windows: What curriculum theorists of the 1960s can teach us about schools and society today*. Charlotte, NC: Information Age.

Poetter, T. (2010). Taking the leap, mentoring doctoral students as scholars: A great and fruitful morass. *Teaching & Learning: The Journal of Natural Inquiry & Reflective Practice, 24*(1), 22–29.

Poetter, T., Wegwert, J., & Haerr, C. (Eds.). (2006). *No child left behind and the illusion of reform: Critical essays by educators*. Lanham, MD: University Press of America.

Poetter, T., Bird, J., & Goodney, T. (Eds.). (2004). *Critical perspectives on the curriculum of teacher education*. Lanham, MD: University Press of America.

Schubert, W., & Lopez, A., Thomas, T., & Carroll, W. (2002). *Curriculum books: The first hundred years* (2nd Ed.). New York, NY: Routledge.

Tyler, R. (1970). *Basic principles of curriculum and instruction*. Chicago, IL: University of Chicago Press.

CHAPTER 1

THREE DECADES OF AMERICAN-STYLE SEX ED

Even Though Seasons Change, The View Out the Windows Remains the Same ... Time to Open the Door

Richelle Frabotta

sexuality education becomes critical and analytical and thus both personally and socially empowering. This.... is the only way of restoring academic
respectability and pedagogic integrity to a discipline that has been relegated
to "family life education" and "life adjustment education" for far too long.
(Carlson, 1992, as cited in Sears, 1992, p. 57)

I went to Catholic school for 13 years and grew up with a strict "abstinence-only" education. My parents and school always taught me that sex
was strictly off limits until I was married. Honestly, the majority of people
I went to school with—myself included—did not benefit whatsoever from
this education. We used each other as resources for Sex Education instead and experienced guilt when we did it because we were terrified that
our parents would find out. This guilt and fear did not, however, stop us
from doing it. Basically, the better approach would have been to be hon-

*Curriculum Windows: What Curriculum Theorists of the 1990s Can Teach Us
About Schools and Society Today,* pp. 1–15
Copyright © 2017 by Information Age Publishing
All rights of reproduction in any form reserved.

est and open about sex and to present us with different options we could
have chosen regarding it. Being more open about sex likely would have
given us all better attitudes about it instead of feelings of guilt and fear.
(Personal communication, FSW 365 undergraduate at Miami University)

Where do you go to sit and think? As I sit in the woo-hoo room, my thinking
space, aptly named for its natural earth-toned, organic décor and peaceful zen feel, I soak up the serene scene that surrounds me; three walls of
windows and a vaulted ceiling with skylights offer a landscaped, country
view with a wide sky. Ahhhh … relaxing. My mind is on this assignment. I
begin to contemplate the contemptuous and disparaging comments, the
pervasive and systemic demolition, and the misinformation with dogged
single-minded intention, and lack of ethical behavior that has historically
plagued the work that is sexuality education. *My work*, that is sexuality
education (Sex Ed), was an unplanned and beloved career birthed in 1992.

The same year that I began my career in Sex Ed, James T. Sears (1992)
offered the world his edited volume: *Sexuality and the Curriculum: The Politics
and Practices of Sexuality Education*. This text reads like a diary from my 23+
years in the field. Two forewords, one introduction, 4 parts, 15 chapters,
and 4 commentaries later, the reader can boast a thorough, nourishing,
and critical examination of the field of Sex Ed. Sears called on curriculum
scholars to review, critique, analyze, report, discuss, and present from their
respective lenses to facilitate a robust roadmap of what the field of Sex Ed
has been and a point from which scholars in Sex Ed can analyze, inform,
and discuss the current climate and future work of the field.

A noisy fire crackling in the wood burning stove and the odiferous salmon
colored blooms of hibiscus are my faithful cheerleaders. They offer me
hope; surviving indoors and thriving like there's no winter outside. I look
up to see ladybugs scurry and flit and fly with purpose on the windows. The
ladybugs want to be outside and work diligently walking the glass seeking
exit and persevere in the direct warmth of the sunlight. They prompt me
to action and remind me that I have work to do.

Using the woo-hoo room's walls of windows, skylights, and doors as metaphorical spaces to gaze into, insightful quotes from masters in the field
from Sears' (1992) text, the reality of undergraduate student voices, and
my experiences in the trenches, I will examine several aspects of Sex Ed
that facilitate *seeing* sex/ual/ity in pedagogy and practice. In order to keep
a broad sense of the subject matter, I denote the three major components
of Sex Ed by defining the term sex/ual/ity: sex (behaviors, things we do) +
sexual (emotions, energy we feel) + sexuality (identity, who we are). So grab
a cuppa and settle into your woo-hoo room because it is time to read about
SEX ED: A PAST (1992, and the windows facing North, East, and South)
so we can inform SEX ED: A PRESENT (2015, and the skylights that offer

a limitless view) and contemplate SEX ED: A FUTURE (no window, an open set of glass paneled French doors beckons the reader to walk through toward the West) in order to teach what is *the most universal, applicable, and human subject matter on the plane*t.

SEX ED: A PASTLlooking to the North, South, and East

> The modernist trick was to "sublimate" desire, particularly sexual desire, into "healthy" channels and guide it in the direction of marriage, "normal" family, and "healthy living." From the start, sexuality education would be defined as a health concern, and one that attached itself to the adolescent body in particular, as a problem body. (Carlson, 2012, p. iii)

> **I've sat through numerous classes pertaining to topics I will never re-visit, or apply, or probably even recall. However, the subject matter of sex, which is so relevant to every breathing human on the planet Earth, is practically ignored. And if sex is not being completely ignored, it's be-ing taught with a scary and unpleasant undertone. I think the only way to combat this injustice is similar to all major movements throughout time— taken in baby steps. And I think it starts with adults. This is because the adults are the ones left to educate the younger masses. (Personal commu-nication, FSW 365 undergraduate at Miami University)**

From my workspace in the woo-hoo room looking out of the floor to ceiling windows, the window the north reveals frost covering the creeping thyme and wintergreen. The zombie skeletons, stoically holding watch over the herb garden, are frozen with somber anticipation of the spring to come. Their roles: sentinels or guardians? With their chipping paint clothes, sly smiles, and steely eyes alert and never wavering, they are turgid reminders of the passing seasons. Why didn't we bring in the herb garden dignitaries? There's no need; they are hardy, well-weathered, and serve as reminders of persistence, enduring through adverse changes.

Sears (1992) opens Part I, "Foundations for Sexual Inquiry," of his book, *Sexuality and the Curriculum*, with an honest presentation of "Dilemmas and Possibilities of Sex Education Reproducing the Body Politic." Sears calls it like he sees it—for real. He proffers an account of the state of Sex Ed and it is disconcertingly accurate. Sears states precisely, "Sexuality education in schools of education should be not only a terrain for personal and social enquiry but also a place to raise fundamental questions among competing sexual ideologies" (p. 28). He goes on to credit Earls, Fraser, and Sumpter (1992) with the insightful declaration that, "such dialogue is lacking in con-temporary discourse on sexuality and the curriculum because of consensus held by sexuality education forces" (as cited in Sears, 1992, p. 28). The consensus Earls et al. refer to is the conspicuously absent "critical conversation revolving around how we conceptualize sexual knowledge, what kind of sexual knowledge is of most worth, and who should have access to what types of sexual knowledge" (as cited in Sears, 1992, p. 28).

There are numerous ways to analyze and dissect issues that are not allowing Sex Ed to meet its true and full mission. Sears (1992) reminds the reader, "we approach sexuality from a technorational worldview ... we can marry critical thinking and heartfelt discussions to the sexuality curriculum by encouraging students to examine the origins of their sexuality" (p. 27). He then goes on to take the reader to the next level of analysis by excerpting from a Sadker, Sadker, and Shakeshaft (1989) piece and offers this:

> But sexual silence dominates schools of education and "Since teachers and administrators typically have little or no formal training in this hidden curriculum, they are often baffled about what to do when they confront sex and sexism in their classroom and schools." (p. 214, as cited in Sears, 1992, p. 28)

Sears (1992) identifies a hidden curriculum, "the overemphasis on rational decision making and the failure to explore eroticism ... and the language of intimate sexual communication" (p. 13). This is a key concept that should not be ignored.

It is within this hidden curriculum, the lack of critical conversation, and a technorational worldview that we find a path forward: educators, most notably preservice educators, need instruction about sex/ual/ity in order to engage learners with knowledge about sexual development and a model comfort level that allows for the natural process of sexual development. It is appropriate for students in K–12th grades to seek sexual authenticity as a course of development. Responding is better than reacting. Professional educators should not utilize personal values and experiences as the foundation for curriculum. We must work to make the hidden curriculum transparent so that the erotic has a place in conversation. In a perfect world, trained professional educators would deliver a curriculum about human sexuality that is culturally aware, developmentally relevant, evidence-based, medically accurate, and sex-positive. This is the means for an effective Sex Ed pedagogy and praxis. Why didn't this happen in 1992 and why doesn't it happen in contemporary times?

Dr. Dennis Carlson (1992) in his essay, "Ideological Conflict and Change in the Sexuality Curriculum," reminds the reader that there are indeed political ideologies involved with access to and delivery of sex/ual/ity information. He takes a critical view so that the reader can literally envision the pros, cons, strategies, and goals associated with each ideology. This in turn provides an opportunity to discuss a best path forward. Carlson states, "sexuality education itself needs to be reconceptualized" (as cited in Sears,

1992, p. 56). He hand holds the reader through what sex/ual/ity Ed isn't nor ought to be and then lands squarely on his own argument:

> I would suggest that it be defined as a subfield of cultural studies, liberal arts, or history … although "liberal arts" tends to imply a traditionalist perspective on the "great books," while "cultural studies" implies a deconstructive analysis of contemporary culture, including mass culture. We learn much about the social meaning assigned to human sexuality through both approaches…. History … is the study of culture over time and thus not fully separable from cultural studies…. So conceived, sexuality education becomes critical and analytical and thus both personally and socially empowering. (Carlson, 1992, as cited in Sears, 1992, p. 56)

Carlson (1992) offers us a unique lens from which to be able to discern that the political *is* personal and it is in our collective best interest to never, ever forget.

Mariamne Whatley (1992) sums up Part I by offering concise language that delineates the multisided challenges that prevent effective delivery of sex/ual/ity Ed:

> Many critics see in it not what is actually there but what they fear, and supporters, instead of arguing for a thoughtful, comprehensive curriculum, try to avoid including anything that might trigger one of those fears…. Perhaps as sexuality educators, we need to do more values clarification for ourselves in terms of our teaching. We need to develop our view of sexuality education from opposition in which we have clearly identified what we want it to be in its ideal form, not what we can "get away with" before the watchdogs of the Right bite us. (as cited in Sears, 1992, p. 83)

This is the necessary set-up for the next concept Sears presents: "Gender and Sexuality." If Sex Ed were to remain reactionary in response to what are some people's narrow-minded, perhaps religiously informed, views, many students—such as gay, lesbian, bisexual, asexual, gender-nonconforming, queer, and those questioning traditional presentations of male/female heterosexuality—would always be left out of the conversation. This is unethical and educators with integrity would never stand for this.

> **I would like to point out that neither men nor women are actually great at intimacy, so it is not accurate to describe women as much more intimate than men. It is important to note that some women may want to have multiple sexual experiences with random men, and some men want to have monogamous relationships with women. And we cannot dismiss same gender sex relations and relationships! I think it is crucial to explore our own lives and relationships because it can be damaging to believe such stereotypical thinking. (Personal communication, FSW 365 undergraduate at Miami University)**

I'm back in the woo-hoo room looking out of the floor to ceiling windows. To the East, the bold rising sun which, as it continues its daily arc, will make the room too hot to bear so that even in midwinter, windows will open. I anticipate the sweaty challenge from the sun, but I don't know how to change it. I accept that the room will become too stuffy and I will be uncomfortable. And then it happens. Seeking liberation from the oppressive confines of physical and emotional discomfort that disallows me to focus on my writing efforts, I choose to act and I move to open the windows. The windows won't budge, no one is around to help, and I am left with no alternatives but to suffer through the day until the sun sets and nighttime brings cool relief.

Although Part II, "Gender and Sexuality," and III, "Making Meaning of Sexuality in the Schools," feature seemingly unrelated topics under different subject headings, both parts are actually are tied together with a single theme: Sex Ed, currently informed, structured, and implemented, marginalizes specific demographics of students and teachers. This absence of key and diverse voices disallows a candid, reality-based presentation of human sexuality and human sexual experience. Those marginalized voices are absent from the authoring of sexuality pedagogy, from the instruction of curricula, the content of lesson plans, and from the seats in the classrooms. Fonow and Marty (1992) state that:

> the paradox cannot be resolved on hegemonic terrain. Given that categories of sexual identity brand everyone and accurately describe no one, it seems evident that we must resist the dominant ideology that places us in intolerable hierarchies while making practical the adage "Until all of us are free, none of us are free." (as cited in Sears, 1992, p. 167)

Along these lines, Ward and Taylor (1992) in their essay, "Sexuality Education for Immigrant and Minority Students," suggest that students who fall under labels such as immigrant and minority are further marginalized in Sex Ed curricula. Therefore, their particular needs are not getting met and they deserve better treatment. Overall, these authors recommend an outcome that is relatively common and a typical expectation associated with learning: "Effective curricula must include an acknowledgement of the context of teens lives and prepare them for the social, cultural, political, and economic realities they will encounter in the world" (Ward & Taylor, 1992, as cited in Sears, 1992, p. 198). Working with students where they are and for an identified outcome constitutes strong education. In the insightful and progressive essay, "Learning to Be the Opposite Sex: Sexuality Education and Sexual Scripting in Early Adolescence," Sapon-Shevin and Goodman (as cited in Sears, 1992) employ story-telling and cold-hard truths to remind the reader that *teaching* gender can be as challenging as a young person *developing* one's gender.

Phillips and Fine (1992) in their commentary, the last entry in Part III "Making Meaning of Sexuality in Schools," further offers this nugget of truth:

> While we must continue to assert our responsibility to infuse considerations of ethnicity and culture, student voices, and activism into sexuality education, such assertions won't replace deep, ongoing, and transformative conversations about the powers of silencing, language, and social change as they lace with our lived sexualities. (as cited in Sears, 1992, p. 248)

Utilizing feminist scholars' lenses, the authors underscore the idea of inclusion of diversity by looking "critically at social arrangements, to chart out spaces for rigorous analyses of power, and to seek out intellectual and political surprises" (Phillips & Fine, 1992, as cited in Sears, 1992, p. 249).

Not dissimilar from Sears (1992) and Carlson's (1992) messages, intersectionality, critical review, and awareness of the political are necessary for moving students forward towards quality Sex Ed programming. Klein (1992) notes at the end of Part II that "Educational researchers and curriculum developers have a continuing responsibility to increase their understanding of how these factors influence all aspects of education" (as cited in Sears, 1992, p. 178). This responsibility is uber important because inequality is rampant. "sexuality education will promote sex-equitable attitudes and behaviors" (Klein, 1992, as cited in Sears, 1992, p. 178).

The fact that the first real information I received about sex was from Cosmopolitan magazine makes me angry. I had to go to a popular media magazine to learn answers to my questions, and in doing so, I felt uncomfortable and guilty for being curious. (Personal communication, FSW 365 undergraduate at Miami University)

Once again, I'm back in the woo-hoo room looking out of the floor to ceiling windows. And to the South, cardinals, blue jays, starlings, finches, and robins are holding court in the evergreens, flitting to the ground, and chirping with high energy. They come and go from nooks, and nests, and hidden places seemingly busy with necessary and important tasks. They are building, feeding, tussling, and vying for perches that offer the safest respite. They struggle in the breeze, never quite flying directly from point A to point B. They are wary of the cat who never quite looks full enough from the food placed in the bowl every morning. The birds never fully relax, but accept that their life is truly in the balance.

Just like the organized chaos of the birds, Part IV, "Problematics of Change," tells us that sometimes gathering more twigs and re-feathering the nest creates opportunity for comfort that has never been quite actualized. Getting busy and re-thinking, re-working, re-forming has got to happen to progress the paradigm. Identifying elements of alternative curricular approaches can only effect a positive outcome! What are barriers to quality Sex Ed?

Patricia Koch (1992) in her chapter titled, "Integrating Cognitive, Affective, and Behavioral Approaches into Learning Experiences for Sexuality Education," asserts that the "formal and informal sexuality education that an individual receives in our society is inaccurate, fragmented, and diminishing" and that "such incomplete and negative sexuality education has taken its physical, emotional, and social toll on individuals, as well as our society collectively" (as cited in Sears, 1992, p. 253). It is also noted that the limited Sex Ed that parents provide is lacking. There is a void and teachers in established education systems can fill it! By utilizing approaches to learning grounded in the cognitive, affective, and behavioral domains, teachers can create growth-enhancing learning experiences. When developing these approaches, Koch (1992) cautions:

> The creation of learning experiences must be guided by the needs and interests of the students and teacher and not the political agendas of school boards or the "moral" agendas of vocal conservative groups. Teachers must battle against the deskilling aspects of restrictive, mechanistic curricula developed by those far removed from classrooms and must recapture their leadership in development of curricula and learning experiences for sexuality education. (as cited in Sears, 1992, p. 262)

Although emphasis is placed on teachers and curricula, the real gatekeepers are in different roles and not necessarily in classrooms nor do they have classroom experience.

Earls et al. (1992) drive home the idea that Sex Ed implementation lies within the political power structure of the state legislative process. Often the dominant or majority political party influences curricula and what gets taught in public schools. These authors caution that "recognizing whose interests are served by various actions can lead to the critically reflective community and liberating models needed to create sexuality education in the interest of all" (Earls et al., 1992, as cited in Sears, 1992, p. 324). In the final commentary of the text, Shakeshaft (1992, as cited in Sears, 1992) adds to the challenges of implementing an inclusive Sex Ed curricula by warning that administrators may be barriers to change. Like many, she notes that administrators (especially males) are not comfortable with the subjects of human sex/ual/ity. She strongly urges administrators take part on a team when considering Sex Ed so as to minimize the discomfort and maximize the awareness of how that "ucky feeling" can affect students' learning.

SEX ED: A PRESENT … Looking Up and Out Through the Skylights

This culture-industry "curriculum" of sexuality education, which has been reterritorialized to public schooling, is now so pervasive that it begins to make what currently passes for sexuality education largely irrelevant. If popular culture is the new text which adolescents draw upon to construct a sexual self, sexuality education must become about media literacy. (Carlson, 2012, p. 173)

As a 22-year-old woman I found myself learning things about my body and sexuality that I had never been told; and many of the things I did know I learned myself the hard way. Sexuality is something that is an inevitable aspect of human nature, yet our society treats it as something we should be embarrassed about and something that should be kept private. As a result, many people feel ashamed of their bodies and their sexuality. Throughout our lives we receive messages about sex from many different sources: our parents, the health teacher, the media, our friends, and maybe an issue of Cosmo. Most people can probably agree that these messages are all very different and mostly negative. Our parents tell us sex is strictly for making babies with whomever you marry. The health teacher tells us not to engage in sex at all. And the media tells us that sex is an act between two 6-feet-tall super-humans with flawless physiques. This leaves everyone on their own messy and often disappointing journey to discover what sex is by themselves. (Personal communication, FSW 365 undergraduate at Miami University)

While sitting in the woo-hoo room looking out of the floor to ceiling windows. Something catches my eye and I look up. The ladybugs have found their way to the precipice! I believe that they think that are almost outside. They are gathered in force, walking, walking, walking around, pushing to move beyond the glass dome. The sky is a mixture of white fluffy and heavy darkening clouds. The wind is present, combative, and moving clouds through quickly. It appears that inclement weather is either coming in or has just passed by. Clearly the weather is tumultuous and with an air of unpredictability, yet blue sky pervades in spots. If I look to the farthest part of the skylights, I can see sunbeams on the periphery.

In 2015, Sears' (1992) choice of content for the four parts of the text is particularly poignant as they are just as relevant today. "Foundations for Sexual Inquiry," "Gender and Sexuality," "Making Meaning of Sexuality in Schools," and "Problematics of Change" continue to be areas of scholarly inquiry, the foci of those delivering Sex Ed, and they are also on-going controversies in our national discourse. All four parts are currently being legislated, funded in some manner by government dollars, and fueled by people with differing agendas. Therefore, these authors' multi-cultured and often radical voices from Sears' (1992) text, continue to ring true a clarion bell of wisdom and warning into the present.

My professional sex/ual/ity educator's perspective is a primary voice from which I will write in this section on the current state of Sex Ed. I have taught thousands of students in over 100 public and private schools in 6 counties in southern Ohio. And it is from this in-the-trenches view that I can say not much has changed. Sears (1992) and his contributors are informed storytellers who remind us that how to do Sex Ed is a conversation that bears revisiting. The current state of Sex Ed confirms: history does repeat. It is a prudent master who recognizes that to look to the future, one must attend to the past.

Sex Ed has been a topic of great debate and controversy in national discourse for two centuries, since the settlers (Puritans, Calvinists, adventurers, and criminals alike) landed on our shores. Just to want to teach about human sexuality can provoke a heated debate where vitriolic declarations, and rigid proclamations, are flung with determined aim. This debate is found at all levels of government, from the executive branch to local community school boards, and all houses of public policy in between. Citizens in every sociopolitical demographic throughout the United States can locate themselves somewhere on the continuum of public opinion about Sex Ed.

The contemporary Sex Ed debate is based in differing and opposing values systems which are essentially (a) respecting a thoroughly informed, individual empowerment, personal choices approach rooted in self-determined sexual wellness and (b) respecting a "one size fits all," traditionally and historically conservative, religious values approach to determining sexual behavior for all individuals. These most frequently discussed pedagogies reflect only two schools of thought. Both are outcomes driven, but utilize philosophical approaches and reasoned curricula with methods that are dissimilar. Medically accurate, risk-reduction models inform comprehensive sexuality education (CSE) whereas values laden, risk-avoidance models inform abstinence-only until marriage (AOUM) programming.

There are focused, intense, and emotionally fueled reactions to sexuality subject matter in both CSE and AOUM models; however, after decades of valid and reliable research, CSE has been *proven* to meet numerous sexual health identified outcomes. Those outcomes are typically qualified as delaying sexual debut and not acquiring a medical concern (such as pregnancy or sexually transmitted infection). Loud and vocal minority voices, who intentionally insight endless politicizing and utilize smoke and mirrors combined with raging and shaming to avoid any rational attempt at finding common ground, are typically the extremists that support AOUM and conversely condemn CSE. This vocal minority tends to cite national adolescent social problems statistics, especially the fiscal and moral costs, in order to win rhetorical favor from those who feel that "legs closed until marriage" is a viable mandate for citizens up to age 27.

The blocking of developmentally relevant, age-appropriate, culturally aware, and medically accurate—literally—life changing information from the minds of those who need it *ultimately hurts us all*. There is no conceivable factual benefit or rational argument for barring access to sexual health and wellness information and strategies grounded in risk-reduction teaching methods. There is no conceivable benefit to the continuation of demeaning the traditionally disempowered (children, adolescents, young adults) or marginalizing minority groups (such as gays, lesbians, and transgender folks or people with disabilities or those with nontraditional gender expression).

When divorce rates in the United States have rested at right around 50% for over 3 decades and the single and unmarried identity demographic is rapidly increasing, there is no conceivable benefit to centering curriculum on a heterosexist, homogenous model of intimate partner relationships. To blatantly avoid conversations about eroticism in a culture that emphasizes virginity until marriage and where pornography is the new accessible teaching tool for teens, leaves generations of confused, guilt-ridden, and shamed and is representative of the hidden curriculum that Sears (1992) wrote about in *Sexuality and the Curriculum*. However, providing access to medically accurate, developmentally relevant, age-appropriate, culturally aware, and empowerment oriented Sex Ed for all is a pro-CSE approach and our public policies from national to local should reflect such.

Indeed, to be able to access medically accurate, developmentally relevant, culturally aware, and empowerment oriented sexuality information that speaks directly to each citizen is a civil liberties and social justice conversation. Marty Klein (2012) reminds us that:

> Our law affords constitutional protection to personal decisions relating to marriage, procreation, contraception, family relationship, childrearing, and education.... Our precedents "have respected the private realm of family life which the state cannot enter." ... At the heart of liberty is the right to define one's own concept of existence, of meaning, of the universe, and of the mystery of human life. (p. xiv)

There is considerable power in having an educated and well-informed polis aware of its constitutional rights. However, an informed and empowered polis can be considered dangerous by folks who have a rigid agenda. Thus, the seasons change, but the view out of the windows stays the same.

SEX ED: A FUTURE ... Looking at the Door to the West and Walking Through

eros was not to be freed so much as educated in an ethic and a discipline of "care of the self," aimed at maintaining physical and psychic health and healthy relations with others. This might be considered an individual project, but it is also, in its most democratic forms, a collective public project of education as upbringing...in which the young are "produced" as subjects of particular forms of democratic sexuality and desire, which also means as active subjects of their own desires. (Carlson, 2012, p. 175)

I want my best friends to see their parents' mistakes and make sure they don't repeat them. Scaring kids, intimidating them, and making them feel ashamed of their sexual thoughts and feelings is just unhealthy and promotes low self-esteem and self-confidence. My best friends in both cases never believed they could talk to their parents openly about sex, contraception, or boys in general because they feared being punished. I want my friends to know that it is important that their kids feel like they have a safe environment to talk to them about anything, especially because the book brought up a good point about sexual predators. If a child is led to believe there is only shame and negativity regarding his or her body, how can they ever feel comfortable enough to tell their parents if someone is subjecting them to unhealthy sexual behavior? This is why I want my friends to know the importance of creating a health environment for their children to be able to explore their sexuality. (Personal communication, FSW 365 undergraduate at Miami University)

Meanwhile, back in the woo-hoo room, I note that all three sets of windows and the skylights are large and yield different views of the same outdoors! The subject matter that is human sexuality is just like the outdoors. The windows each show a different aspect, just as the lenses used here show differing views of Sex Ed in pedagogy and praxis. Maybe we have run out of time to stare longingly out of the windows. Hanging out in the same room, albeit with different views, is not really progress. Perhaps it is time to leave the room and actually head outside? The door is directly behind me, to the West.

When I think of the West, I think of the American old West: wild, unsettled, and rife with opportunities for anyone with know-how and ambition to make it happen. Although boldly striking out on one's own is a noble undertaking, many pioneers find themselves lost to the harsh terrain in need of specific tools, skill-sets that would tighten the odds for survival. The American West found itself inundated with groups of ambitiously minded, but differently skilled settlers and homesteaders who recognized that survival might be for the fittest, but thriving was for those who could work together. In other words: it takes a village, people. This is the future of Sex Ed.

It is absolutely imperative to pay attention to the extremists; vocal minorities who champion personal agendas or who ignore the professional standards incorporated into our public education system and are not interested in finding common ground. Often these folks are reactionaries, holding views related to a moralizing stance about sex/ual/ity and who give little credence to the construct of public education where hired teachers deliver lesson plans from a proven curriculum. These vocal minorities, as well as the occasionally outspoken majority, can and do affect Sex Ed policy. Those whose job it is to make policy can have a significant impact on personal health and public health. In Sex Ed, whether it is a policy creation discussion or a policy implementation or delivery discussion, the personal is truly political.

We continue to be challenged in 2015 in partisan ways. There are lessons to learn, and relearn, and learn again. Such is my professional take-away from reading Sears' (1992) *Sexuality and the Curriculum: The Politics and Practices of Sexuality Education*. It is a candid and reality-based entreaty from some erudite folks who were speaking the capital T-truth of the times. What contemporary sexuality educators are struggling with, public discourse does not address. Where do we go next? There are two other models of sexuality education: the abstinence-plus and the rights-based approaches. Both are essentially the "next generation" of AOUM and CSE and tend to appeal to more moderate groups of folks who are knowledgeable about and engaged in this discourse.

In the spirit of pioneering the wild West, *Already Doing It: Intellectual Disability and Sexual Agency*, by Michael Gill (2015), unabashedly and unequivocally calls for sexual and reproductive justice for people with intellectual disabilities (ID) on the grounds that sexuality, sexual expression, and choices about such are indeed human experiences. "When we assume to know what is best for others, this knowledge can often actively hide or deny individual sexual self-determinism" (p. 194). This reflects the challenges that Sears identified in 1992!

Gill's (2015) contemporary assertions are not rights oriented, but justice centered. He contends that, "sexual ableism is the system of imbuing with determinations of qualification to be sexual based on criteria of ability, intellect, morality, physicality, appearance, age, race, social acceptability, and gender conformity" (p. 2). From this lens, Gill explores a historically ignored, denied, condemned, and pathologized concept too dangerous to utter, let alone embrace: to be human is to be sexual and to be sexual is to be human. Drawing on Siebers' (2008) work, Gill demonstrates that individuals have consistently found, *né persevered*, through obstacles constructed by medicine, rehabilitative processes, parental authority, popular culture, and those who provide residential support to be creatively sexual, thus expressing an "artfulness of disability" (p. 148, as cited in Gill, 2015, p. 6). Gill removes what is considered a most progressive "rights" argument and simply contends that the "artfulness of disability" is reason enough for accepting the sexuality of individuals.

Not unlike the disabilities population that Gill (2015) specifically discusses, students in AOUM and CSE programs from the 1990s also have had to navigate challenges! The struggle is real for students who have been not been receiving sex/ual/ity Ed, receiving inadequate sex/ual/ity Ed, and marginalized students who have been intentionally overlooked in sex/ual/ity Ed.

Gill (2015) references a discourse of protectionism which also (most insultingly) denies an innate expression of human desire by folks with intellectual disabilities. Looking to feminist theorists, disability studies, and queer theory to critically dismantle the overt protections of individuals' sexual expression, Gill "envision[s] a future where disabled individuals and their sexual and reproductive lives are not constructed as "special" or in need of regulation" (p. 192). He states that, "The challenge is to continue to forward sexual pleasure and desire in sex education materials, to continue partnerships with disability justice and reproductive justice, [and] to advocate for and believe in coalitions that enable equitable and accessible futures" (p. 194).

What Is It "to do" Sex Ed?

Citizens must have policy, both at federal and state levels, that affirms delivery of CSE with an empowered social justice approach! CSE should be honed so that it is in the most research supported, and inclusive form, plus it should be taught in an affirming, skill-building format. Furthermore, it should be taught by academically prepared and trained educators in order for our students and our citizens in society, to be sexually healthy and well. It is time to move beyond AOUM, which is a narrow, agenda-driven, morals-only model, We need to take the pathology-focus away from sex/ual/ity. We are no longer served from a public health-only approach, nor can the risk reductionists, so harried and overworked from being in the streets night after night, tackle the complexity of sex/ual/ity challenges.

The religious, the medical practitioners, the clinicians, the community-based workers walk into a bar … no, there's no joke here. In all sincerity, perhaps a round or two of darts can be the catalyst for the building of a super team? It is *essential* that we achieve intersectionality among these knowledgeable and invested disciplines. We can all move one step forward and identify, own, exclaim: human sex/ual/ity and expression is normal! It is not a simple right, but simply right. It is imperative that this society reach the conclusion: all people should have access to and be provided a quality, well-defined, research supported and medically accurate curriculum in Sex Ed. This should be taught by a trained, certified sexuality educators so that praxis is employed via personal reflection, critical thinking, decision making, and skill building for empowered students advancing an agenda of a sexually healthy life. This is the clarion call that James T. Sears (1992) and those whose informed work are featured in *Sexuality and the Curriculum*. This is the determined battle cry that Dennis Carlson voiced over the decades that he reviewed history and analyzed political ideologies. This is the call to arms that Marty Klein's (2012) book, *America's War on Sex* demands. Who will lead the charge now?

The last word belongs to one of my most amazing undergraduate students. I believe this insight candidly speaks to who needs to lead.

> **Instead of making kids feel embarrassed about sex or timid about it, we should encourage parents to be open-minded and honest about the topic. I feel like I missed out on so much because my parents never sat me down to have the sex talk explain the process of puberty. I am grateful that they were not psychotic parents who had one view and only one view about sex, but I am definitely frustrated that they did not have any opinions about it that they shared with me. How was I supposed to form my own opinions and thoughts about sex when I was not even informed about the topic from my own parents? Aren't parents supposed to be your primary sex educators? In my situation, my primary sex educator was my sixth grade science teacher. In sum, the extent of my sex education was my sixth grade Health class and some occasional discussions with my older sisters. As a result, I still feel like there are many things regarding sex that I am completely unfamiliar with. Because of this, when I have children of my own, I will be sure to be open and honest with them when it comes to discussing puberty and sex so they can be both informed and comfortable with the topics. (Personal communication, FSW 365 undergraduate at Miami University)**

REFERENCES

Carlson, D. L. (2012). *The education of Eros: A history of education and the problem of adolescent sexuality*. New York, NY: Routledge.

Gill, M. (2015). *Already doing it: Intellectual disability and sexual agency*. Minneapolis, MN: University of Minnesota Press.

Klein, M. (2012). *America's war on sex: The continuing attack on law, lust, and liberty*. Santa Barbara, CA: Praeger.

Sears, J. T. (Ed.). (1992). *Sexuality and the curriculum: The politics and practices of sexuality Education*. New York, NY: Teachers College Press.

CHAPTER 2

OUR CHILDREN ARE NOT FOR SALE

How the "Manufactured Crises" Has Commodified Our Public Schools and Students

Cleighton J. Weiland

"The ideal of oppression was realized by this dismal servitude.... When they find themselves in such condition at the dawn of existence- so young, so feeble, struggling among men- what passes in these souls fresh from God?"

Hugo and Wilbour (1992)

THE CURRICULA OF CHILD LABOR

The structural similarities between school buildings and old factories are strikingly similar, with their brick exteriors and tall edifices. What secrets do your walls hide, old factory? What jobs did your industrial workers perform? What defining events transpired within you from yesteryear? Peer into the windows of the factory as whispers from the past take shape.

Curriculum Windows: What Curriculum Theorists of the 1990s Can Teach Us About Schools and Society Today, pp. 17–30
Copyright © 2017 by Information Age Publishing
All rights of reproduction in any form reserved.

17

See the work floor of Indiana Glassworks, where hundreds of small bodies navigate a web of pipes and gears. Many of these "career-ready" employees are not yet shaving but work late into the night, their dangerous employ illuminated by a single weak and flickering bulb … slivers of glass surround their still growing feet. Or think on the weed of a youth under 14, a young cigar maker at Engelhardt & Company, sampling his factory's wares. And let us take a look at the young female knitters of London Hosiery Mills in Tennessee deftly weaving thread through the crunchy, crushing, killing gears of unforgiving machines (Freedman & Hine, 1994).

A quiet murmur is heard. Like a forgotten memory the conscience is pricked. Look away from the window of the factory and the repulsion within. Listen to the voice of one crying out in the wilderness. Can we not see "the withering of child lips in the poisoned air of factories; the strained look of child eyes that never dance to the glad music of souls tuned to Nature's symphonies… [?]"; Indeed, who would ever dare "tally the death of childhood's hopes, ambitions and dreams" stillborn on the floors of industry (John Spargo, 1906 as cited by Goldstein, 1976, p. 48).

As the gears of time spin and wear on, so the needs of business grow and evolve. Mercy arrived and industry no longer demands such dismal indentureship and shameless exploitation in the United States. Yet if we peer long enough into childhood, we find that the horrors of the factory floors have begun to sneak back into children's life experiences through new educational legislation and practice. Hidden in the circumlocutions of reform, government policies have gladly marched big business into the hallways and classrooms of our public schools, consequently commodifying our children's education and wilting democratic principles of citizenry. Public schools have slowly become transformed from placid learning communities into automatized meritocratic systems of achievement that award those most privileged and punish those dwelling in poverty. Similar to child labor, schools must offer children up at the altar of big business. Berliner and Biddle's book, *The Manufactured Crisis* (1995), draws back the curtains of corporate greed and government rhetoric to reveal a triple-paned window: the pane of extensive government propaganda; a complex pane using the word play of inequity and iniquity; and a final pane culminating in the workings of big business and its financial interests in schools.

A WINDOW PANE OF PROPAGANDA

"They seem not men, but forms fashioned of the living dark…. What is required to exorcise these goblins? Light. Light in floods! No bat resists the dawn. Illuminate the bottom of society."

Hugo and Wilbour (1992)

Like many children, I relished the moment when my father walked through the front door of our house at the end of his workday. After greeting his children, my dad would gather up the newspaper and sit down on the couch or at the dining room table to read the latest headlines, scan the op-eds, and learn about local happenings. I chuckle as I think about how we would hang around his neck, pestering him for attention until he set aside the headlines and read us the latest iterations of *Family Circus* or *Garfield*. These interactions bleed into a hybrid of reminiscence, perhaps a snapshot of days long past that are relegated to the corners of my thoughts. Undeniably, many of these events occurred while I was barely old enough to hold onto a memory. However, one particular instance of this newspaper routine remains etched into my mind.

I recall my father reading through an article on education that provoked verbal consternation and indignation on his part. The article likely nuanced the failings of schools, the incompetence of teachers, and the economic fallout of poor educative experiences. One moment I certainly recall with clarity was when my father voiced his disgust at the academic ineptitudes of students born out of a futile public school system. In retrospect, I believe the information contained in the newspaper at least partially guided my parents' decision-making in respect to my own schooling experiences. My parents forwent my kindergarten year completely and ordered a packaged homeschool curriculum, converting a room in our basement into a classroom complete with charts, desks, and books. I soon learned that school meant endless hours lost in confusing workbooks and few social interactions with the outside world: a functional incarceration. After two mind-numbing years of boredom and verbal spats with my teacher (i.e., my mom), my parents raised the white flag and enrolled me in a private, sectarian school. Entering third grade, I felt nearly illiterate, unable to read grade level text with any degree of confidence or fluidity. For our family the homeschool experiment was a failure, perhaps caused by a misplaced trust in what turned out to be government propaganda.

Irrespective of the actual source of information my parents used to make their decisions regarding my schooling, very likely the education critiques they read sprang from the report titled *A Nation at Risk* (United States National Commission on Excellence in Education, 1983). *A Nation at Risk* is a document commissioned by then-President Reagan based on "the widespread public perception that something is seriously remiss in our educational system" (n.p.). As described by McIntush (2000), *A Nation at Risk* inserted new vocabulary into the conversation playing on metaphors of war and peril, impending doom, and urgency. A subtle shift of dogma was inserted in public discourse including free-market ideology and the introduction of education serving individual interests as opposed to a public or democratic good. The purposes of public schools were forever altered from a lever of social and political equalization to a means of achieving economic prosperity. Indeed, the results of the report captured the public's imagination and legitimized federal efforts to reform the public school system. Certainly, *A Nation at Risk*, its related studies, and reports armed ideologues and reform advocates for decades with rhetorical ammunition with which to dismantle and reformulate public schooling through the 1990s and beyond. And as we have seen, the U.S. Department of Education has played an important role in advancing the neoliberal reform agenda spawned by *A Nation at Risk*.

Although addressed as "An Open Letter to the American People," what was the real purpose and design behind the document? After all, then Secretary of Education T. H. Bell initially thought his cabinet appointment would be short-lived as President Reagan had vowed during his electoral campaign to dismantle the U.S. Department of Education, an institution that still thrives today. I propose that the document served as an agent of propaganda, ground zero in reforming education to reflect new principles to fuel and feed economic engines of private enterprise.

As Vlăduțescu (2014) submits, propaganda is subtle, but clear. It is a form of persuasion coupled with approximations, followed by manipulations and disinformation. Propaganda is what fueled child labor proponents to suggest that economic profits rested on the shoulders of child workers. And similar to the shame of child labor, *A Nation at Risk* plays the same sickening melody used to justify the merry-go-round of injustice, encumbering schools and children with irrelevant economic statistics and findings that simply have no substance. Propaganda hides itself in the facts or behind seemingly objective information. The motor of propaganda is suggestion and the more suggestive the presentation of information, the better.

Vlăduțescu (2014) delineates several aspects required for the presentation of ideas to be regarded as propaganda including: a doctrine, a program, a synthesis of information culminating into a slogan, all of which become symbolic platforms to make policy. *A Nation at Risk* was as Orwellian as they come as the report took facts and threaded them with ideology. For propaganda to truly have an impact, the form must be realized as a contagion that exasperates an already innate desire or feeling within the public at large. During the 1960s and 1970s, public schools were flooded with monies in order to combat numerous social problems; the perceived failure of economic investment in public schools brought disillusionment and dissatisfaction (Berliner & Biddle, 1995). Propaganda is mono-thematic, functioning as a set of sequenced messages on a single topic or set of facts (Vlăduțescu, 2014). *A Nation at Risk* was the progenitor of numerous subsequent reports, all of which fostered a perception of schools as failing. Finally, when the doctrine is reified through slogans, it forms a trend of public opinion. The Presidential Commission was wildly successful in reifying the term "at-risk" as a slogan implying a need for change. With this report the public's conception of schools was blanketed as violent, unsafe, unsuccessful, inept, and needing federal intervention in order to preserve society and economic prosperity. In a sense, *A Nation at Risk* was its own curriculum for the masses, serving to foster the belief that our schools and consequently society are perishing, and that educational decisions were better made by the social elites. These slogans continue to litter the highways and byways of education through reform movements such as *No Child Left Behind* and *Race to the Top*, which provide provocative images that engender uncertainty, and deflate the public's will to question, critique, and resist new reforms.

Propaganda loses its power and momentum when confronted with counter-propaganda. Counter-propaganda locates the thesis, attacks its weaknesses, and places the opponent's propaganda in contradiction with the facts (Vlăduţescu, 2014). Such was the work by Berliner and Biddle (1995) in their opus, *The Manufactured Crisis*. According to Berliner and Biddle, the phrase "manufactured crisis" is a reference to a campaign of public school criticisms and reproaches launched by the American government. Written "in outrage," Berliner and Biddle used their book to address the "myths, half-truths, and sometimes outright lies" of the propaganda launched at American's schools through "reason and displays of relevant evidence" (p. 4). Using an array of graphs, tables, asides, narratives, stories, and other artifacts, Berliner and Biddle's work served as an apologetic for the effectiveness of public schools. Yet, their work was more than counter-propaganda. Berliner and Biddle's book uncovered the realities of public schools through careful scholarship, empirical research, and data analysis; revealing a maligned but dynamic and efficacious educational system.

Berliner and Biddle (1995) also attacked governmental propaganda by refocusing America's attention back on the real problems of public schools such as income and wealth inequities; racial, religious, and linguistic diversity; prejudice, discrimination, unequal access to rigorous academic courses for students of color; and social problems such as violence and drugs. In addition, they critiqued weak reform ideas and offer their own suggestions for school improvement, all of which will be discussed in this chapter. Although the work served as a shining light in the dark rhetoric foisted on the public by *A Nation at Risk*, ultimately public opinion had already been determined. Schools had lost their credibility through a well-crafted governmental campaign. However, the conversation still matters as the missteps of the 1990s continue to plague today's education policies, heaping injustice and inequities on the shoulders of our children...much like we always have.

A WINDOW PANE OF INEQUITY/INIQUITY

"Motivated by pity, compassion, and a sense of patriotism, they argued that, for the child, labor was a delusion; for industry it was a fallacy; and for society, a menace. Child labor means the spread of illiteracy and ignorance … the perpetuation of poverty … and in the end, racial degeneracy."

Trattner (1970)

As a child, there are indelible moments that stain and remain fixed in my consciousness. Although not always preeminent, memories emerge at the oddest of times, as if waiting to be exhumed and puzzled over. The summer of 1994 was one such time where I can only think, reflect, and wonder at the events of my own life. From my recollection, my family had just finished a garage sale where we sold off much of our furniture, toys, and other household essentials. We also moved some other things into storage and had what might appear to be a traditional moving day, when we packed numerous items into cars and left our house. Later that night, surrounded by darkness, rain, and lightening we put up our tents and embarked on a new type of living that no one wants to talk about: homelessness.

Our move to the campground was not our first brush with poverty. My late elementary and middle school years were marked with changes in schools, late notices from utility companies, variable access to healthcare, and frenzied court proceedings regarding child custody during and after my parents' divorce. Even today as I stand in the check-out line at the grocery store, I still am periodically immersed in the image of my 10 and 11 year-old self with the family's groceries in one hand and food stamps in the other. Government subsidies were how my family survived during those years. However, even with welfare income, the effects of poverty enveloped even mundane events. When I was about 12, I was bitten by a dog and required treatment at the doctor's office. I grabbed the Medicaid card and walked five miles to receive treatment. Such are the life and times of nearly a quarter of our nation's children living below the poverty line.

My eventual educational resiliency was not catalyzed by more rigorous academic standards, better teachers, more efficient pedagogies, or increasing accountability measures and government surveillance. My personal successes and failings in school were prompted by the numerous social conditions and perhaps internal qualities that had little to do with the school I attended or the public education I received. Despite the economic difficulties I endured, there were assets available to me that served as bulwarks to stymie some of the alienation of poverty, including a rich verbal familial environment, parents who valued literacy, a home emphasis on character development, participation in a religious community, my own latent academic potential, and a fundamental acceptance that educational success could translate into a more flourishing life. I understand conditions of poverty because I have experienced the effects and have emerged as an exception due to social assets beyond my control. Educational reform obfuscates the destructive nature of poverty that fuels our plutocracy, subtracting robust democratic experiences that would otherwise energize the struggle for critical analysis and our communal responsibility for one another.

Berliner and Biddle's (1995) book *The Manufactured Crisis* attempted to change the conversation from disingenuous test scores and data to the inherent inequities in resources for families in schools. According to a recent report from National Center for Children in Poverty (2015), "Among all children, 44 percent live in low-income families and approximately one in every five (22 percent) live in poor families" (n.p.). Currently, a family qualifies as "poor" if total earning for a familial unit of four with two children is $23,624 or less. A family of four including two children earning less than $47,248 land below the "low-income" threshold. The significance of these statistics stems from the strong correlation between academic achievement and poverty. Here is where Berliner and Biddle (1995) make their strongest case regarding America's schools: "some American schools are terrible places. This is certainly true, but it is largely true because those schools lack resources and must contend with some of society's worst social problems" (p. 144). Like my own experiences of poverty, Berliner and Biddle clearly articulate that poor academic experiences are the result of social issues such as poverty that exist beyond the scope and influence of classrooms. Their contestations continue to echo in contemporary scholarship, including Stern (2013) who suggests good schools have:

> children who have parents with fair-wages, [who] have access to healthcare and nutrition, live in safe neighborhoods, aren't racially profiled ... [have] access to early childhood care and pre-kindergarten ... [and] have well paid teachers who work in decent environments and are encouraged to collaborate. (p. 217)

Yet, these are not the policy reforms that lie on the desks of politicians, as they are expensive and require a reconceptualization as to how our economy operates as well as how we determine the value of children. It's simply easier and more efficient to draw up a set of common standards and design high-stakes tests to show students' skill at filling in the bubbles.

I posit that the very failings of our low income students and the current high stakes standards (suggested by some as "minimum proficiencies") produce the result they are designed for; low test scores that translate into corporate profits ... racketeering to the nines. In light of *Race to the Top*, our nation's most recent educational reform, Ravitch (2013) noted:

the Race to the Top competition abandoned the traditional idea of equality of educational opportunity ... the new billions of federal funding encouraged entrepreneurs to enter the education market. Almost overnight, consultants and venders offered their services to advise districts and states on how to design teacher evaluation systems, how to train teachers, how to train principals, how to turn around failing schools. (p. 15)

Corporate greed and avarice yearns for a slice of the 500 billion dollar plus a year budgets appropriated to schools. This is simply the nature of capitalism as it "demands a growing spiral of investment, production, distribution, and sales ... [indeed] the capitalist economy will collapse unless mass populations purchase a constantly increasing volume of consumer products and services" (Kersplebedeb, 2014, n.p.). For capitalism to survive, doors must be opened to new horizons, or in other words, the privatization of public sectors lends itself to corporate profit. For us, the public sector encapsulates the lives of our children. The "For Sale" sign is in the window and commercial vendors have come a-calling. How did schools come to be in such a dark place? How did progressive ideals of education get swallowed up by big business? Where did those values come from?

A WINDOW PANE OF CORPORATE INTERESTS

During the late 1800s America had an agenda. The plan involved the capturing of munificent riches and natural resources of the land through a westward expansion. The luring promise of wealth and the potential for affluence and power served as lubricant for motorizing the engines of industry and capitalism. However, corporate and national interests could only be realized if the labor could be supplied. As Hindman (2001) purports, this opportunity posed a particular dilemma for America as the labor supply was generally filtered to meet the demands of agriculture as the shadow of "free" labor had been eviscerated through the emancipation of black slaves during the Civil War. A natural solution to the problem arose through the arrival of little hands to run big machines. As the value of education arose in the consciousness of society, the question of what constituted true educative experience was often interlaced with corporate interests.

Many of the early manufactories were called "spinning schools" and received their public support on account of their alleged educational value. The curriculum involved bringing girls in to learn the arts of industrial spinning and, when they had become proficient, putting them out to homework to spin. (p. 58)

Presently, one would be hard-pressed to find a college or university that offers a major in spinning as the idea certainly seems anachronistic. However, if we fast forward 125 years to the present day, the ideal of spinning schools still exists, the metaphor and practice shrouded by "accepted" modern day terminology such as "career-readiness". In other words, today's political milieu has repurposed public schools into technical and corporate training sites as opposed to thoughtful learning communities, guided by the notion of human capital theory.

Human capital theory served as the driving force in the redesign of curricula in America's schools during the 1990s. According to Berliner and Biddle (1995), human capital proper is the notion that "education should be thought of as 'investing' in human resources and that appropriate investments in education can benefit industry and fuel the national economy" (p. 141). Corporations and businesses embraced the idea of having schools produce equipped workers who could more readily enter the workforce without a need for additional professional training and/ or internships. Supposedly, public schools should bear this responsibility by providing curricular experiences that were heavy in the math and sciences in order to alleviate the cost of industry training and insure a more competitive workforce in the global marketplace. According to Berliner and Biddle, these extensive instructional modifications are expensive and bound to become unfunded mandates. Berliner and Biddle assert that there is virtually no evidence to suggest that human capital theory can be effectively used as a tool to train children for the workforce. Once again, we have businesses hoping to recapitulate the ideas of spinning schools, which were only "schools" in the most duplicitous sense. Our national heritage is to profit from children any way we can, however the form has changed in order to protect our sentimentalities and our consciences.

In Joel Spring's book (1972) *Education and the Rise of the Corporate State*, he describes how schools evolved to reflect highly organized cooperate structures as they emerged out of the industrial revolution. Individuals were conceptualized as "whirring gears" and "specialized cogs" (p. 167) constructed to passively fill assigned roles and duties within a vast corporate machine. According to Spring, faith in technological and mechanical efficiency powered government reform efforts in schools. Although Spring's book is over 40 years old, it described the continual evolution of schools existing in "streamlined form of scientific management" (p. 169) where children can follow a "predictive chart" (p. 169) flowing smoothly through school like computerized automatons, much like the labor in factories. Although efficient, the cost of living in a technocratic and mechanized society are steep, requiring students to become "things" as the "needs of the system determine the form of [sic] his behavior" (p. 171).

Elliot Eisner (2001) claimed that for a school activity to be educational, it must support the unfolding of a child's development. He channels John Dewey as he notes that education must "increase the organism's ability to secure meaning from experience and to act in ways that are instrumental to the achievement of inherently worthwhile ends" (p. 37). Berliner and Biddle (1995) note that meaningful education includes various components including depth, duration, and complexity of curricular experiences, features of which are absent in a narrow curricula that feeds corporate interests. Currently our nation's schools use a banking model of education where instruction is dropped into repository of the student's mind to be later spewed out onto the scantron test (Freire, 1970). Curricular experiences for students should encompass experiences that are complex, fully-orbed, profound, dynamic, and beautiful; that is reflective of real life. Education viewed through the lens of test preparation is a serious distortion of legitimate learning, as it reduces education to a simple datum and excludes other experiences that are worthwhile and morally defensible.

In contrast to the human capital theory that inculcates students into becoming resources that benefit the national economy, Berliner and Biddle (1995) suggest that public schools should provide curricular experiences that are contextualized, sequenced, and accommodate a broad base of student interests. That is to say, students are not designed for rigid sequences of instruction, but instruction should be designed for the learner to unearth and showcase his or her unique qualities since human life cannot be constrained to paper and pencil tests. Berliner and Biddle point out the obvious which has been lost in our national conversation when they suggest, "studies have shown that students are more likely to achieve when they are offered materials that are interesting and relevant to their needs than when they are coerced" (p. 131). Neoliberal reformers love prepackaged curricula as it provides a uniform and predictable outcome; a child filling in the correct bubbles on a standardized test using a click of the mouse. However, this type of test prep training has the unintended consequence of restricting the classroom experience to the acquisition of dead knowledge and fill-in the blank automation. Furthermore, this lifeless information never contextualizes or actualizes into anything meaningful in a child's life, but depersonalizes children by pressing them into standardized molds that are powered by the impersonal ideology of neoliberalism.

Berliner and Biddle (1995) also champion educative experiences that promote constructive and creative use of leisure time, which lies in stark contrast to current policies emphasizing math and language arts over other educative experiences. As students and adults are engaging in an increasing number of hours connected to media comprised of television, Smartphones, YouTube, and social media, this recommendation is perhaps even more apropos in today's milieu. Educational experiences that promote responsible use of leisure time and activities would likely pose a side benefit to society and employers by decreasing social fragmentation and isolation and promoting richer, more flourishing lives through responsible activity.

CLOSING THOUGHTS

"Resolved...that childhood is endowed with certain inherent and inalienable rights, among which are freedom from toil for daily bread; the right to play and dream... the right to an education that we may have equality of opportunity for developing all that there is in us of mind and heart."

McKelway (1913 as cited by Trattner, 1970)

The 1990s ended and the era of No Child Left Behind, Common Core State Standards, and national high-stakes standardized testing have continued in earnest. These initiatives have usurped local control and radically changed the landscape of public schools. I believe that many of Berliner and Biddle's (1995) deepest fears regarding public schools in 1995 have been realized now 20 years later. Our schools have become test prep factories, where information is downloaded onto students' computerized brains for later output on high-stakes, high-stress, artificial tests that may have nothing to do with students' realized lives. This conception of students assumes that a passive, receptive, and imitative learning style is superior to learning that is active, creative, and socially conscious (Tienken, 2013). Paulo Freire fittingly asserted, "Education should be used as a transformational mechanism to improve lives rather than a tool to train and inculcate people to imitate and be subservient to the dominant culture" (p. 304, as cited by Tienken, 2013). Education is not simply transferring or downloading information to the minds of children as our current Common Core Standards reflect. To suppose it as such demeans children and robs them of their human dignity and basic rights as individuals. Grant and Gibson (2010) reflect:

> we see a mandate for education that contributes to self-realization and to a flourishing and whole life. This vision not only reframes education as a public good rather than a marketable commodity; it also demands that education be directed toward cultivating an informed and democratic citizenry. (p. 95)

Berliner and Biddle (1995) attempted to confront ideology and defend the value of children as they accurately laid out the neoliberal battle plan that would quickly hijack U.S. public education. Essentially, the strategy included free market reforms, privatization, and nationalized standards (i.e., nationalized curricula by default), coupled with national tests of student achievement. In addition, sanctions against school districts and individual teachers (through value-added evaluations) would serve as a "cattle prod" to help insure higher test scores. In the current zeitgeist, these reforms have infiltrated our psyche and appear as common sense approaches to improving schools. However, as Berliner and Biddle accurately assert, these reforms are catalysts to greater inequities among students, particular those who are regarded as disadvantaged.

I often wonder how our nation with its current norms could have ever endured the notion of child labor. How could we have normalized such a deep moral affront to our most vulnerable members? Indeed, normalization and rationalization often serve as components of oppression. Perhaps there was a degree of groupthink that occurred where morally intolerable views became accepted as part of the self-enhancing process of the group. Prilleltensky and Gonick (1996) state, "By portraying members of subordinate groups as undeserving, agents of domination morally exclude them from norms of behavior that the agents would apply to themselves" (p. 137). Or maybe our progenitors supposed they were doing a social good by employing these children, despite such harsh and inhumane conditions? Such self-taught lies often serve as a form of cognitive dissonance whereas individuals will seek consistency regarding their beliefs. When one's beliefs are out of balance with their associated actions, one has to change or deal with continuous tensions. Conceivably in the event of child labor, these employers of children believed that the poor have somehow merited mistreatment. Such justifications sound hollow to our modern ears, as indeed they do not reflect the truths of these children or the nature of their oppression, particularly when confronted with the reality:

> Chained, belted, harnessed like dogs in a go-cart, black, saturated with wet, and more than half-naked—crawling upon their hands and feet, and dragging their heavy loads behind them—[the children] ... present an appearance indescribably disgusting and unnatural. (D'Avolio, 2004, p. 115)

At times, the activities of past generations often appear barbaric, naive, and calloused. How will our treatment of children today in test-prep schools be judged by future generations? What will our educative legacy be? Will our emphasis on testing, accountability, and rigid standardization be interpreted along the same lines as child labor; an embarrassing chapter of injustice shelved in the library of history?

According to Pinar (2004), "Writing behavioral objectives, evaluating with standardized tests, presenting material in linear, lock-step fashion ... these solutions have failed" (p. 7). Educational mechanization and efficiency have blossomed into an obsession with quantification which reduces educational experiences to a decontextualized set of bottom-line test scores. Prepackaged curricular standards superimpose values that commandeer more important detours that have potential to foster meaningful childhood experiences. The reform movement has led our nation's schools into a dead-end curricula ally that is an inch wide and an inch thick with respect to democratic spaces and critical discourse. Rather than reform, we need a revolution of curricular experiences that spark exploration, expression, and experimentation. Berliner and Biddle (1995) close their book, by suggesting that "compassion in education is an utter necessity if we in America are to realize our long-held aspirations for equality, justice, true democracy, and a decent standard of living for us all" (p. 350). Berliner and Biddle's legacy is clear: it's time to take down the "For Sale" sign from our school windows and pursue a new agenda that values children, and stands in solidarity against forces that seek to manipulate and exploit our heritage. After all, we eliminated child labor as a normalized aspect of our capitalist economy. We have the moral understanding to stop the same trend in our public schools. Can we return to providing our children true educative experiences? Do we have the moral will to end the abuse and champion the lives of our children?

REFERENCES

Berliner, D. C., & Biddle, B. J. (1995). *The manufactured crisis: Myths, fraud, and the attack on America's public schools*. Reading, MA: Addison-Wesley.

D'Avolio, M. (2004). Child labor and cultural relativism: From 19th century America to 21st century Nepal. *Pace. Int'l L. Rev.*, *16*, 109.

Eisner, E. W. (2001). *The educational imagination: On the design and evaluation of school programs* (3rd ed.). Upper Saddle River, NJ: Prentice-Hall.

Freire, P. (1970). *Pedagogy of the oppressed*. New York, NY: Continuum.

Freedman, R., & Hine, L. W. (1994). *Kids at work: Lewis Hine and the crusade against child labor*. Boston, MA: Houghton Mifflin Harcourt.

Goldstein, H. (1976). Child labor in America's history. *Journal of Clinical Child Psychology*, 47–50.

Grant, C. A., & Gibson, M. L. (2013). "The path of social justice": A human rights history of social justice education. *Equity & Excellence in Education*, *46*(1), 81–99.

Hindman, H. D. (2002). *Child labor: An American history*. Armonk, NY: M. E. Sharpe.

Hugo, V., & Wilbour, C. (1992). *Les misérables* (Modern Library ed.). New York, NY: Modern Library.

Jiang, Y., Ekono, M., & Skiller, C. (2015). Basic facts about low income children. New York, NY: National Center for Children in Poverty. Retrieved from http://www.nccp.org/publications/pub

Kersplebedeb. (2014, May 1). The worker elite: Notes on the "Labor Aristocracy" [Text]. Retrieved April 7, 2015, from https://www.leftwingbooks.net/book/content/worker-elite-notes-%E2%80%9Clabor-aristocracy%E2%80%9D

McIntush, H. G. (2000). Defining education: The rhetorical enactment of ideology in A Nation at Risk. *Rhetoric & Public Affairs, 3*(3), 419–443.

Pinar, W. (2004). *Understanding curriculum: An introduction to the study of historical and contemporary curriculum discourses.* New York, NY: Lang.

Prilleltensky, I., & Gonick, L. (1996). Polities change, oppression remains: On the psychology and politics of oppression. *Political Psychology,* 127–127.

Vlăduțescu, Ş. (2014). Twelve communicational principles of propaganda. *International Letters of Social and Humanistic Sciences,* (23), 71–80.

Ravitch, D. (2013). *Reign of error: The hoax of the privatization movement and the danger to America's public schools* (1st ed.). New York, NY: Alfred A. Knopf.

Spring, J. (1972). *Education and the rise of the corporate state.* Boston, MA: Beacon Press.

Stern, M. (2013). Bad teacher: What race to the top learned from the "race to the bottom." *Journal for Critical Education Policy Studies, 11*(3), 194–229.

Tienken, C. H. (2013). Neoliberalism, social Darwinism, and consumerism masquerading as school reform. *Interchange, 43*(4), 295–316.

Trattner, W. I. (1970). *Crusade for the children: a history of the National Child Labor Committee and child labor reform in America.* Chicago, IL: Quadrangle Books.

United States National Commission on Excellence in Education. (1983). *A nation at risk: The imperative for educational reform: a report to the Nation and the Secretary of Education, United States Department of Education.* Washington, DC: National Commission on Excellence in Education.

CHAPTER 3

THE STORIES OF RALPH TYLER AND ELLIOT EISNER

Contesting Accountability Job Creep Into the Field of Curriculum

Kurtz Miller

This is the second consecutive year I have served as a curriculum special-ist in a large, urban school district in the State of Ohio. During the past couple of school years, I have contemplated the field of curriculum, what it encompasses, what it excludes, and its apparent nuances, and I have also reflected upon how the pressures of school-accountability have inhibited the important work curriculum directors and specialists should be doing to improve the practice of professional teaching. For four weeks in February and March of 2015, I monitored a high-stakes, Partnership for Assessment of Readiness for College and Careers (PARCC) testing room at one of our district's PK–8 buildings. Almost every day started out the same way, by reading the standard testing script about what the students should do and what they should not do during the timed testing period. Thankfully, I was armed with a detailed 200-page long PARCC testing manual to help me

Curriculum Windows: What Curriculum Theorists of the 1990s Can Teach Us About Schools and Society Today, pp. 31–49
Copyright © 2017 by Information Age Publishing
All rights of reproduction in any form reserved.

to identify solutions to the hundreds of possible error codes that could be generated in the online testing environment.

Many of the students and teachers were unprepared for the new format of the online, high-stakes testing environment, so I was prepared to troubleshoot technology problems, solve error codes, adjust settings on the computers, aide students in understanding how to use the on-screen features, and even help teachers learn how to log into the testing system for the first time. Beyond putting out numerous fires for 4 weeks, I had plenty of time to read Marsh and Willis' (1995) classic, well-circulated, synoptic text, *Curriculum Alternative Approaches, Ongoing Issues*. I spent time reflecting upon the contours of the modern curriculum world behind the tapestry of the evolving high-stakes testing environment of PARCC. It is my hope that this chapter will provide a venue for me to critique the current status of the curriculum field in public education by using Marsh and Willis' work through the insightful lens of the curriculum work being conducted at the National Art Educators' Association (NAEA).

I chose the Marsh and Willis (1995) text because I have an interest in critiquing and understanding the field of curriculum in our modern age of accountability. Although I work in the curriculum field on a daily basis and have a Curriculum, Instruction, and Professional Development (CIPD) license through the Ohio Department of Education, I was never actually required to take a formal course in curriculum studies. So, I was pleased to read an accessible textbook with a solid treatment of the curriculum field for practitioners like myself. According to Schubert, Schubert, Thomas, and Carroll (2012), the Marsh and Willis text speaks directly to classroom teachers and curriculum practitioners in school districts. Further, Marsh and Willis used straight-forward language and easy-to-read diagrams throughout the text without losing the discipline-specific language and important themes in the field of curriculum studies.

Overall, the text is balanced and fair in its treatment of the approaches of curriculum planning, the history of curriculum studies, curriculum theorizing, how to go about curriculum development and change, how to plan curriculum, the process of implementing curriculum, and how to evaluate curriculum (Schubert et al., 2012). Further, the textbook also expounded upon how curriculum is a deliberative process conducted by numerous stakeholders, and it also detailed how the curriculum filed is constantly buffeted by ongoing political activity (Schubert et al., 2012). The Marsh and Willis (1995) text has made a significant contribution to the field of curriculum studies as evidenced by the fact that it is currently in its fourth edition. This text continues to be used in curriculum courses around the country to prepare practitioners and scholars to thoughtfully consider diverse approaches to planning, implementing, evaluating, and understanding curriculum (T. Poetter, personal communication, 2015).

The accountability measures associated with the No Child Left Behind (NCLB) Act of 2002 have continued to force curriculum directors and specialists into a "neoliberal straightjacket" (Klaf & Khan, 2010, p. 194) of evaluating, measuring, and testing behavioral objectives, which has inhibited them from engaging in professional curriculum work. The "job creep" of accountability into the field of curriculum was noted by Eisner (1994) in the 1990s when the federal *America 2000* agenda was initiated in an effort to expand the reporting of education data to a wary public. As will be discussed later, Tyler's (1949) rational-linear approach to curriculum planning has had an immense influence upon the state and federal reporting of the successes and failures of public education. Although Tyler's approach initially helped to advance the field of curriculum studies forward, it has been overused by policymakers to support one-dimensional accountability systems, such as those outlined in the NCLB Act of 2002. Further, I will make the argument that the overextension and over usage of the "Tyler rationale" is slowing eroding the professional field of curriculum work.

It is time for a significant paradigm shift in educational accountability to modify one-dimensional testing measures toward a more holistic system, such as that described by Eisner (1994) in *The Educational Imagination: On the Design and Evaluation of School Programs*. The National Arts Education Association (NAEA) has utilized Eisner's artistic approach to curriculum planning to develop nontraditional ways of promoting the expansion of visual and performing arts education across the United States. Through the NAEA curriculum window, along with the support of the classic Marsh and Willis (1995) text, I hope to lay the foundation of an alternative approach to curriculum work in public schools in the United States. With the right forethought and planning, public school curriculum directors and specialists along with the support of those in higher education, private citizens, and advocates in the political arena, can collaborate to reclaim the professional field of curriculum and promote high-quality learning for all students.

EDUCATION IN THE 1990s

Much of the decade of the 1990s the American public was discontent with the public education system. The general public, including business leaders, parents, and politicians, viewed the education system as a failed relic of the past. Folks in higher education and business leaders lamented that students graduating from high school could barely read, write, and think for themselves (Eisner, 1994). Experts around the country vehemently argued that the failure of the public education system could actually threaten the economic competitiveness and vitality of our country. Before the 1990s began, the National Commission on Educational Excellence

(1983) released the ground-shaking report, *A Nation at Risk: The Imperative for Educational Reform*, which had a monumental influence upon public school reform in the 1980s, the 1990s, and beyond. Throughout the 1990s, the public generally supported the expansion of state and federal accountability systems as a means to force improvement upon the education system including the *America 2000* initiative.

America 2000 was a federal reform initiative developed in 1990 by President George H. W. Bush, state governors, and the U.S. Department of Education (Eisner, 1994). This long-term strategy was intended to bring much-needed reform to public education by setting up national goals. Based upon the logic of Tyler's rational-linear approach to curriculum planning, the establishment of national goals for education would help address the apparent shortcomings of public schools by outlining where they should be by the year 2000 (Eisner, 1994). Based upon this argument, public schools could be adequately reformed only if administrators, curriculum leaders, politicians, and teachers had a roadmap of expectations. Further, it would then be possible for leaders in public education to determine if the curriculum goals were being achieved, which, in return, would provide data about the current status of the entire public education system in the United States. Two of the trademarks of the *America 2000* initiative were "the public report card" and "The American Achievement Test" (Eisner, 1994, p. 4). One of the many unintended consequences of the *America 2000* initiative was the exclusion of the arts from the public school curriculum.

The idea behind "the public report card" is strongly connected to Tyler's rational-linear approach to curriculum planning, because it is intimately connected to identifying behavioral objectives and then measuring whether or not students have mastered them (Eisner, 1994, p. 4). Most recently, "the public report card" has been mandated by the reauthorization of the Elementary and Secondary Education Act (ESEA) of 1965, otherwise known as the NCLB Act of 2002. States are now required to have accountability and reporting systems in place to clearly document how public school buildings and districts are performing in terms of student achievement, as well as value-added calculations separated by exceptionality, gender, race, and other factors (Jacobsen, Snyder, & Saultz, 2014). Since NCLB did not stipulate the format of the state-level reporting system, there has been a considerable amount of diversity in how states have decided to organize building and district report cards. Further, a body of evidence suggests that how the report cards are organized has had a large impact upon public perceptions of the quality of schools (Jacobsen, Snyder, & Saultz, 2014). The NCLB-era accountability systems just described can be traced back to the 1990s and the *America 2000* initiative.

The idea of "The American Achievement Test" (Eisner, 1994, p. 4) was also a concept strongly connected to Tyler's rational-linear approach to curriculum planning, because assessment information was deemed necessary to adequately judge whether students were learning and performing at grade-level. Standardized, national tests were needed to demonstrate that the content-specific learning standards were being taught and learned across the country. Such an assessment system would help to collect data about the status of the public education system, which students were learning the content standards, and what buildings/districts were performing at acceptable levels. Both "the public report card" and "The American Achievement Test" were aimed at improving accountability and reporting systems in public education in order to improve student achievement and performance. Most recently, the NCLB Act of 2002 stipulated that states must develop rigorous state assessments to measure student achievement. States have either developed state achievement tests with the help of vendors or joined multi-state assessment consortiums, such as PARCC, to meet the requirements of the NCLB Act of 2002 (Miller, 2014).

The intentions of "the public report card" and high-stakes assessments in the 1990s were good, but there were intrinsic problems with the logic of how they were supposed to work. First of all, there were tens of thousands of school districts across the country, and there was no uniformity in educational courses or programs between districts, so standardized measuring instruments (i.e., high-stakes tests) could not tell the complete story of student achievement and performance (Eisner, 1994). Next, the notion of local control over curriculum stipulates that building and district administrators and teachers have a significant amount of latitude in prescribing what to teach and how to teach it (Eisner, 1994). Without taking into account the reality of the local control of curriculum, accountability systems, such as the *America 2000* initiative and NCLB, are doomed in their attempt to accurately reflect the complexities of the public education system. Finally, in the 1990s, there were monumental differences in community support for education from school building to school building and district to district across the United States. Some children came to school well prepared, while others were multiple grade-levels behind due to a host of reasons from socioeconomic issues to parental involvement.

Unfortunately, according to Eisner (1994), the initial framework for *America 2000* did not mention the arts and how they should be taught in public schools. This oversight generated a backlash and a major lobbying effort from the arts education community. Thankfully, the *America 2000* initiative was later updated to include the arts, but, as Eisner (1994) noted, this addition appeared to be "a reluctant afterthought" (p. 4). In a similar way, the NCLB Act of 2002 did not stress the need for arts education in our nation's schools ("Learning in a Visual Age," n.d.). While it makes sense that there are no mandated testing requirements in the arts areas, this has caused school districts, especially those in urban city centers, to drop art and music classes and programs. Few of my district's twenty elementary school buildings have art or music teachers. Unfortunately, the expansion of state and federal accountability programs between the early-1990s and mid-2000s has resulted in millions of children around the country losing the opportunity to develop skills in creativity, observation, and problem-solving through studying the arts.

The 1990s were a period of time when a lot of policy changes were being formulated to alter the trajectory of public education into the next century. During the late 1980s and early 1990s, before the bull market of the 1990s, there was popular discontent with the economic conditions in America, and the public education system was an easy target for criticism. Business leaders, citizens, and politicians, as they have often done in the past, placed increasing pressure on the public education system to assume responsibility for the lack of highly-qualified workers in the private sector (Pinar, 2011).

A CRITIQUE/REVIEW OF MARSH AND WILLIS

Marsh and Wills' (1995) text is a solid overview of the curriculum field for the school curriculum practitioner. The treatment of the topics in the textbook is not a weak, unscholarly "how to" approach to curriculum, but rather, the authors provided a solid, foundational understanding of the frameworks and theoretical underpinnings of modern curriculum work. The textbook can easily be broken down into three major parts, which outline the central themes of curriculum studies. Part one explains concepts of curriculum planning, the history of the field of curriculum, and curriculum theorizing. The next part details curriculum development, including curriculum change, curriculum planning in action, curriculum implementation, and curriculum evaluation. The final part describes a whole list of ongoing debates and issues taking place in the curriculum field, such as the politics of curriculum work, curriculum decision making, education reform and curriculum, and current trends in curriculum. The Marsh and Willis' (1995) textbook is filled with important contentions, directions, frameworks, and theories about curriculum, so it is impossible to critique and review all aspects of the text. However, I hope to provide a critique of some of the most important points from the work.

The book describes three alternative approaches to curriculum planning, namely the Tyler rational-linear approach, Walker's deliberative approach, and Eisner's artistic approach. Some level of planning is required to prepare educators for teaching, and there are multiple competing frameworks about how to conduct the curriculum planning process.

Probably the most influential framework in the history of the curriculum field is Tyler's rational-linear approach (Tyler, 1949), which was later commonly referred to as "The Tyler Rationale." Tyler (1949) warned readers that his book should not be used as "a manual" about how plan a curriculum (Hlebowitsh, 1992). Unfortunately, "The Tyler Rationale" and its insistence on measuring behavioral objectives has become the standard-operating procedure for nearly all public schools across the entire country and has been institutionalized in the form of high-stakes testing.

According to "The Tyler Rationale," there are four major parts of the curriculum process, and they include identifying objectives, selecting learning experiences, organizing learning experiences, and evaluation (Tyler, 1949). The purpose of the objectives is to formulate the educational purposes for learning. Once the objectives are identified, the curriculum planner is better able to select the most appropriate learning experiences (e.g., lecture, reading, writing, class discussion, etc.) to allow the students to learn the intended content, processes, and/or skills. The curriculum planner or teacher can use the objectives to determine how to best organize or sequence the instructional segments. Upon the completion of the instruction, curriculum planners should evaluate the process to determine what the students learned. The evaluation process, according to Tyler (1949), should move beyond traditional paper and pencil tests to include things such as observations, interviews, questionnaires, and samples of students' work (Marsh & Willis, 1995). Tyler initially identified a whole host of possible avenues for evaluating the "planned curriculum," yet most of the emphasis in the last half century has been upon traditional achievement tests such as state graduation tests and end-of-course exams.

Marsh and Willis (1995) also described the three focal points for making curriculum decisions: the nature of subject matter, the nature of society, and the nature of the individual. The nature of the subject matter pertains to "the content of the curriculum, and choices about what subject matter to include within the curriculum and also choices about what to leave out" (p. 40). Students are usually at school for less than 185 school days per year, and they may interact, for instance, with a physics teacher for only 45 minutes per day for a total of 140 direct instructional hours per academic year. Curriculum planners and teachers must carefully choose what to teach (and what not to teach) during this short instructional window in terms of academic content. Also, curriculum planners and teachers must consider how to most appropriately select the content based on the accuracy of the information, the representation of ideas within the specific disciplines, and the connections between multiple disciplines (Marsh & Willis, 1995). Beyond the academic content, curriculum should also reflect some level of utilitarian value by making the content knowledge applicable to living in society, helping to provide for students' material needs, and making

meaning in a constantly changing world (Marsh & Willis, 1995). The immediate and long-term usefulness of a curriculum is "an important question
in curriculum planning" (Marsh & Willis, 1995, p. 42). Finally, curriculum
planners must contend with the need to help students to grow, personally. School curriculum should aim to help students to develop things
such as artistic skills, attitudes, career interests, spatial relationships, and
values (Marsh & Willis, 1995). Curriculum planners and classroom teachers should identify and organize balanced learning outcomes for a course
on the basis of the nature of subject matter, the nature of society, and the
nature of the individual to maximize the impact on students.

Marsh and Willis (1995) highlighted the process of curriculum implementation. Curriculum development is no doubt an important process, but
actually executing what was planned is just as important. Marsh and Willis
defined curriculum implementation as "the translation of a written curriculum into classroom practices" (p. 205). The planned curriculum is typically
the content of a textbook, as well as what has been written in state content
standards, course syllabi, regular lesson plans, along with what has been
communicated to stakeholders such as parents and students. It is fair to say
that the planned curriculum is almost never followed in its entirety because
teachers must "interpret [and] enact" (p. 206) the planned curriculum.
Because teachers and classroom contexts are unique, there are numerous
ways to enact the planned curriculum. Classroom teachers are constantly
making instructional decisions to adjust to students' individual needs.

Marsh and Willis (1995) echo Eisner (1994) in outlining three types of
curricula, namely the experienced curriculum, the null curriculum, and the
hidden curriculum. The experienced curriculum is how students interpret
the enacted curriculum through classroom learning activities, how the
teachers convey information, and how the students interact with each other.
A classroom of thirty students could potentially produce different learning experiences for each student. Although it may be too time consuming
to constantly monitor the experienced curriculum for a large number of
students, curriculum developers and classroom teachers should at least
consider whether a package is biased against ethnic or minority groups
through bias committee reviews. Next, the null curriculum usually refers
to what is not taught in schools. Because educators do not have enough
instructional time to teach every piece of pertinent knowledge there is a
need to leave information out of the curriculum. Finally, the term "hidden
curriculum" was coined by Philip W. Jackson (1968), and it describes what
is taught but is not part of the formal planned curriculum. The hidden
curriculum may be actively concealed, or it may be entirely unintended
and conveyed through curricular and instructional practices. For instance,
educators may inadvertently teach that girls are not good at science by
calling on boys more often or that compliance is more important than what

is learned by praising those who work quietly more than those whose work is superior. The multiple forms of curriculum require that practitioners and scholars be cognizant of what is being planned, implemented, and evaluated whether it is the planned, experienced, null, or hidden curriculum.

The curriculum evaluation process is another important part of this field of work that can involve formal or informal activities used to determine the effectiveness of curricula applied to a small scale such as a classroom environment or a large scale such as a statewide textbook adoption (Marsh & Willis, 1995). Program evaluations should be conducted using the following principles to keep the data collection process highly focused: (1) Limit data to a few specific foci, (2) Collect only essential data, (3) Use information that is already collected, and (4) Consider the needs of all stakeholders when evaluating data (Marsh & Willis, 1995). Further, program evaluations can provide valuable information if they include artifacts such as " an analysis of the interests, motivations, reactions, and achievements of the students experiencing the curriculum" (Marsh & Willis, 1995, p. 253). Program evaluations should evaluate curriculum questions connected to the teacher, the learner, the subject matter, and/or the milieu (the physical and social setting of the curriculum). Since curriculum is an intellectual as well as a social endeavor, considering the milieu is a powerful way of evaluating its impact on the students and teachers. Unfortunately, according to Marsh and Willis (1995), "the milieu has often been entirely left out of evaluations that focus on objectives and student behaviors" (p. 257).

Marsh and Willis (1995) discuss several models of curriculum evalutation. Tyler's objectives model, which has been the most influential of the models, was derived from Tyler's (1949) *Basic Principles of Curriculum and Instruction*. This model has been the most popular method of curriculum and program evaluation by far because it is a relatively simple design that often utilizes a pre-test and a post-test to measure student learning objectives. Tyler's objectives model has been popular because it emphasizes scientific measurement, objectivity, validity, and reliability which are all considered to be indicators of rigorous evaluation (Marsh & Willis, 1995). According to Marsh and Willis (1995), this model is based upon the logic of the "rational-linear approach to curriculum planning" (p. 277) and a "strict ends-means rationale" (p. 278). Tyler's objectives model is grounded in the notion that "evaluation cannot be done soundly unless based on scientific measurements that precede it" (p. 279). Tyler's objectives model has had a monumental influence upon curriculum program evaluation for the past 60 years, and it is also strongly connected to the logic of high-stakes testing in the modern era of NCLB.

There are some inherent problems and shortcomings of Tyler's objectives model, such as the fact that it does not provide evaluators with the power to make value judgments about the learning objectives (Marsh &

Willis, 1995). Evaluators are not given the flexibility to draw conclusions or make recommendations about the most appropriate learning objectives. Evaluators may also find it difficult to develop recommendations about what changes to make to curricula because the changes in pre and post-test scores can't be fully attributed to the curriculum. Curriculum implementation is a social endeavor involving multiple stakeholders, such as administrators, parents, students, and teachers, who communicate and interact with curricular and instructional materials and pedagogical methods. Because curriculum implementation is such a complex, dynamic process, it is difficult to draw major conclusions about the usefulness of a package by using a single indicator, such as normalized gain scores collected from pre- and posttests or other data analyses. Additionally, Marsh and Willis (1995) contend that using Tyler's objectives model "can [sometimes] lead to sound curricula being altered and unsound curricula being left unchanged" (p. 280).

Marsh and Willis (1995) explored the politics and decision-making within the field of curriculum, as well as historical and current issues connected to curriculum. Three key points pertain to the thesis of this book chapter: the connections between accountability and curriculum, the unfortunate messages curriculum work relays to teachers, and the question about whether curriculum development should be a top down or bottom up process (Marsh & Willis, 1995). The three themes were important in the 1990s, and they continue to be imperative to classroom teachers today.

At first consideration, accountability systems seem reasonable because teachers should have some form of responsibility for high-quality teaching and sound practice. However, as Marsh and Willis (1995) argued, teachers should not be held accountable for what students do not learn, but they should be responsible for good teaching. Modern accountability measures continue to stress the important of holding educators responsible for student achievement as indicated by high-stakes testing scores. Unfortunately, accountability measures often obscure the importance of high quality teaching (Temes, 2003). Further, accountability is creeping in upon real curriculum work because curriculum directors and specialists are spending increasingly large amounts of time working with assessment data, managing testing rooms, and preparing teachers for high-stakes tests like the PARCC. Testing is also increasingly driving instruction in classrooms around the country (Popham, 2014). Data-based decision making and school improvement processes (e.g., the Ohio Improvement Process (OIP) are two ways educators are being required to use linear-rational logic and the fundamentals of accountability measures to force fit curricular and instructional changes.

Next, curriculum work is sending classroom teachers a number of unfortunate messages, including (1) The idea that curriculum development is not the responsibility of the teacher, (2) Testing should drive instruction, (3) It is more important to teach all of the content standards instead of making sure students learn the material, (4) A minimal level of competence is the target, (5) Educational leaders do not trust classroom teachers to develop curriculum, (6) Local programs, innovations, and cultural variations in schools are viewed with little value compared to uniformity, and (7) It is fine for some standards to not be developmentally appropriate for all students (Marsh & Willis, 1995). Like in other fields, such as economics, history and public policy, the law of unintended consequences suggests that initiatives may sometimes result in inadvertent, unplanned problems. Adopting Tyler's rational-linear approach over the past 60 years has resulted in a number of unintended consequences including the unfortunate messages detailed by Marsh and Willis (1995). Adopting any one of the curriculum development or evaluation models has potential to have unintended consequences.

A final ongoing issue connected to the curriculum field is whether this important work should be conducted as a top-down or bottom-up process (Marsh & Willis, 1995). In some circles classroom teachers have a significant level of control over curriculum implementation, but in other areas, teachers feel they do not have the power to adapt content standards to meet the needs of the local community and diverse student populations (Marsh & Willis, 1995). When state and national standards are developed, a small number of classroom teachers typically serve on committees to provide feedback about the draft version before they are released. However, teachers still feel they lack voices and choices because "centralized curriculum planning limits the opportunities teachers have to develop and exercise professional knowledge and skills" (Marsh & Willis, 1995, p. 332). One possible solution to centralized curriculum planning is to empower teachers to exercise "long-term curriculum planning" (Marsh & Willis, 1995, p. 332) so this process can become more balanced as both top-down and bottom up. Although classroom teachers have some professional latitude about how to enact the planned curriculum some rebalancing is needed to give them additional professional freedoms to build bottom up processes for ongoing curriculum development, implementation, and evaluation.

Marsh and Willis' (1995) synoptic text, *Curriculum Alternative Approaches, Ongoing Issues,* is a classic read for practitioners working in the field of curriculum studies. The text is far from a "how to" guide about working in this important field of study. In fact, the treatment of the frameworks, models, and theories is transparent and well-balanced so the readers can determine the best avenue for curriculum development, implementation, and/or evaluation. Tyler's rational-linear approach is detailed in understandable language, and its shortcomings are clearly articulated. Although Tyler's rational-linear approach is ingrained into the fabric of public education, there are alternative approaches to curriculum development and evaluation that should be considered to better balance the accountability pressures on schools.

THE NAEA AS A CURRICULUM WINDOW

The curriculum window for this chapter is the National Art Education Association (NAEA), which is the primary professional organization for art educators in the United States. The NAEA, founded in 1947, boasts over 20,000 elementary, middle school, high school, postsecondary, and museum members in all 50 states. The NAEA empowers art educators with opportunities for advocacy and a voice pertaining to issues in public education, as well as informal learning environments such as after-school programs and museums. Since art education has often been neglected in the realm of public policy, the NAEA has served as an important source for information about how to increase awareness of the arts. Further, the NAEA has also promoted advocacy for the arts through activities such as conferences, community discussion forums, and through formal work of commissions (e.g., the NAEA Commission on Art Education). The NAEA is an excellent example about how activists, administrators, business leaders, citizens, nonprofit organization leaders, and teachers can work together through professional associations to advocate for students in the "digital age" (NAEA, 1978).

One of the most famous and highly respected scholars and supporters of arts education, as well as the NAEA, was Elliot Eisner who was Professor Emeritus of Child Education at Stanford University (Marsh & Willis, 1995). Eisner was one of the most powerful supporters and voices for art education through his research on curriculum and his advocacy work with the NAEA. Eisner was trained as a painter, served as an art teacher, and was also a graduate of the University of Chicago where he interacted with some of the greatest thinkers in the fields of curriculum, education, and evaluation during the 20th century. Eisner published about issues in art education, curriculum development, curriculum evaluation, and the history of the field of curriculum studies (Eisner, 1967, 1994; Marsh & Willis, 1995). Also, Eisner influenced a whole generation of educational scholars about how to study curriculum by advising dozens of doctoral students at Stanford University (Eisner, 1994). During Eisner's life he was intimately linked to the NAEA, and the organization continues to hold his advocacy, scholarship, and work in exceptionally high esteem. The NAEA web site, as well as many of its publications, continue to display evidence of Eisner's lasting influence upon art education in the United States.

A significant body of Eisner's research in the 1960s attacked and challenged curriculum and education scholarship for "overemphasizing such things as behavioral objectives and traditional academic subjects within the school curriculum" (Marsh & Willis, 1995, p. 23). His publications also helped to demonstrate the logical shortcomings of the dominant paradigm of curriculum planning, implementation, and evaluation by exposing its faulty assumptions and inabilities to measure all of the variables in an educational setting. Through much of Eisner's career, there was relatively little qualitative evaluation and research taking place in the educational establishment, and he contested the dominant "empirical-analytic model of educational research" (Marsh & Willis, 1995, p. 23). Eisner's believed there were many ways to plan, implement, learn, and evaluate. Further, he strongly believed that there was a significant artistic component of curriculum development and teaching. In Eisner's view, curriculum practitioners and teachers were like artists, because they had many decisions about how to approach planning, teaching, and evaluating (Marsh & Willis, 1995).

By the 1970s Eisner began to synthesize his ideas on curriculum by publishing a well-acclaimed book titled, *The Educational Imagination: On the Design and Evaluation of School Programs* (Eisner, 1994). The volume is an edited book, but Eisner wrote most of the chapters in it. The book lay out the framework for his artistic approach to curriculum and education (Marsh & Willis, 1995). Eisner's artistic approach to curriculum planning had a total of seven steps, as follows: (1) Goals and their priorities, (2) Content of the curriculum, (3) Types of learning opportunities, (4) Organization of learning opportunities, (5) Organization of content areas, (6) Mode of presentation and mode of response, and (7) Types of evaluation procedures (Marsh & Willis, 1995). As Marsh and Willis (1995) pointed out, the steps in Eisner's artistic approach to curriculum planning looked like the steps in Tyler's rational-linear approach until the steps are fully deconstructed. The differences in the two approaches become apparent in Step 6 (Mode of presentation and mode of response) and Step 7 (Types of evaluation procedures). In Eisner's artistic approach to curriculum planning, students have many diverse opportunities to learn through multiple modalities. Further, Eisner believed that evaluation should take place during the entire process of curriculum implementation instead of just at the end of the instructional segment, which was divergent from the traditions of Tyler's rational-linear approach (Marsh & Willis, 1995). To have a full understanding of the importance of Eisner's work it is also necessary to investigate his educational connoisseurship model for curriculum evaluation.

Traditional models of evaluation, especially those identified as scientifically rigorous, were built around the idea that an evaluator is an objective, passive observer of educational processes. However, Eisner's educational connoisseurship model is different because it empowers the evaluator to become an active participant with those in the field (Marsh & Willis, 1995). In fact, this model is the first to clearly articulate and explain the objectivity-subjectivity debate in program evaluation (Marsh & Willis, 1995). Educational evaluators who subscribe to the positivist paradigm claim to be "objective" while those who use models such as Eisner's are fine with the evaluator interacting and participating with both students and teachers who are being studied without having concerns about "subjectivity." Eisner's educational connoisseurship model may be more powerful than Tyler's objectives model for program evaluation because it allows the evaluator to "apprehend reality available [to him or her]" (Marsh & Willis, 1995, p. 292). Although the evaluator's reality may have some level of subjectivity, a lot of useful contextual information can be obtained by allowing the evaluator the latitude to step outside of the traditional mold she is expected to stay within.

Eisner's model of evaluation is different than Tyler's because it utilizes a divergent means of assessing what takes place in classrooms, as well as new ways of summarizing the major themes of classroom life. According to Marsh and Willis (1995) connoisseurship is "the art of appreciation, especially the ability to make fine discriminations between different qualities" (p. 292). An educational connoisseur, therefore, must be a person who is comfortable and experienced with observing active learning environments in classrooms. It is safe to assume that Eisner would likely argue that a curriculum evaluator using Tyler's objectives model could be a measurement expert but may also lack the necessary experience and skills to successfully act as an educational connoisseur. There are three basic questions an evaluator within the educational connoisseurship paradigm must consider: (1) What do I see in the classroom?, (2) What reflections can I make about what I have experienced?, and (3) How can I render my reflections to others? (Marsh & Willis, 1995). These questions can be used as the starting point for Eisner's three stages of inquiry. The first stage involves observing what happens in the classroom while also comparing it to other classrooms. Next, the second stage allows the connoisseur to identify the "most noteworthy" (Marsh & Willis, 1995, p. 293) traits of the classroom through the process of reflection. The third stage of Eisner's model involves "recreat[ing] in words the various qualities and meanings they have encountered in the classroom" (Marsh & Willis, 1995, p. 293). The third and final stage introduces what Eisner termed educational criticism.

Eisner derived the idea of educational criticism from the art community, because artists are typically well-trained at disclosing, explaining, and judging the merits of artwork. According to Eisner (1985), "the art of disclosing the qualities of events or objects that connoisseurship perceives" is educational criticism (p. 223). Educational criticism has three separate but interrelated processes and they are description, interpretation, and appraisal (Marsh & Willis, 1995). Description involves describing in written form what the evaluator experienced in a classroom setting. Interpretation is connected to the attribution of the meanings and specifics within a classroom. Appraisal is the process of judging the quality of experience the evaluator had in the classroom. An interesting aspect of educational criticism is that it is linguistic and fundamentally qualitative in nature. In fact, educational criticism is a form of constructivist research that has slowly become a more popular method of inquiry within the educational establishment since the 1970s (Marsh & Willis, 1995). Unlike other models of evaluation, it allows the evaluator to use figurative language, artistic expressions, and the latitude to make value judgments about what is observed (Marsh & Willis, 1995). Both educational connoisseurship and educational criticism empower evaluators to make use of qualitative methods and techniques such as structural corroboration, referential adequacy, and triangulation to develop a fuller understanding of what takes place in classrooms (Marsh & Willis, 1995).

Educational practitioners and scholars have argued that teaching is not only a scientific endeavor, but it is also an artistic enterprise (Marazano, 2007). Scientific testing and measurement has its time and place in informing policymakers and educators about what students know and how certain programs are performing. However, there are certain limitations to scientific testing and measurement and the value it adds to the field of curriculum studies. Further, curriculum practitioners and educators must cautiously use data to make decisions because it can sometimes be overused and actually cause more harm than good. The usage of accountability data, such as value-added measures, to make curricular and/or instructional decisions can have long-term, negative, unintended consequences in classrooms and school buildings. The unintended consequences for misusing accountability data in the realm of curriculum and instruction can have significant repercussions on student learning, as well as other important variables, such as improving the conditions of school climate/culture. For instance, high-stakes testing and school accountability data typically do not measure knowledge or skills in the arts, which suggests that these fields are not an important part of school curriculum. Since scientific testing and measurement has its limitations, it is more important now than ever to consider alternative approaches to curriculum planning, implementation, and evaluation, such as the models developed by Eisner.

The curriculum window of the NAEA provides a critical look at how a professional community, namely art educators in the United States, view the current status of public education in the era of NCLB ("Learning in a Visual Age," n.d.). Art educators are disillusioned with the accountability systems of NCLB, but they have not lost hope in promoting the value and the importance of high-quality arts programming. In fact, the arts educa-tion community in the United States, under the auspices of the NAEA, has promoted a series of forums in the 2000s to empower art teachers and community activists to discuss the future of the arts. The commu-nity meetings allowed all voices to be heard in spite of the fact that the education research establishment is set on promoting one central form of evaluation and measurement: those connected to the rigors of scien-tific testing. Eisner's influence upon the art education community and the NAEA serves as an excellent demonstration that there is more than one way to plan, implement, and evaluate school curriculum. Mathematics educators, policymakers, and science education researchers may prefer to rely upon quantitative methods of curriculum planning and evaluation, but specialists in art education and workers in the critical study fields should have the freedom to choose the most appropriate model to use in practical applications and/or in scholarly studies. Unfortunately, classroom teachers, curriculum practitioners, and school district administrators typically do not have any choices about how accountability and evaluation systems are established. Eisner's models for curriculum planning and evaluation gen-erally remain unused in classrooms, school districts, in state departments of education, and at the federal level. The NAEA is an excellent example of how certain segments of educators have embraced alternative frameworks of curriculum planning and evaluation, although the dominant framework used in school districts, states, and at the federal level continues to be those primarily proposed by Tyler.

The NAEA serves an insightful curriculum window to allow educators to see that there are multiple models about how to plan, implement, and evaluate school curriculum. Many curriculum practitioners and educators are not even aware of the fact that there are research-based methods of conducting curriculum work because there is honestly very little curriculum work taking place in public schools today. Before reading Marsh and Willis' (1995) text *Curriculum Alternative Approaches, Ongoing Issues* I was unaware of the various models of curriculum development, implementation, and evaluation, and I have a Curriculum, Instruction, and Professional Devel-opment (CIPD) license! Curriculum directors and specialists are consumed with issues and work connected to accountability, data-based decision making, measurement, and testing which prevents these important people from functioning as developers, implementers, and evaluators of authen-tic, high-quality school curriculum. It is time for activists, administrators, parents, policymakers, and teachers to come together to discuss ways of rebalancing school accountability programs to free up educators around the country to focus upon the important work of promoting high-quality teaching, instruction, and curriculum work in the interest of all students succeeding in the 21st century.

CONCLUSIONS

Tyler, who was "The Father of Educational Evaluation" (Nowakowski, 1983, p. 24) and one of the most prominent education researchers in the 20th century, may be best known in the field of curriculum studies for his models for curriculum planning and evaluation. Tyler's rational-linear approach to curriculum planning and his objectives model for curriculum evaluation have had the greatest impact upon the field of curriculum studies because they are the basis for almost all curriculum work in public schools in the United States. Although there are alternative frameworks and models (e.g., Eisner's educational connoisseurship model) available in the literature for planning, implementing, and evaluating curriculum, Tyler's lasting influence has been monumental in comparison to the others. What has been called "The Tyler Rationale" is intimately connected to the identification and evaluation of behavioral objectives in school curriculum. The curriculum window of the NAEA and the scholarship of Eisner represent a much-needed alternative method of planning and evaluating school curriculum in the United States. The usage of "The Tyler Rationale" needs to be remolded to fix the severe problem of accountability job creep, which is encroaching into the field of curriculum studies. Continuing to rely upon the "The Tyler Rationale" as the silver bullet in public school accountability may result in the complete destruction of the field of curriculum in public education.

In the first several paragraphs of this chapter I introduced the situation I faced in early 2015 where I was required to sit in a PARCC testing room for a total of 4 weeks. It was unfortunate that I lost 4 weeks of the school year by sitting in a PARCC testing room because I was (and still am) behind in updating the high school science pacing guides. Further, during these four weeks, I was essentially unable to serve as an instructional coach or to plan, implement, or evaluate science curriculum programs at my school district as described by Marsh and Willis (1995). My experiences are not unique, as other curriculum specialists and instructional coaches, in my school district and elsewhere, have expressed similar concerns to me. From my experiences as a high school curriculum specialist, accountability continues to be the chief concern of district administrators, state education agency officials, and politicians. Thus, curriculum work and instructional coaching is taking a back seat to data-based decision making. The pressures of school accountability and the increasing external demands on districts are responsible for generating a fog that is obscuring the importance of individualized student differentiation over the coverage of content standards (Daggett, 2014). Helping students on a one-on-one basis should always trump the coverage of all content standards, in spite of the pressures being applied by district administrators, state education agency officials, and/or politicans.

Politicians, practitioners, and scholars must identify possible solutions to the current crisis in school curriculum. Otherwise, the field will continue to suffer immensely.

It is easy to point out a problem (or multiple problems), but it is much more difficult to propose a series of manageable solutions. The first solution is probably the least likely to happen because it would require a significant amount of political will on the part of all stakeholders including activists, administrators, citizens, parents, politicians, students, and teachers. The first solution is to eliminate all state and federal accountability measures and then to repurpose the designated money to instructional coaching, the monitoring of instructional delivery, and to 21st century curriculum development for all teachers. A second proposed solution is to purposely divide district responsibilities to include a separation between the jobs of accountability and curriculum, so accountability job creep would be minimized to its fullest extent. In this scenario, there would probably be an ongoing need for accountability and curriculum administrators to collaborate on specific projects, but such a division would empower curriculum directors and specialists to devote a significant amount of time to planning, implementing, and evaluating school curriculum programs. A final solution would be to modify current accountability systems to include qualitative modes of evaluation to enhance the information being analyzed by including a more diverse set of variables not already being considered. I am hopeful that this chapter, the voices of other curriculum advocates, and future scholarship will help to further identify the causes of the current crisis in public school curriculum, so additional solutions will be offered to save the field of curriculum studies from accountability job creep.

REFERENCES

Daggett, B. (2014). Finding clarity amid the fog of external demands: How rapidly improving schools and districts are taking control and putting students first [White paper]. Retrieved May 17, 2015, from International Center for Leadership in Education: www.leadered.com/pdf/FindingClarityAmidtheFog.pdf

Eisner, E. W. (1967). Franklin Bobbitt and the "science" of curriculum making. *The School Review, 75*(1), 29–47.

Eisner, E. (1985). *The educational imagination: On the design and evaluation of school programs* (2nd ed.). New York, NY: Macmillan.

Eisner, E. W. (1994). *The educational imagination: On the design and evaluation of school programs* (3rd ed.). New York, NY: Macmillan.

Hlebowitsh, P. S. (1992). Amid-behavioural and behavioruristic objectives: Reappraising appraisals of the Tyler rationale. *Journal of Curriculum Studies, 24*(6), 533–547.

Jackson, P. W. (1968). *Life in classrooms*. New York, NY: Teachers College Press.

Jacobsen, R., Snyder, J. W., & Saultz, A. (2014). Informing or shaping public opinion? The influence on school accountability data format on public perceptions of school quality. *American Journal of Education*, *121*(1), 1–27.

Klaf, S., & Khan, M. P. (2010). The neoliberal straightjacket and public education in the U.S.: Understanding contemporary education reform and its implication for urban contexts. *Urban Geography*, *31*(2), 194–210.

Learning in a visual age: The critical importance of visual arts education [Brochure]. (n.d.) Reston, VA: National Art Education Association.

Marazano, R. J. (2007). *The art and science of teaching: A comprehensive framework for effective instruction*. Alexandria, VA: Association for Supervision and Curriculum Development.

Marsh, C., & Willis, G. (1995). *Curriculum alternative approaches, ongoing issues*. Columbus, OH: Merrill.

Miller, K. K. (2014). NGSS: Three resonating themes for geoscience educators. *In The Trenches*, *4*(4), 13–14.

National Commission on Excellence in Education. (1983). *A nation at risk: The imperative for educational reform*. Washington, DC: U.S. Government Printing Office.

Nowakowski, J. R. (1983). On educational evaluation: A conversation with Ralph Tyler. *Educational Leadership*, *40*(8), 24–29.

Pinar, W. (2011). *What is curriculum theory?* New York, NY: Routledge.

Popham, W. J. (2014). *Classroom assessment: What teachers need to know*. Columbus, OH: Pearson.

Report of the NAEA Commission on Art Education [Brochure]. (1978) Reston, VA: National Art Education Association.

Schubert, W. H., Schubert, A. L. L., Thomas, T. P., & Carroll, W. M. (2012). *Curriculum books: The first hundred years*. New York, NY: Peter Lang.

Temes, P. S. (2003). *Against school reform (And in praise of great teaching)*. Chicago, IL: Ivan R. Dee.

Tyler, R. W. (1949). *Basic principles of curriculum and instruction*. Chicago, IL: University of Chicago Press.

CHAPTER 4

"REFLECTIVE ECLECTICISM"

In the Windows to Curricula, I See Myself

Thao A. Nguyen-Horowitz

"We don't learn from experience. We learn from reflecting on experience."

– John Dewey (1933, p. 78)

Reflection is an art, an ability that can be honed with patience and persistence. It is a process of internal growth that opens doors to insightful action. George J. Posner's (1992) *Analyzing the Curriculum* pushes students of education to think critically about all forms of curricula We learn from intellectual giants, reflect on circumstance, and then move forward purposefully. The book begins with introductions to the varied definitions and several major theories of the curriculum field so that we may become familiar with them. Posner skillfully weaves throughout the text several case studies of well-known U.S. curricula to make our newfound knowledge practical. Thought provoking questions at the end of each chapter guide us to look critically at our own curricula and help us understand that all curriculum topics are deeply multifaceted. By following the way Posner structures his synoptic text (curriculum documentation and origins, curriculum proper, curriculum in use, curriculum critique) with reflections

Curriculum Windows: What Curriculum Theorists of the 1990s Can Teach Us About Schools and Society Today, pp. 51–65
Copyright © 2017 by Information Age Publishing

51

of my own thoughts and experiences, I hope to model how a thinker of education may throw open the windows through which we view schools and societies of the past, present, and future.

CURRICULUM ORIGINS

It began as a question: How do students learn? While in college, I worked as a tutor for a nationally known test prep company. My assignment was to conduct twice weekly drill and review sessions at a local Title I elementary school. Like many other schools in the area, this school was struggling to meet the state's Adequate Yearly Progress (AYP) requirements and feared the harsh consequences under the No Child Left Behind Act (NCLB). The administration hoped that bringing in college-aged tutors with fresh teaching materials and methods would improve the school's performance on standardized tests. I taught with confidence; I would be the difference. Listen, explain, practice, and repeat.... Improve, they did! Over the year, as I grew more comfortable teaching, I began to look critically at the greater picture. What was impacting the students? Was it the material? Me? The nontraditional training and new culture from young tutors? Was something lacking from their traditional classroom? Curiosity mounted and these issues loomed in my mind.

Years later, I found myself enjoying an early career in college counseling. Time was spent pouring over student files and eliciting deep discussions about likes, dislikes, and wants in academic life. I advised my students that they had the power of choice, and that being informed would allow them to weigh their options and make the best possible decisions for themselves. Whatever their goals, I often pondered students' situations—what factors shaped their academic experience and influenced their future lives? These students came from a variety of backgrounds that were often quite different from the impoverished families at Title I schools. Their wants and needs for the future revealed their various backgrounds.

The practice of those formative years as an educator, while I served and learned from students, is curricula. Lived curriculum is an experience one learns, whether intended or unintended. It is the uniqueness of daily occurrences, the distinctiveness of being (Aoki, 1993, p. 258). To begin our journey of analysis and reflection, Posner (1992) directs us to examine background and origins. These are the frameworks of new curricula, the structuring theoretical perspectives that shade every assumption and practice. Education is so much more than hard facts written into a plan. As students and future consumers of curricula, we are reminded of the plethora of views about the purpose of education, the way people learn, what should be taught, and so forth. By understanding this and recognizing the distinctiveness of every situation, we are more capable of selecting or adapting curricula. After all, if we can apply some detective work, find the vantage point of a curriculum, and identify its strengths and weaknesses, then we can modify it to create a better, lasting impression on our students. Curriculum is more than information gained in the classroom; it is also the process, organization, and emotions of learning that leave lasting imprints on all of us. Events and choices designed by educators shape the thoughts and opinions of later days. My involvement with Title I students, then later with college counseling, has shaped my pedagogy and altered my consciousness.

George J. Posner (1992) seeks to inform us that best practices for schools today cannot conform to any single, standardized, national curriculum. Believing that a singularly prescribed written plan could serve the interests of all students today and tomorrow serves as a great injustice to all. We each adhere to deep-rooted values and systems of beliefs formed from growth and experience, each person different from the next. Curriculum designs will reflect one's particular theoretical perspective while turning a blind eye to differing views (p. 47). This is the reason for curriculum analysis and the heart of Posner's "reflective eclecticism" (p. 23). Local administrators and teachers will better serve their students if given the space and freedom to choose or modify curriculum.

Posner's (1992) philosophies may have been conceived in his years studying psychology and teaching physics at Union College. He later continued his studies at the State University of New York, Albany, where he earned an EdD in curriculum and instruction. If early schooling influences later thinking, then his course of study is telling. Students of psychology dig deeply into the way people process the world around them, how they think, how they acquire knowledge, how they interpret surroundings, how they process memory, and so forth. His experience teaching science and mathematics gave him much to consider in regards to how curricula could be situated to achieve best learning outcomes.

Analyzing the Curriculum was formulated while Posner (1992) taught Education Studies and Teacher Preparation at Cornell. Twelve years of teaching and listening to his students cultivated the materials for his writing projects. Students seeking careers as teachers or administrators of education demanded learning beyond theories and history; their search for practical applications allowed *Analyzing the Curriculum* to come to fruition (p. xv). In this book, Posner presents us with a timelessly valuable tool. Not only does he provide easily accessible scope and history of the curriculum field, he makes the material practical by delving into case studies with us riding along as novice critics. Knowing his audience, aspiring teachers along with graduate students of education, it was important to first delve into the major theoretical perspectives that form educational practices: traditional, experiential, structure of the disciplines, behavioral, and cognitive. Advocates of each have fundamental differences in how they view educational purposes, develop curricula, and seek reform. Understanding these influences on decision making is crucial to curriculum analysis and thoughtful reflection of things that be.

As readers consume *Analyzing the Curriculum*, they are shown ways they can think for themselves, understand conflicts, and better recognize education and reform. Posner (1992) underlines the implicit assumptions in curriculum development and gives us an overview of three considerations in curriculum thinking: how learners learn, how teachers teach, and the focus of reform, all collegially based with research applications or in consideration of political contexts and societal needs. Great care is taken so that we may be able to see through the many windows of education with clarity and understanding. It is important for those responsible for shaping the next generation to be able to criticize what is given rather than to follow blindly. Even in test-dominated schooling, Posner (2015)aknesses in the curriculum, which would allow them to make modifications to better serve the needs of their students (G. Posner, personal communication, April 20, 2015). The ultimate goal is attentiveness to the diverse needs and goals of every student. All children deserve care and attention from the adults who surround them and a positive learning experience.

CURRICULUM PROPER

How do students learn? What can I do to better prepare my students for their experiences to come? I entered graduate school to seek answers to these questions, to understand the learning process, and to be educated about the forces that impact learning. The first courses loaded my mind with theories of learning and society that offered possible explanations for how education came to be. Professors lectured of deeply rooted social and political institutions and students discussed ways to combat achievement gaps. We read expert opinions of whom to blame and what to change, all the while learning that injustices are so entrenched in society that attempts to make change are like flickering flies nudging an enormous elephant. Full of conflict, I grew frustrated by the seeming impossibility of it all. A student of Posner's (1992) shared the same aggravation:

> I'm totally confused! I came to Cornell to find out how to make curriculum decisions, and all I am learning is that different experts have different answers to basic questions. Now I have more problems than when I started. What are we supposed to do when the so-called experts disagree? (p. 3)

My realization—There is no answer! There are just more questions on the path to seeking answers. Problems in American education are as glaring today as they were 100 years ago. These problems are impossible to fix with one person or any single policy change. Posner (1992) offers "reflective eclecticism," a solution to this frustration that directs us to decisive action:

> Reflective eclecticism is based on the assumption that, much as we would like to deny it, there is no panacea in education. People who are looking for "the answer" to our educational problems are looking in vain. Different situations require different practices. (p. 3)

Posner reminds us that education reflects humanity; there is no one-size-fits-all but rather a rich harvest of diversity, many approaches that might work in a given context.

We need to keep these lessons in mind when we look at the current state of education. Political demands for quantitative data and account-ability measures have greatly evolved school culture. Constant pressure to perform adequately on standardized tests has evolved the student experi-ence and classroom focus. The ideals of No Child Left Behind (NCLB) and Race to the Top (RTT) are rooted in *Brown v. Board of Education* and the Elementary and Secondary Education Act of 1965. All four pieces of legis-lation, upon creation, sought to equalize access and protect those who are economically disadvantaged. The principles of NCLB and RTT also seek to improve academic achievement of marginalized groups (U.S. Depart-ment of Education, 2004). However, as with all federal decisions, there is a much more complicated story. Time reveals if federally mandated pro-grams are effective in achieving their goals. NCLB funded my college job and gave me a wonderful experience working with children, but graduate study, along with *Analyzing the Curriculum*, has directed me to question and explore the complex issues regarding the effects of legislation, the curricula of high stakes testing, and their impact on all involved.

"Teaching to the test" is a frequently used phrase that describes teach-ing methods where the primary objective is to raise a particular test score. With current political trends assigning heavy significance to quantifiable data, it is not surprising to see classroom priorities shift towards training students to be better test takers. Schooling in the context of training focuses on teaching specific material that will categorically be reapplied—in this instance, nationwide, on standardized tests. In the meantime, subjects that offer practice in processing skills, such as the arts and humanities, get pushed aside. Schooling in an educational context teaches students how to think and interpret the world; these abilities cannot be measured quantifi-ably through testing, nor can it be determined when and how students may eventually utilize those capacities. As we think of how to find a balance, consider the sociological message conveyed when one is prioritized over the other. Posner (1992) asks us to ponder the purpose of schooling, "How much of schooling and what proportion of each subject should we conceive of as education, and how much should we conceive of as training?" (p. 74). The argument should not be which context of education is more important. Rather, there is value in both and we should focus on finding a way to provide a balance of both in school curricula.

No matter student developmental status, diversity, or class size, teachers are under tremendous pressure to have all students reach 'proficiency' standing in all test subjects. This need looms over every decision when planning lessons and shaping activities. Tony Scott (2008) explains, "virtually every aspect of students' writing was in some way subsumed by the state-wide assessment and system of accountability" (p. 147). Rather than drawing from years of experience working with students or academic training in lesson planning and critical thinking, teachers are restricted to the genres and evaluation process defined by the state. They are bound by time and expectations, leaving no room for exploration of what may be of personal interest to student or teacher alike. Today's data driven climate threatens our ability to foster balance in order to meet state standards.

During my stint as an after-school tutor and "teaching to the test," it was easy to judge how boring and mundane lessons were by the glazed look on the students' faces. Since our only purpose was to raise test scores, we were bound to particular lessons; we had to be resourceful in retaining student attention during drill and review sessions. Tutors drew on a variety of antics dependent on the age of the students. These included making spectacles of themselves in front of the classroom, linking teaching to a performance art, or drawing from their role as mentor rather than traditional teacher to relate, enchant, and garner student devotion. Imagine the boredom of teaching to the test throughout a full school day! By the end of the term, all my students met proficiency standards; drill and review tactics were justified to achieve this end. However, here we ponder the messages those students received. What did they learn? They learned tips and tricks on how to eliminate multiple-choice answers. They learned how to be good at guessing. Then I understood ... doing well is important to school data and accountability policies. But what is the impact on students' perspectives when this form of training is the majority of the school experience? Students' perceptions of themselves and their abilities are shaded by how well they test. Their trust in school wanes when classroom practices are rigid and hegemonic rather than fluid and diverse. As for teachers, working in an environment that does not trust one's abilities, training, and creative talents is cumbersome; it's no wonder why many new teachers quit and seasoned teachers grow weary of their jobs. It is easy to disengage from mundane work; stringent state standards constrict lessons, taking away space to connect to familiar issues, ultimately making lessons trivial and often repetitive.

In his study of large-scale testing, Scott (2008) found that assessment and policy influences run so deep that even classroom language has changed. In his transcripts of Kentucky high school classes, the vocabulary used reflected that of the state scoring guides. When discussing writing assignments, students would have individual copies of the state scoring guide on hand, which described the differences between the four scoring levels— novice, apprentice, proficient, and distinguished. Teachers questioned the high school senior class in a manner that exemplified their familiarity with the state guide. In response, the students could describe and critique any of the five forms of writing required by the state. The language the students used in open discussion was language directly learned from the grading criteria. For writing projects, the students would write, peer edit, and reflect on several drafts. They strived for a "proficient" draft because they all understood that once that was achieved, the editing process was over and they could move on to their next project (p. 148). This idea of working towards "proficient" seemed to give the students a stop sign or end point in their evolution as writers. In reality, writing is a process that constantly evolves; there are always more critical ideas to add, grammar to edit, and structures to debate. When students to have a predetermined minimum standard, it takes away from their need to be critical thinkers in the writing process. "Most students discussed the ownership of their work in terms of the pressure to meet state requirements, rather than in terms of their own desires to grow as writers or explore specific topics of interest" (p. 157). What message is being conveyed here? Are we molding a generation that works towards just enough? With everyday class lessons like this, how do we teach young people to strive towards innovation and excellence?

A history of progressive educational aims shows us how U.S. interests change over time. Keeping mindful of current educational aims, we can recognize strengths and weaknesses in available curricula to make appropriate classroom adjustments (Posner, 1992, p. 79). Data driven curriculum, like in Scott's (2008) Kentucky high school classes, result in behavioral changes rather than cognitive development. Students find quick ways to achieve the minimum work required in order to move on. To practice reflective eclecticism, let us muse over adjustments that could add critical thinking and allow students to feel a sense of ownership in their work. The language of state standards was all too familiar because passing became the primary purpose of the work. In this case, we could assign a greater purpose to the writing while housing state standards within the project. Posner (1992) would remind us here that no approach is less important. "The strengths of the top-down approach are its uncompromising attempt to respect the structure of the disciplines and to respect the student as a neophyte member of the community of scholars" (p. 182). Popular venues for writing such as blogging or website publishing may stimulate students to produce higher quality work. The expectation that they follow proper grammar and structure satisfies requirements from testing standards; yet, the individualistic nature of this work lets students feel emotionally invested. Creative freedom offers a counter balance to the top-down practices of writing to achieve "proficiency."

It is easy to ruminate about how the classroom could be handled differently. The reality is much more harsh. Pressure on teachers and administrators mounts daily; they face constant threats of loss of funding for their schools and, even worse, loss of jobs. This stress trickles down to staff, teachers, and rests upon students.

> Teachers and administrators have fewer degrees of freedom in adapting the curriculum to the students or to the community, because of high-stakes testing. The domination of tests and the tendency to teach to the test can be overwhelming. However, by analyzing the curriculum the teacher still can identify its blind spots and its assumptions. This kind of analysis can help teachers adapt the curriculum to the needs of students and make modifications in the curriculum to address its weaknesses. (G. Posner, e-mail communications, 2015)

Posner believes analysis and mindfulness of curriculum, reflective eclecticism, should be practiced by all but should begin with administrators. They hold control over what teachers are held accountable for and are in positions to offer support. Especially in urban school settings, educational leaders must be attentive to the fact that students enter each school year lacking fundamentals. Therefore, teachers will struggle with bringing students to grade level expectations before tackling new concepts. With backing and encouragement from administrators, teachers may work around the test, adapting the curriculum and making modifications, rather than falling into the trap of teaching to the test.

Educational leaders are at odds with policymakers over what changes need to be made to address student performance and enhance overall U.S. academic achievement. Bureaucrats in Washington fight the noble cause of improving education, but who defines those goals and how to achieve them? It is not far fetched to say that comfortable, white-collar, career politicians lack a connection to the needs of impoverished children who live in troubled communities, and to the teachers who teach them. Acts that implement curricular change over the entire nation denote hegemony; objectives of the dominant group are validated through messages and activities students receive. Posner (1992) explains, "Objectives that embody racial, ethnic, social, or sex stereotypes may be hegemonic in this direct sense, serving as a means to reinforce a social order that serves the interests of those in power" (p. 120). We should, perhaps, take a look into what policies have had an impact on education, how they have molded this generation, and if there are alternatives for teachers and administrators to choose rather than let a misplaced emphasis on testing and accountability take over our schools. Armed with "reflective eclecticism," teachers and administrators can understand the necessity of being flexible as they respond to the needs of students and the community. To understand the assumptions made by test makers is to identify weaknesses in today's schools.

CURRICULUM IN USE

Better decisions are made when educators have a deep understanding of options. As a parent, I am constantly looking for the best options for my children. In which preschool should we enroll? Are our family meals setting them up for long-term health? What is the best way to handle this toddler tantrum? What rules and guidelines should be firm and which may be more lenient? In many ways, my experiences working with students and their parents influence the way I parent. I love choices! But how do I know I am making the right choice?

The students I counseled through college applications came from a middle class, suburban area and the majority were from only a few ethnic groups: Caucasian, Vietnamese, Korean, and Chinese. Scholarships brought in students from impoverished families, but most of my students fit a particular middle to upper middle class mold. In this sense, there was a lack of diversity, but I quickly learned that even though the students had similar backgrounds, streamlining the application process and cookie cutter advice would be lazy and inadequate.

To give thoughtful, effective advice that would be well-received by parents and students alike, I had to truly listen. My approach to college counseling was to first collect data: quantitative data in the form of questionnaires and qualitative data from conferences. Then, I would pore over myriad college information sources or draw from colleagues in the field. Finally, college matches would be presented and discussed over a series of meetings in conjunction with helping students dig deep within themselves to write thoughtful and imaginative personal statements. Colleges and universities each have something different to offer. My students had diverse needs. Programs, school environments, student bodies, faculty, and so forth, come in every shape and size under the sun. No one choice could promise the perfect college experience, but guidance and information would allow students to make informed decisions for themselves.

I wanted all the success and happiness of the world for my students. Like all educators I have met, I passionately want to help children succeed. I have been fortunate enough to work for institutions that allow many freedoms, unrestricted by the limitations and controls facing public schools. I could differentiate curriculum and offer students what I saw fit without considering how that would conform to looming state tests; these students had a wholly different schooling experience. Schools are budding societies where young people learn what to expect from the greater world and, in turn, what is expected of them as citizens. Public schools should be focusing on the big picture: creating a society and a culture where people may accommodate and respect differences, thereby affording all of us opportunities to blossom. There is no single, correct form of parenting or growing into adulthood. So then, why are public school teachers and students expected to conform to someone else's standards?

During my early years of graduate school, I harbored a teenage angst against the American public school system. It was near and dear to me, and I wanted badly for a complete overhaul worthy of Sir Thomas More's Utopia. Whether through maturation or a better understanding of the powers at play, I have come to be more mindful that even as we fight the status quo, what matters most in a single day is the impact we have on the children present. Rather than the complete overhaul I dreamed of, by adjusting and adapting curricula, we create imperceptible waves of justice that are transported by our students to the public. Reflective eclecticism forces us to analyze the effects of power over what is learned so that we can better serve our students. Posner (1992) would have us understand that dominating groups place a filter on all aspects taken away from schooling. The lessons students learn go beyond the "official curriculum;" what they carry with them is more than basic sentence formation and essay structure. Lives are influenced by classroom language used, teacher interactions, images from a text, and issues that are left untouched. The "hidden" and "null" curricula have deep implications on student lives (Eisner, 2002).

When standardized tests play such a large role on the student experience, the topics included are legitimated, while those stories and skills not included are sidelined, important elements like lessons of influential African Americans other than Martin Luther King, Jr., large corporate control over politics, stories of other countries' views on American politics, moral and leadership skills, citizenship, soft skills on building relationships, and so forth, all conspicuously missing. Those lessons that cannot be measured and computed on graphs and scales are easily dismissed (Eastman, 2006, p. 306). Examinations cause schools to fixate on what is measureable, which is often simplistic and acts as a disservice in preparing students to be creative, critical and motivated adults. Eastman (2006) explains:

But the way we generally teach students isn't by allowing them to pursue their own interests. Teachers invert the process so that students are made to feel interested, or to feign interest, in institutional prerogatives; that is, institutions teach by opening students' attitudes and motivation—in short, their personality—to interference so that institutional knowledge meets little psychic resistance; the institutional body forecloses on knowledge which might threaten its mission of social regimentation. (p. 304)

The student loses agency; the teacher is not trusted and grows disenfranchised from his or her passionate work. Neoliberal politics and its need for data would have us create a nation of drones.

Recognition of the powers at play fortifies people with the ability to critique and question further policy change. Educational leadership programs have an important duty to create this awareness so that future teachers can strive for some level of justice in their classrooms and future leaders may fight for the democracy our children deserve. With *Analyzing the Curriculum*, Posner (1992) has created the tool to achieve exactly this. Giroux (2010) explains that in a flourishing democracy, public schools are the political nucleus for producing upright citizens (p. 357). He argues that President Obama's administration is still stuck in neoliberal politics. Although we have taken a step away from NCLB, the administration's introduction of Race to the Top (RTT) is still based on free-market principles, especially that of competition. Furthermore, RTT continues to crumble a weakening educational system by highlighting accountability measures over faculty protections. We are more in need of Posner's work today than ever before. Trust of teachers is essential. The risk of losing one's job due to a failure to comply to state measures is changing the educational environment. Curricula that maintain emphasis on basic and measureable knowledge must be stopped before making it into the classroom. Too little room is left for teachers to engage students with political, cultural, and ethical discourse; these are the skills and knowledge that will allow students opportunity for upward mobility (Giroux, 2010, p. 351).

To break beyond the confines of neoliberal politics, we must strengthen discourse that deemphasizes current data driven culture in classroom practices. Before testing and accountability mandates, teachers and administrators held themselves accountable. The teaching profession was given high regard and educators worked with enduring passion and commitment. Knowing their influence, teachers sought to arm their students with life skills and academic lessons. We need to once again trust teachers' abilities and allow them the space to explore critical pedagogy and time to draw out student creativity, "validating the discourse of public purpose over self-interest, embracing critical thinking over a culture of conformity, and viewing pedagogy as a productive force that creates particular modes of knowledge, agency, values, and social relations" (Giroux, 2010, p. 353).

Teaching once was and should always be a profession of passion and principles. It should not be the monotonous task of drill and review that it has
become. Our nation will continue to suffer if students are not taught to find
their political voices, fight for personal values, and validate their identities.
Politics promoting minority groups should be the norm in a nation that was
built on diversity; instead, actual policy and institutions exist to perpetuate
the dominance of a political minority at the expense of a diverse majority.

In a very thought-provoking TED Talk, Chimamanda Adichie (2009)
shared her childhood experience in Nigeria and her love of storybooks. She
reflected on the characters she saw and the subtle messages the stories gave.
Most were blond-haired and blue-eyed, and acted in a manner foreign to a
child in Nigeria. Like our classroom textbooks, they were written to reflect
culture and customs of the dominant group. Minority groups take away the
message that their identities are "wrong" or are not significant enough to
learn in schools. "Power is the ability not just to tell the story of another
person, but to make it the definitive story of that person" (Adichie, 2009).
I learned from my own students that connection to lessons along with a
deep level of self-reflection is vital to quality education. Posner's reflective
eclecticism follows critical pedagogy, the philosophy of great thinkers like
Paulo Freire (1970) and Henry Giroux (2011). "It is important to stress that
teachers must take active responsibility for raising serious questions about
what they teach, how they are to teach, and what the larger goals are for
which they are striving" (p. 48). If we can expose the ideological curtains
draped over them, students may be able to see through clearer windows.

To strengthen the student experience and mold citizens capable of pro-
tecting our democracy, teachers should try to help their students critique
the curriculum. Teachers need room for flexibility and to customize based
on student backgrounds. Since it is not plausible to completely do away
with all standardized tests, reflective eclecticism would enable teachers
to teach around the test, showing students valuable lessons while using
test material. We can make students more aware of what is happening
to and around them so that they do not remain the blind "camels" from
Nietzsche's three metamorphoses of Zarathustra. Rather, their knowledge
of the powers of the dominant culture would rally groups who are "othered"
to act as a "lion" and fight to validate their own identities (Carlson, 2002,
p. 109). The examination itself could be analyzed and critiqued. Students
can deconstruct who wrote the test, what purposes it serves, the "hidden"
and "null" curriculum, and then evaluate.

Gerald, McEvoy, and Whitfield (2004) share experiences that

> using tenets of feminist pedagogy to open our students' minds, teaching
> them to be resisting readers, critical writers, and empowered speakers [would]
> enable our students to do more than memorize unquestioned information;

students become the kind of critical thinkers and rhetors who excel across disciplines inside and outside the academy. (p. 48)

While students address skills that would bring them up to "proficiency," they can self reflect on their experience in schooling, validating their thoughts and words. Students empowered with the role as master rather than minion would have a more vested interest in learning. Harold Wenglinsky (2004) explored international test data to show that "students demand autonomy in how to improve that achievement. And as the NAEP data suggest, the best way for school leaders to raise student achievement is by placing more emphasis on teaching for meaning" (p. 35). The emphasis on data collection further proves that teachers need space to use critical thinking and creativity in order to reach their goals.

Teachers able to see beyond the surface of curriculum are more apt to address the plethora of student backgrounds, situations, needs, etc. Standardized tests express intellectualism of the dominant culture, but educators must try to redefine the daily student experience.

CURRICULUM CRITIQUE

Teacher education programs continue to fight against government mandates to standardize how a teacher is trained. Giroux (2010) explains that "Education remains one of the most important spheres left for creating critical and engaged citizens capable of challenging a material and symbolic order that blindly legitimates a culture of corruption, greed, and inequality" (p. 342). Therefore, texts such as *Analyzing the Curriculum* are of paramount importance to future teachers and administrators. Educating minds to be critical of societal influences and flexible to choices of action will bring a more potent classroom experience. Minds enlightened by educational theory can identify the values and social relations conveyed to the children (p. 371). Teachers should regain the respect they once had from policymakers; they deserve to be trusted in the decision making for the betterment of our future generation.

An important part of teacher education is bringing about an understanding of diversity. Educators armed with knowledge about diverse cultures in American society will better connect with their students who have "fallen through the cracks." Posner (1992) tells us, "Perspectives not only provide vantage points that increase our educational vision but also may influence and be influenced by our views of reality" (p. 68). I hold Posner's lesson close to heart. Once I return to serving the educational community, I will create moments that ask students to reflect on their lived experiences and bring awareness of "hegemonic macrostructures" to enlighten their understanding of our existence (Tobin, 2009, p. 511). Traditional curriculum marginalizes many minority groups and devalues their differences. Programs that build value in student identities will create a more successful generation and stimulate the American public to greater participation (Sefton-Green, 2011, p. 61).

Those who have a true passion to provide American youth with exceptional care in instruction and experience are worth time and attention. Consider Diane Ravitch's (2010) about-face upon studying the social conditions caused by NCLB. She speaks with honesty and from experience when she turns a critical eye on her own policy stances to say that the accountability measures had failed to achieve their goals. Ravitch recognized that current educational studies revealed a system where students succumbed to test preparation of math and English skills that require little thought.

Moving towards a better future, it is important to sustain the idealism that we can change American education to make it the greatest experience for all. We can improve schools to reflect the big picture of community education, allowing us to respectfully raise each others' children. Even with slow momentum, working toward democratic ideals, we can make positive changes in society. Educational policy should not be reformed to return to the way things once were but rather evolve and continue to work towards greater equity and social justice.

Staring at melting snow drip off tree branches, I sit by the living room window with *Analyzing the Curriculum* in hand. I quietly muse over my own path from schooling to teaching and counseling, then back again to graduate school. By chance or by curricular omnipotence, Dr. Poetter's (2009) pairing of Posner's thorough explanations, analytic voice, and reflective style was a perfect fit for this point in my scholarship. Posner answers my question, "How do students learn?" with more questions to consider, but at this moment, I am satisfied. There is always more to mull over as I continue course work in transformative education at Miami University. Reading *Analyzing the Curriculum* has given me tools and space to reflect. It has opened a window from my inner being to the space of today and all future educational contexts.

REFERENCES

Adichie, C. (2009, October). Chimamanda Ngozi Adichie: The danger of a single story [Video file]. Retrieved from https://www.youtube.com/watch?v=D9Ihs241zeg&t=59s

Aoki, T. T. (1993). Legitimating lived curriculum: Towards a curricular landscape of multiplicity. *Journal of Curriculum and Supervision, 8*(3), 255–268.

Carlson, D. (2002). *Leaving safe harbors: Toward a new progressivism in American education and public life.* New York, NY: Routledge Falmer.

Dewey, J. (1933). *How we think*. Boston, MA: D. C. Heath & Co.

Eastman, N. (2006). Our institutions, our selves: Rethinking classroom performance and signification. *Review of Education, Pedagogy, and Cultural Studies, 28*(3–4), 297–308.

Eisner, E. (2002). *The educational imagination* (3rd ed.). Upper Saddle River, NJ: Prentice Hall.

Freire, P. (1970). *Pedagogy of the oppressed*. New York, NY: Continuum.

Gerald, A. S., McEvoy, K., & Whitfield, P. (2004). Transforming student literacies: Three feminists (re)teach reading, writing, and speaking. *Feminist Teacher, 15*(1), 48–65.

Giroux, H. A. (2010). Dumbing down teachers: Rethinking the crisis of public education and the demise of the social state. *Review of Education, Pedagogy, and Cultural Studies, 32*(4–5), 339–381.

Giroux, H. (2011). *Teachers as transformatory intellectuals*. Retrieved April 01, 2015, from Sindh Education Foundation: http://www.sef.org.pk/old/Educate/education/Teachers%20as%20Transformatory%20Intellectuals%20by%20Henry%20Giroux.pdf

Poetter, T. S. (2009). Taking the leap, mentoring doctoral students as scholars: A great and fruitful morass. *Teaching & Learning, 24*(1), 22–29.

Posner, G. J. (1992). *Analyzing the curriculum*. New York, NY: McGraw-Hill.

Ravitch, D. (2010). *The death and life of the great American school system: How testing and choice are undermining education*. New York, NY: Basic Books.

Scott, T. (2008). "Happy to comply": Writing assessment, fast-capitalism, and the cultural logic of control. *Review of Education, Pedagogy, and Cultural Studies, 30*(2), 140–161.

Sefton-Green, J. (2011). Cultural studies and education: Reflecting on differences, impacts, effects and change. *Cultural Studies, 25*(1), 55–70.

Tobin, K. (2009). Tuning into others' voices: Radical listening, learning from difference, and escaping oppression. *Cultural Studies of Science Education, 4*, 505–511.

U.S. Department of Education. (2004, October 01). *U.S. Department of Education*. Retrieved May 01, 2015, from A Guide to Education and No Child Left Behind: www2.ed.gov/nclb

Wenglinsky, H. (2004). Facts or critical thinking skills? What NAEP results say. *Educational Leadership, 62*(1), 32–35.

CHAPTER 5

THE LOST ART OF DELIBERATION

Ryan Graham

In the United States, we hold deliberation as the pinnacle of decision making, the backbone of our legal system, and the process through which laws come into existence. When the prosecution and the defense rest, the jurors are excused to their chambers to deliberate in an unbiased manner and decide the fate of the defendant. Local, state, and federal politicians are constantly creating and proposing bills that are ultimately signed into law or rejected after the legislative branch deliberates the merits and consequences of said bill. Deliberation seems so simple, so straightforward, and so ideal.

The reality of the situation is that jury deliberations or passing bills is only simple, straightforward, and ideal until human actors get involved in the process. Jurors are incredibly biased, often consider flawed evidence, are expected to disregard any bit of information that was not presented in court, and are compelled to forfeit their daily activities for as long as it takes to reach consensus. Members of Congress attempt to push personal and partisan agendas through dense documents with ambiguous wording, hidden stipulations, and purposeful loopholes. Often, fellow members of Congress need only to know which side of the partisan line the sponsoring member falls on to decide whether they will support or reject a bill.

Curriculum Windows: What Curriculum Theorists of the 1990s Can Teach Us About Schools and Society Today, pp. 67–80
Copyright © 2017 by Information Age Publishing
All rights of reproduction in any form reserved.

Unless, of course, the party in control of Congress takes advantage of its majority and passes as many bills as possible with as little resistance as possible. Then, of course, the executive branch can exercise the veto power and kill a bill, which then must be sent back to Congress to be revised, or repassed by a two-thirds vote in both chambers to override the executive veto. Perhaps deliberation is more of a quixotic aspiration than a given in any decision-making process.

Unfortunately, curriculum decision makers face many of the most significant pitfalls of the human error-filled jury deliberations, and the political dog and pony show that passes for legislative deliberation. There are also aspects of curriculum decision making that are unique. Even considering the flawed nature of jury and political deliberation process, the potential outcomes are so limited in number that the process retains an element of simplicity, and results can be reasonably expected. The flaws or even corruption inherent in the process do not prevent decisions when the only possible conclusions are guilty, not guilty, unable to reach a consensus, or pass, reject, no vote. When considering curriculum, however, the potential ends are innumerable, and each end can be approached by equally innumerable means. In light of this consideration, it is much easier to see why results in curriculum decisions are much more difficult to come by. Added to the myriad different approaches to curriculum is the complexity of engaging in deliberation in a culture that approaches conflict with extreme trepidation.

Gail McCutcheon (1995) was abundantly aware of the necessary role that conflict plays in deliberation when she wrote *Developing the Curriculum: Solo and Group Deliberation*. McCutcheon points out that a defining feature of group deliberation is often the avoidance of conflict. The attempt to avoid conflict is futile, however, as it is an essential aspect in deliberation. Without conflict there would be no reason to deliberate in the first place. If everybody started with a shared vision and agreed with their colleagues, then decisions would simply be declarations rather than a process. McCutcheon situated conflict, deliberation, and her treatment of the curriculum within the context of being between teachers and education professionals. While I agree with McCutcheon that teachers are the most important parties in curriculum implementation, and I am in favor of increasing teacher autonomy in curriculum development, it is becoming increasingly obvious that this is a contested issue. In 2016, we are at a point where larger group deliberations dictate the extent to which teachers are allowed to deliberate and make curriculum decisions. This wider group deliberation is the arena through which systematic change is made possible. Teachers can act as solo deliberators operating under the cloak of invisibility within their own classroom, influencing children, possibly inspiring them to go forth and educate, but until the deliberation is brought into the light and pursued amongst larger groups, teachers will always be fighting against the system, rather than working towards emancipation.

REENGAGING DELIBERATION

The recent trends within education leave little doubt that the role of the teacher in contemporary schools is that of an implementer, rather than a creator of curriculum. In this climate it is crucially important for not just teachers, but every individual involved in education, to recognize the importance of finding their voice and insisting that they are included in conversations. Learning to deliberate with other teachers and education professionals is important, but they must first reestablish their position as the rightful decision makers before they can utilize their skills to engage each other. The only way that they can reestablish this position is through conflict-laden deliberation with the policymakers who are stripping them of their autonomy. If educators are going to reclaim the schools, they need to get very comfortable with conflict and practice true deliberation.

Those of us fortunate enough to enjoy the contested spaces of doctoral classrooms may be somewhat insulated from the general public's contentious relationship with conflict, but not immune to it. The initial foray into Doctoral work could be thought of as a resocialization, but might be more aptly thought of as a desocialization. I am not referring to the ideas, beliefs, and values that are espoused in these classrooms, although they do often lead to desocialization. Rather, I am referring to the process through which learning, and personal growth occurs. Individuals who are intellectually honest appreciate the necessity and usefulness of good old fashioned conflict. The best method for learning a topic at a deeper level is approaching a true understanding of why you hold the views you do pertaining to said topic and why others disagree, and engaging in dialogue regarding the disagreements. There are still occasions when even those of us who accept the inherent conflict of learning shrink into ourselves and shy away from taking on contested issues. These occasions are not particularly rare. Unfortunately, it is often the issues that we are the most passionate about that we shy away from. This is reasonable, given our broader cultural context, and given that it is exactly those issues that we are most passionate about that are indivisible from our sense of self. In other words, even those of us who are trained to accept conflict, have experience with and often a fondness for engaging in disagreement, are susceptible to conflating an attack on an idea we hold with an attack on our personhood. Individuals in other contexts outside of higher education are much less prepared to engage in conflict-laden deliberation, and often avoid it at all costs.

DEBILITATION OR DELIBERATION

This avoidance of deliberation broadly, and conflict specifically, is especially counterproductive given the rapidly changing nature of our contemporary world. There is a notion within the law community regarding the difficulty that the law has keeping up with technology. The implication is that technology is growing and changing at a pace that causes gaps within existing laws. The law is not unique in this situation. New technology is outpacing every other aspect of our society and we are all rushing to keep up. There is no doubt that our 21st century world is one in which the only consistency rests in its constant change. In such a world, where change is the only constant, it should be expected that conflict will arise when making decisions on how to best meet this change. In order to appropriately meet the demands of this dynamic world, we need to be engaging in ongoing, ever-changing dialogue focused on collaboration. This, however, is the complete opposite of our typical approach.

I believe that deliberation is the most appropriate and possibly only method of changing society. This is where I feel that deliberation has become a lost art. In our contemporary society it seems as if we only know how to symbolically adopt change through compulsory legislation. Compulsory legislation does not change society, does not bring about progress. Some legislation is absolutely necessary, but in order for true progress to happen on a wide-scale we must rely on deliberation, conflict, and resolution. People cannot be compelled to change. They cannot be compelled to progress. They must be convinced that changing, progressing, is the appropriate course of action. Our country has a strong history of deliberation, where if an argument were compelling enough then it would be accepted into practice. Somewhere along the line, we became incredibly uncomfortable with having our values and beliefs questioned, became personally offended by conflict, and fell into a deeply entrenched partisan rut in which arguments are primarily examined on the political affiliation of the arguer rather than the merits of the points being argued. From this approach we replace true deliberation, true discussion with mutual disrespect, vilification, and ultimately compulsory edicts that drive us apart rather than bring us together. As McCutcheon (1995) assesses, solo deliberation is the process by which individuals determine an approach to a given task, but only through true group deliberation can we determine how to collectively approach a task. There may have been a time when this type of group deliberation could have been achieved by conscientious educators getting together and making decisions, but now these educators must reaffirm themselves as the rightful decision makers. They must make their argument and convince society that they, not legislators, are best suited for making educational decisions. But what might this amorphous group deliberation look like in practice?

BUILDING BRIDGES

If we were to visualize the contemporary deliberation process, we could think of it as two large groups of people on opposite sides of an abyss. Each group vehemently believes that it knows for certain the appropriate manner in which to construct a bridge to span the abyss. Each group begins construction of its bridge, but every time that it makes progress the opposite group does its best to sabotage the foundation. The groups persevere, however, and despite the best efforts of its rivals, each group manages to construct its own shaky, ominous looking bridge swaying in the wind that leads to the opposite side of the abyss. So now each group has a bridge that might allow its members to risk life and limb to cross the abyss. Crossing the abyss was never the group's intention, however. Now that each has its bridge, both try their best to lure their rivals over with tricks, false promises, and personal incentives. The endgame is to secure a large enough group that will allow one group to forcibly drag those remaining in the other group to its side. Some are swayed from one side to the other, but the abyss remains with each group competing to see who can yell the loudest across it.

It is obvious that this visualization can be characterized by danger, lack of productivity, and an impenetrable divisiveness. So what would the visualization look like if true deliberation were taking place? You might imagine that there are the two groups on opposite sides of the abyss and each group works to construct a bridge that will meet in the middle. Decisions are made on either side that determines how best to reach this middle ground in which a solid bridge will span the abyss. This scenario is certainly much tidier and arguably more productive, but it is not true to the aims, the process, or the nature of true deliberation. This scenario of placating, compromising, and falsely cooperating is what we have come to accept as the gold standard for establishing best practices, but it is only through our flawed visualization of reality that this standard is granted gold status.

THE BRIDGE OF TRUE DELIBERATION

If we were to visualize this scenario through the lens of true deliberation, it would look much different than the previous examples. In true deliberation, both of our groups are on the same side of the abyss. They are being pushed ever closer to the precipice and the more time that passes the less time they have to act before falling into the abyss. They cling to their group membership and spend precious time shouting at the rival group, certain that they know the appropriate solution to avoid disaster. Their first impulse is to build their own bridge because they know the best approach. They quickly realize that they do not have the time or resources to implement their solution without the collaboration of the other group. Necessity breeds collaboration, and eventually the two groups are now indistinguishable from one big group working toward a common goal. There are intense disagreements, strong opinions, and frequent setbacks, but moving forward necessitates integrating their designs and making decisions. The group realizes that there are numerous strengths in each other's designs and appreciates their usefulness in the situation. Even more important, the collaboration leads to the realization of fatal flaws in each group's initial design that could have led to catastrophe had they not been pointed out.

Amazingly, the collaborative process has allowed everybody involved to see the problem they are facing from a whole new perspective. They now understand that there never were two groups working toward two different goals, but a bunch of individuals who believed that there was only one path to achieve a goal because they did not allow themselves to see alternatives. In the end, they realize that through collaboration they are able to achieve their common goal via a path that would not have been available in the absence of collaboration. Thanks to the wealth of ideas and resources that they discovered while deliberating as a big group with a common goal they realized that building an archaic, run of the mill bridge was not the appropriate path. Instead, they had all the knowledge, skill, and cumulative material needed to construct an innovative, state of the art aircraft capable of not only traveling safely across this abyss, but every subsequent abyss the group encounters.

DELIBERATION IN CURRICULUM

Building bridges and safely spanning abysses is all well and good, but we are not engineers, architects, or city planners. We are educators and we must figure out how deliberation tends to play out in curriculum. Following the tradition of McCutcheon (1995), I believe that the best approach to bringing the deliberation conversation to curriculum is through a few case studies. Unlike McCutcheon, however, I will rely on fictitious case studies and examine how the various deliberative models impact life within the fictitious F.W. Nietzsche Middle School.

McCutcheon (1995) illustrated her most effective points regarding solo and group deliberation by exploring the deliberation process within the real experiences of educators. Whether it was an individual teacher engaging in solo deliberation while deciding which lessons to include in the classroom and how to best engage with students, or a group of teachers deliberating in an effort to formulate curriculum that works in an authentically educative way, McCutcheon presented compelling real-world examples. This worked well for her goal, which was to address the crucial role that deliberation played in educational decision making at the level of educators. For McCutcheon, deliberation was the process through which educators made decisions, both mundane and exceptional. In order to illustrate my point, that we are in a situation that requires us to think of deliberation beyond teachers deciding the best course of action behind closed doors, I am going to relocate my aforementioned abyss right into the middle of my fictional school.

LEVIATHAN SMILES

The teachers and students at F.W. Nietzsche Middle School are sitting silently in the main auditorium. The room is large and monochromatic. The slightest sound echoes off the barren walls. The only adornment whatsoever is the school mission statement, which just so happens to be the mission statement of every school: "Decisions are better committed to one than many." Suddenly, static booms from the intercom system and bounces around the cavernous room. Every person in the room comes to attention and awaits the daily prerecorded instructions from the Sovereign Tom Hobbes. The Sovereign's tone is noticeably harsh as he begins admonishing dissenters:

Unfortunately, a number of students and teachers at Central High School took it upon themselves to make decisions. These decisions were in direct opposition to our national aims. Luckily, the National Compliance Council has stepped in to run the day-to-day operations of Central and removed the dissenting teachers and students before their damaging messages could be spread. It is essential that every teacher remembers the necessity of complying with the National Compliance Council Standards when dealing with students. Students, it is crucial that you remember your role in ensuring peaceful interactions, and bringing the Sovereign's goals to fruition. My pledge to you as Sovereign is that I will provide you with all the knowledge you need. And remember, knowledge is power.

A second round of static pinballs around the auditorium as the teachers and students stand and move toward the doors docilely. F.W. Nietzsche Middle school goes about business as usual.

Later that day, during lunch, Mr. Smith is conversing with Ms. Jones while they monitor the students' cafeteria behavior. The smell of the National Compliance Council (NCC) mandated meal for the day filled the air. "I knew a few of the teachers over at Central who were dismissed," remarks Mr. Smith. Ms. Jones answers, "I heard that they hadn't been following the NCC Standards, and that they were encouraging their students to look for outside material to use in their studies." The use of non NCC approved and supplied materials is expressly prohibited in schools under Sovereign Hobbes. "Yes, they were encouraging their students to question the Sovereign and his goals," Mr. Smith replies shaking his head. "They were probably More supporters," sneers Ms. Jones. Tom More was an aspiring National leader who looked to oppose Tom Hobbes and gain enough support to take control of the Sovereignty. More has been garnering support among those who are tired of Hobbes and believe that the Sovereignty needs to adopt new goals for the Nation. Hobbes has been aggressively working to quell sources of opposition and suppress pro-More propaganda while simultaneously running a media campaign highlighting all the good that his decisions have brought to the Nation.

The lunch bell rings and the students begin to clean up their mess and move toward the tray return. Mr. Smith and Ms. Jones stand and survey the cafeteria to ensure that every student was complying with cleanup. "Yeah, a few of them were More supporters. Others were just tired of the Sovereign's Standards. They thought that maybe More's standards would be better for them and their school so they went along with the More supporters," explains Mr. Smith. "Yeah, I did hear that More wants new standards. I actually heard that he wants to include more classic literature in his standards which would be great for our students," remarks Ms. Jones optimistically. "Our students probably could benefit from some of More's standards. Maybe More would be a better Sovereign. But let's be realistic … look what happened to those teachers at Central High who were suspected of opposing Sovereign Hobbes. Besides, do you remember the upheaval and chaos when Sovereign Hobbes took power from Sovereign Harrington? The school days are just now starting to feel like routine. How are the students going to learn the standards if the standards keep changing?" Mr. Smith asks while he and Ms. Jones head to the door to form a line for their respective classes to fall into. Ms. Jones tidies her students and turns to head down the hallway to her classroom and agrees with Mr. Smith, "You're right. The students don't need new standards. I'm still trying to memorize the NCC Standards. The last thing I need is a new 1,000 page manual to learn."

That evening the National News Station reported the breaking news that Tom More had been jailed for treason and conspiracy to support disobedience. In Capital City, Sovereign Hobbes met with the head of the NCC to discuss the recent dissent. "Good news, your Sovereignty. The daily compliance report indicates that the events at Central High were localized and compliance officers from other schools are confident that your standards are being supported," reports the NCC official. "I trust that if anybody had illusions of disobedience, they were quelled by the news of the dismissals at Central. I am certain that Tom More will not be getting them agitated with his rabble-rousing anytime soon. I just hope the ideas fade away with the man," replies Sovereign Hobbes. "Well, whether his ideas spread or not, all indications are that compliance can be expected. We can't force them to agree with you, but they're not going to oppose you. Not a chance," the official chuckles. Sovereign Hobbes grins, "The more they disagree, but comply the more satisfied I am. I relish their reluctant submission. And leviathan smiles!"

THANK YOU FOR THE STANDARDS

The teachers and administrators of F.W. Nietzsche Middle School are all gathering in the teachers' lounge for a faculty meeting. Winston Smith, the sixth grade literature teacher enters the lounge and walks around the long Grecian conference table. He sits down next to Frank Parker who teaches literature to the seventh and eighth grade students. Winston leans over and quietly asks, "Do you have any idea what's on the agenda for this meeting?" Frank responds, "Not yet." Just then, Principal Polly Marcus stood up from her seat at the head of the table, "Good afternoon everybody. Thank you for your punctuality. I know that this is not a regularly scheduled meeting, and I appreciate everybody showing up. We are honored to have Representatives Adeimantus and Cephalus here from Kallipolis to share the most recent standards for best practices." The standards were ratified at the most recent meeting of the Philosopher-Kings. The Philosopher-Kings are a select group of the most well-groomed, technically trained citizens who are endowed with the power to make decisions on behalf of the public. The Philosopher-kings are comprised almost exclusively of Platonians and Glaucons. These two groups hold ideological differences, but are jointly tasked with determining a unified set of best practices. "There's no reason for me to stand up here and talk your ear off when we can hear from the Representatives," Principal Marcus explains as she shuffles back to her seat.

Representative Cephalus, representing the Platonians and Representative Adeimantus, representing the Glaucons each stand from their respective seats on opposite sides of the table and walk up to the head of the table meeting in the middle. "Good afternoon. We are pleased to be here to report the joint efforts of the Philosopher-Kings regarding the best practices for educating our children," Cephalus greets cordially. Adeimantus follows up, "Firstly, I think we should take a moment to thank the Philosopher-Kings for all of their hard work in creating these standards. The process was not without conflict, but in the end the Philosopher-Kings agreed that compromise was necessary. We all know how busy you teachers are, and we do our best to provide you with thorough standards that you should be able to implement without too much extra work. So thank you to all of the Philosopher-Kings for their tireless devotion to improving education." There is an uneasy silence, before Principal Marcus begins to clap and the teachers slowly join in to the round of applause.

The representatives proceed to explain how the new standards differ from the existing standards. Occasionally, a hand will raise or a teacher attempts to interject. The Representatives implore the group, "Please hold all questions until the end of our presentation." After a half hour of listening to the Representative, but hearing very little new information, Frank turns to Winston and whispers disapprovingly, "There is absolutely no substance to any of these changes. Nothing is going to change!" Winston replies sarcastically, "Yeah, the way they've been hyping these changes in the news lately you would think all our problems were being solved. Maybe they're saving the best for last. I'm sure that's it."

The representatives drone on for another 45 minutes celebrating the forward-thinking, genuine, caring nature of the Philosopher-Kings' new standards. "In summation, we believe that every student, every teacher, our entire Nation will reap untold benefits thanks to the beneficence of our wise Philosopher-Kings. Now, we will consider your questions," concludes Cephalus proudly. Winston and Frank immediately speak up, cutting each other off. "Go ahead, Winston," Frank says placing his hand on Winston's shoulder. Winston begins, "You didn't mention whether teachers and students will have the freedom to choose learning materials that they find particularly relevant and interesting. Is this something that will be allowed under the new standards?" Adeimantus responds, "The teachers will have a great deal of freedom to make decisions under the new standards. There is a pretty extensive list of materials for each subject at each grade level that the Philosopher-Kings have created. Every teacher will be able to select anything from this list to utilize in their lessons." Frank quickly responds, "But we teach literature, and there is a nearly limitless number of literary works that could be incorporated into our classes." Adeimantus immediately replies, "The Philosopher-Kings thought long and hard before creating the lists of acceptable material. Literature is no exception. The upmost care was taken to provide an impressive selection of literature." Unconvinced, Frank asks, "But if we are interested in incorporating works not on the list, is there a process for adding to the accepted list?" Cephalus interjects with a tone of annoyance, "Again, the Philosopher-Kings put this list together. They know what is best for students to learn. That is all the time we have for questions. Any further questions or concerns can be forwarded in writing to the Kallipolis Capital Building and they will be reviewed when the Philosopher-Kings have time."

The teachers take offense to being cutoff and continue discussions amongst themselves as the Representatives rush out. A voice rises from the back, "I don't think they have ever met a teacher let alone asked a teacher for input." Winston agrees, "I don't think most of them have ever been in a school, but they'll continue patting themselves on the back up in Kallipolis while we deal with their supposed changes here in the trenches."

SPAGHETTI AND SCHOOL REFORM

It is the first Wednesday evening of the month. At F.W. Nietzsche Middle School, this means that the monthly open-forum pasta dinner is under way. The community room is buzzing with energy and the aroma from an array of international cuisine fills the air. Children are running around playing with their friends, parents are enjoying heaping plates of pasta while admiring the new décor in the community room. The students chose "Jungle Under the Sea" as this month's theme and created an impressive menagerie of scuba diving paper mache monkeys, Super Marioesque flying fish, and a large, mosaic mural featuring a rainbow corral forest. Some of the children from the school band are regaling their monthly guests with the latest and greatest hits of Nietzsche Middle.

After everybody has had a chance to partake in the pasta buffet and the brass section of the band ran out of air, Fred August stands up on his chair and waves his hands requesting everybody's attention. Fred is the father of an eighth grade daughter and sixth grade son. He acts as the impromptu monthly meeting coordinator, and a prized member of the Community-School Coalition. He explains warmly, "As always, please continue eating and keep eating until all of this delicious food is gone. I just want to open the floor to discussions, questions, concerns, praise or anything in between. As most of you know, but I do see some new faces—it's great to see all of your new faces, and I hope you will become regular faces – but yeah, we will stay as long as it takes to ensure everybody has an opportunity to address anything they want to address. If you need to leave, we'll be happy to have had you as long as we did, if anybody just wants to eat and run that is fine, too, but those who want/need to discuss anything we'll stay till they shut the lights off on us." Fred steps down from his chair and turns to talk to his children.

Everybody continues to eat and many conversations strike up among and across tables. After a minute or so everybody's attention began to shift to a discussion that is quickly becoming heated between Beth Stanton, a teacher specializing in interpretive performance arts, and Howard Roark, a teacher specializing in architectural application. Beth is upset because she believes that Howard has been attempting to solicit extra funds from

the school's financial committee to bring in a series of professional architects to demonstrate their work to his class. These funds would be from
the same discretionary fund that Beth relies on to fund Nietzsche Variety
Show. The two teachers go back and forth listing the merits of their respective programs and highlighting the essentialness of these experiences for
the students. Both are noticeably agitated. Dagny Taggart, an interested
community member intercedes, "Thank you both for your impassioned
explanations of your programs. This is the first that I am hearing of the
great work that Mr. Roark is doing with the architecture program, but it
sounds fantastic. And I absolutely love the Variety Show. My partner and
I come every year and it is a blast. It would be a shame if you had to cut
back on the show this year. I have a potential solution. My partner and I
own a local transportation company. We design the majority of the elevated
public transportation and employ a dozen architects with a variety of spe-
cialties. It would be my pleasure to encourage them to speak to Mr. Roark's
students on company time. Would that free up the money to devote to the
annual show Ms. Stanton?" Beth and Howard look at one another and then
shake their head in unison and turn to Dagny, "Thank you, Ms. Taggart!"

Everybody in the room seems satisfied with the way that the previous
discussion played out and got resolved. Suddenly Fred Engels, the civics
specialist stands up and asks, "Can we please address my longstanding
proposal to extend the school year to include the summer months? I don't
know the last time any of you checked, but we are not living in an agrar-
ian culture. We don't need our children working the farms in the summer,
and knowledge retention is such a challenge during the year let alone over
the summer. I'm not saying that it would be easy to do, but bottom line
is that the students would benefit from year round school." A number of
parents immediately voice concerns over this proposal. Among them is
Alex Deville who adamantly declares, "I don't know about everybody else,
but my kids have more going on in their lives than just going to school.
My kids are not just vegging out all summer long, and they certainly aren't
out causing trouble. They have activities that are just as important to their
growth as school and they look forward to these activities all year long. We
have sports, day camps, swim lessons, vacations, and a little bit of R and
R every now and then. I think they spend enough time in school already."
A number of parents clap for Alex's thoughts and the vast majority agree
with his concerns. Mr. Galt, the engineering specialist chimes in, "Yeah
Fred, I count on the time off in the summer to fully immerse myself in my
own family and self-care. A lot of us teachers are able to give of ourselves
as much as we do during the year because we know we have the summer
for personal time. Perhaps it would be more reasonable to discuss potential
optional programs for students and teachers who wish to take advantage."

Conversations similar to these continue well into the evening, but for the most part everybody spends their time mingling. Decisions big and small are deliberated every month at the Nietzsche Open-Forum. These events are garnering a great deal of attention and schools across the nation are coordinating similar Community-School Partnerships.

SO, WHERE ARE WE NOW?

Today we are standing at the edge of an ever-expanding abyss hoping for somebody to come and save us. When McCutcheon wrote her text extolling the benefits of deliberation, I am not sure if she was being optimistic or if she was living in a different world. I believe that both are partially true. McCutcheon found great cases of educators participating in group deliberation to make important curriculum decisions for their respective schools. She also cited great examples of individual teachers engaging in solo deliberation in order to continually hone their craft and provide the best possible curriculum to their students. I share McCutcheon's optimism because I have seen teachers engaging in deep solo deliberation in order to master the science and the art of building relationships with and inspiring our children. I have also seen the power of effective group deliberation. Unfortunately, I do not share McCutcheon's world. In my world the community-school partnerships are few and far between, and often superficial where they do exist. In my world, educators, students, parents and the general public feel disenfranchised and voiceless in conversations that directly affect them. In my world we wait for our elected Philosopher-Kings to use their altruism and wisdom to dictate how our schools should be run. The problem is that our grandiose Philosopher-Kings substitute self-interest and short-sighted constituency building for altruism and wisdom.

I would argue, and I believe McCutcheon (1995) would have agreed, that Mendelberg (2002) cited the true nature of deliberation:

> People in conflict will set aside their adversarial, win-lose approach and understand that their fate is linked with the fate of the other, that although their social identities conflict they "are tied to each other in a common recognition of their interdependence. (p. 153)

Individuals and groups participating in this type of deliberation have the unique ability to raise consciousness, encourage empathy, and begin to cooperatively solve problems rather than pull political strings to create edicts that elicit a forced pseudo-cooperation. Embracing the deliberative process allows us to hold individual beliefs and ideals that span the continuum, but still progress collectively. If we are looking to make worthwhile changes in our schools and in our society then we must adopt this ideal rather than recruiting 51% in order to drag the other 49% along against their will.

The real difference between my world and McCutcheon's world is that the opportunities for solo deliberation and true group deliberation are disappearing and being replaced by edicts from above. Educators, students, and parents feel voiceless because conflict-laden deliberation has been replaced with disconnected legislation. We have accepted the fallacious belief that our voice is heard through casting a vote. This is fallacious because our elected officials believe that they know what is best for us, but they are protected from the consequences of their decisions because they are well-served no matter what they decide. It is also fallacious because we all have a voice, a voice that is out of practice, but with the help of deliberation, a voice that cannot be silenced, and a voice that has the potential to change our society.

We are standing at the edge of an abyss. With every passing day the abyss continues to grow. Our Philosopher-Kings only distract us from our true goals with false promises. The situation is dire and we are frightened. Do we stay put and pretend we will not fall in? Do we take the path of decisiveness and authority and look to our Sovereign Master for security on the one-way bridge to submission? Or do we recognize deliberation as the vehicle of salvation and begin the messy process of leaving our bridges in the past and building our aircraft to the future?

REFERENCES

McCutcheon, G. (1995). *Developing the curriculum: Solo and group deliberation.* White Plains, NY: Longman.

Mendelberg T. (2002). The deliberative citizen: theory and evidence. In M. X. Delli Carpini, L. Huddy, & R. Shapiro (Eds.), *Research in micropolitics: Political decision making, deliberation and participation* (pp. 151–93). Greenwich, CT: JAI Press.

CHAPTER 6

UNDERSTANDING BY DESIGN

From Opacity to Transparency

Tasneem Amatullah

To be able to play with the ideas is to feel free to throw them into new combinations, to experiment, and even to "fail."

—Eisner (2002, p. 162)

Everyday a teacher walks into the classroom with numerous goals to achieve. The objectives and the outcomes of the lesson are written on either end of the whiteboard. The teacher explains the objective of the lesson and students take it down in their notebooks reinforcing what they will learn in that 50 minute time frame. The teacher delivers the lesson as planned and scripted on paper. After the lesson, the teacher assesses the students with differentiated questions to confirm that students understand the concepts and the objectives are met.

This procedure happened for almost every lesson I taught as a teacher in international elementary schools in Middle Eastern Countries. I served as a third grade homeroom teacher. There were five sections. As a science teacher by profession, I taught three different sections of third grade students, and the other two sections were taught by another teacher. A science

Curriculum Windows: What Curriculum Theorists of the 1990s Can Teach Us About Schools and Society Today, pp. 81–97
Copyright © 2017 by Information Age Publishing
All rights of reproduction in any form reserved.

coordinator met with both of us weekly to discuss the daily lesson plans, and we shared the objectives, activities, outcomes, and assessments as laid out in the initial yearly plan and the term plan. This happened routinely throughout the year. Yes, the lesson plans did have some differentiated activities for students based on their ability levels, but it was always a question for me as to how different students with different ability levels achieve the *same* objectives! Moreover, these different students are not just different based on their nationality, but they are different socially, economically, racially, and intellectually; yet, they are all subjected to identical assessments. Students then are divided based on their achievement levels and promoted to the next grade.

I was bored with the monotonous activities and imagined that the students probably felt the same way. I started to ask myself, "Am I doing a fair job for my students? Are they learning what they need to learn, not just to face exams, but also for life-long learning? Is teaching just about following goals and preparing students for standardized tests? Are my students enjoying their learning?" These were the questions that kept bothering me, and I decided to further my studies to hone my knowledge and skills and explore the field of teaching and leadership. I joined the Master of Educational Leadership program in Qatar, a small country bordering the Persian Gulf and Saudi Arabia (Brewer et al., 2007). It was there in 2012 that I first came across the book by Grant Wiggins and Jay McTighe (1998), *Understanding by Design* (UbD), for the first time. I was impressed by the way it laid out the need for "understanding," along with the six facets for understanding. My university classroom discussions were rich with ideas of how teachers used these facets in their teaching experience. The first time I read this book back in 2012, all I saw was the positive impact that this book had created with the "backward design" process. My colleagues then shared how powerful it is to implement this backward design in preparing lessons and teaching students.

And now, in 2015, I see the same book in my doctoral level seminar course. Dr. Poetter walked in with the pile of curriculum books of the 1990s on the first day of our seminar course for our project on writing the next volume of *Curriculum Windows: What Curriculum Theorists of the 1990s Can Teach Us about Schools and Society Today*. All students got to choose the top three books that they would like to work on for the 1990s book that will discuss how the curriculum books of 1990s create a window that connects the past, present, and the future to the field of curriculum. I put UbD on my list as my first choice. Luckily, Dr. Poetter assigned me this text to read for the spring semester. Excited, thrilled, and very nervous with mixed emotions, I started reading this book for the second time. To my surprise, this time, my perspective changed, mainly because I learned a lot about the curriculum field from great scholarly works of Eisner (2002) and Pinar,

Reynolds, Slattery, and Taubman (2006) on the reconceptualization of the curriculum field and also from the rich discussion in our seminar course.

Therefore, in this chapter, first, I present my "understanding" of the book *Understanding by Design*. Next, I critique Wiggins and McTighe's concept of backward design using Eisner (2002) and Pinar et al. (2006) which helped me conceive of *Understanding by Design* as an opaque window that does not let teachers look forward, only backward to originally planned objectives. However, I go on to discuss ways for that window to become a transparent window through the use of aesthetic curricular design. Finally, I share interactions with education professors in order to further consider the ways in which UbD might be useful to educators today. This chapter is presented like a short autobiography of a teacher, but the hope is that readers may reflect on their own teaching practices and look forward for transformation. It is never too late!

UNDERSTANDING *UNDERSTANDING BY DESIGN*

Wiggins and McTighe (1998), in their book *Understanding by Design,* present key ideas that facilitate teaching and learning and present a design template for educators to plan lessons. This design template is called backward design. The design has three stages in sequential order: (1) identify desired results; (2) determine acceptable evidence; and (3) plan learning experiences and instruction (Wiggins & McTighe, 1998). It calls for planning in such a way that we have the end goal in mind and plan the assessments and lessons to achieve the end goal.

UbD explains in detail each step that is required to design a lesson in a backward design model. The main idea revolves around demystifying the concept of "understanding" that gives rise to six facets of understanding: explanation, interpretation, application, perspective, empathy, and self-knowledge (Wiggins & McTighe, 1998). These six facets of understanding serve as a foundation for educators to think like an assessor and to justify learning based on these six facets of understanding. After prioritizing goals for learning and enduring understanding, an educator then designs the methods of assessment, finally writing the lesson plans and unit plans. I briefly present here the three stages of backward design.

Stage 1: What Is Worthy and Requiring of Understanding?

Wiggins and McTighe (1998) call for the framing of essential questions and more specific unit questions to aid in determining learning priorities by literally narrowing down the learning goals through a funnel. A teacher has to prioritize a broad essential question for each unit and then narrow it down by framing more specific questions. In this stage, the teacher determines the learning priorities. It is noteworthy that Wiggins and McTighe stress the need of realizing the "expert-novice" gap and advocate that teachers attempt to uncover the learning priorities from the students' perspective. Wiggins and McTighe (argue that there is no clear and finite line between the essential and the unit questions; they need to be seen as flowing on a continuum.

Stage 2: What Is the Evidence of Understanding?

In the second stage, students have to provide evidence for their understanding. It is here that Wiggins and McTighe (1998) unpack the six facets of understanding. They argue that if a student has developed a sound understanding, then the student will be in a position to explain, interpret, apply, have perspective, empathize, and have self-knowledge. Moreover, only when a student is able to provide evidence of all these facets has the student developed a "mature" understanding (p. 45). In addition to these facets, Wiggins and McTighe advocate for the teacher to think and plan like an "assessor" rather than just serve as an "activity designer" (p. 45). Assessing is basically broken down to two basic areas: (1) exploring where to look for understanding and (2) deciding on what needs to be looked for. This ties back to the first stage, and literally, we teach what we want to assess. However, Wiggins and McTighe do mention that assessment, like understanding, is on a continuum and assessments do not merely mean right or wrong; rather, they can be of a wide variety. Wiggins and McTighe argue for teachers to look for more insightful understanding beyond technical knowledge. They also have designed a rubric for assessment based on the six facets. With these two stages set up, next, teachers address enduring understanding and ways to find evidence of such in student learning. Then, in the third stage, the teacher actually designs the curriculum and the instruction.

Stage 3: What Learning Experiences and Teaching Promote Understanding, Interest, and Excellence?

Wiggins and McTighe (1998) posit that the main goal for teachers as designers is to focus on "uncoverage" in contrast to coverage (p. 99). They argue that a lesson ought to be planned in such a way that not only the concept of the unit is understood in "depth," but the lesson should also add another dimension called the "breadth," that will create room for extensions in learning and making connections to enduring understandings (p. 101). Further, Wiggins and McTighe present how the six facets can be applied to the design of units and individual lessons. The authors suggest the use of the acronym "WHERE" while designing lesson plans, which stands for: Where are we headed? Hook the student through engaging and provocative entry points, Explore and enable/equip, Reflect and rethink, Exhibit and evaluate" (p. 115). Overall, Wiggins and McTighe believe that education and learning will improve by beginning with the end in mind and assume this is the best approach to reach the desired goal. The quote below illustrates these authors' thoughts:

> Until we have specified the targeted understanding, the assessment tasks implied, and the enabling knowledge and skill necessary to master such tasks and display understandings, a discussion of learning activities and teaching strategy is immature. (p. 158)

This summarizes the whole idea of UbD. It seems that they are advocating for designing curriculum in a backward process, but my experience is the opposite of this design. We do have broad learning goals for a unit, but not with specific details that would restrict the teacher from creativity. Having an idea of what Wiggins and McTighe present in their UbD book, I rely on scholarly curriculum work from Eisner (2002) and Pinar et al. (2006) to critique UbD in my next section. The main purpose of the following sections is to understand how UbD can be viewed differently. How does a practicing teacher see it? How did I initially see it vs. how do I see it now?

EDUCATIONAL CRITICISM

Criticism is the art of disclosing the qualities of events or objects that connoisseurship perceives. Criticism is the public side of connoisseurship. One can be a connoisseur without the skills of criticism, but one cannot be a critic without the skills of connoisseurship. (Eisner, 1985, p. 223)

I present this section starting with a quote from Eisner (1985) that Pinar and his colleagues (2006) also emphasize in *Understanding Curriculum: An Introduction to the Study of Historical and Contemporary Curriculum Discourses*. We, as educators, need to learn educational connoisseurship: an "art of appreciation" and educational criticism: an "art of disclosure" (Eisner, 2002, p. 215). One key point to mention here is that I do agree with some of the profound thoughts that Wiggins and McTighe (1998) have explained in their UbD book, such as the six facets for understanding. However, the rhetoric in the book attempts to persuade the reader to believe that there is no better option than UbD for teachers. Wiggins and McTighe in each chapter lay out a rigid plan for each stage of backward design, but conclude the chapter saying that it is up to the teacher to embed creativity in it. Like I began to question my teaching in the past, I am also rethinking my unquestioning acceptance of UbD. The idea of working with ends in mind is clearly what has blown my mind. Right in chapter one of UbD, Wiggins and McTighe clearly state that "teaching is a means to an end" (p. 13), and I argue against this. Where does creativity lie when teachers teach with the ends in mind? I argue, in simple terms, they end up teaching to tests! Where is the freedom for teachers to practice progressive education? How could one accurately imagine and pre-plan the whole teaching process? Well, yes, an educator can, of course, anticipate a lesson the way s/he wants to execute it, but one cannot be a progressive educator in this backward design process. Eisner (2002) calls for "expressive outcomes" as the consequences of an educational activity that come into the limelight as the teaching is in progress (p. 118). As a teacher, I think that something good might come out of the teaching process that I never imagined, that I had never planned and anticipated. Hence, there are millions of objectives that teachers meet as unintended learning outcomes that cannot be fully fleshed out in one particular class.

Having about 10 years of teaching experience in international schools and students from diverse populations, I am unable to figure out ways of applying this backward design model with ends preceding the means, yet meet the needs of *all* students. And I am sure many teachers might echo similar concerns with the current education reforms focusing on standardization and high stakes testing, not only in the United States, but globally. Instead, I agree with Eisner (2002) who calls teaching an "art" that reveals itself during the process of teaching and that cannot be completely defined well ahead of time with a clear, concrete road map that has an *end in and of itself*. Eisner states that "teaching is an art in that the ends it achieves are often created in process" (p. 155). Numerous scholars echo Eisner and advocate for "curriculum as an aesthetic text" (Pinar et al., 2006, p. 567). They compare teaching and curriculum to the art of painting on canvas and state that, "curriculum comes to form as art does" (Pinar et al., 2006, p. 567). James Haywood Rolling Jr. (2010) shares these ideas and argues against the traditional curriculum planning. Rolling ironically argues that, by providing students with all these rigid and predefined objectives and outcomes to achieve, we merely subject them to "educational programing" and do not let them grow as responsible citizens. He argues that an "arts based curriculum ... has the flexibility either to spring up from traditional Tylerian objectives-based curriculum architectures or to trickle down from non-traditional practice based pedagogies" (p. 111).

We are all teachers in one way or the other! Well, I claim this from my personal experience as well as my educational experience. I am a teacher by profession, but I am a teacher to my children, too. I was a teacher to my siblings and other community members as well. And, I believe that many may also define "teachers" as I do. In my childhood days, I learned great things just by observing things happening in my surroundings, from my parents and other people living with me. For instance, I have a great passion for embroidery designing, and I learned it by watching my mother do it and by practicing myself. I can imagine that my mother may have had a broad goal that I learn embroidery, but I don't think she had definite end goals in mind that I should be learning certain designs only or specific methods that must be used. She left the doors open for creativity, color schemes, fabric choice, and so forth. The outcomes of such an activity for me are expressive, and this is what I wish to give to my students as well. The quote by Eisner (2002) that begins this chapter relates to teaching as an art, emphasizing the idea that being "able to play with the ideas is to feel free to throw them into new combinations, to experiment, and even to 'fail'" (p. 162). But the question arises, is there any room for teachers today to try new things? If one argues yes, I cannot imagine there is any opportunity for a teacher to *experiment* and *fail*. Reflecting back in the past, as an elementary teacher, I had the least opportunity to bring in any creativity as I was handed a set of standards that my third graders need to learn and on which they would be assessed. Therefore, as a teacher, I was just working to meet those standards and teach students to score well on the test. Even though, I was conscious that my students could learn a lot more that lies outside these sets of standards, I was held to the objectives that I was told to teach. "Superficial accountability," as I will call it, played a big role. I was accountable to my superiors and my students' parents. Teachers were and are evaluated on student achievement scores. So far, in my graduate studies, in Qatar and in the United States, I have heard and have been hearing concerns from teachers about the current educational reforms. I hear the same statement from teachers that learning is not *always* measurable. Reflecting on what UbD has proposed, I question how educators can plan their lessons, units, assessments, and end goals with such specificity that everything can be measured? Is measuring predetermined ends all there is to curriculum planning and teaching?

Further, Wiggins and McTighe (1998) refer to teachers as assessors who need to prepare assessments based on the end goals in mind. This ties back to the second stage of backward design. It reminds me of the same concept of teaching to the test. Eisner (2002) argues that "we look for data with which to determine education" (p. 177). We as educators tend to heavily rely on the information we already have planned to find in the students. In contrast, Eisner calls for a functional means of evaluation in five steps:

"(1) to diagnose the students' needs, (2) revise the curriculum, (3) compare the curriculum, (4) anticipate the educational needs, and (5) determine the objectives that are to be met" (p. 171). This is an artistic way to approach student evaluation, and this speaks to me. I see that evaluation happens in the process of learning, and we are working from means to the ends. This also provides some opportunities for me as a teacher to meet the needs of all students based on *their needs* instead of forcing my defined goals for them to achieve and prove as well.

Another thought that kept me bothering as I was reading UbD was referring students to "clients" (Wiggins & McTighe, 1998, pp. 7, 165). It is hard to imagine and use this metaphor for students who come to school desperate to be educated and not just be treated like "clients" in a business. This is exactly feeding into the current capitalistic economic world. The epistemological questions of who is deciding the curriculum, for whom and for what purposes need to be the central questions that we as educators should explore while designing a curriculum. I see students as citizens, equally important as any other member of the school, but unfortunately, they are the ones who are mostly taken for granted.

The educational criticism on UbD unpacks the metaphor of "window" that the *Curriculum Windows: What Curriculum Theorists of the 1990s Can Teach Us about Schools and Society Today* seeks to open up to all educators, pre-service teachers, curriculum designers, policy makers, and, hopefully, the upper governing bodies as well. I see UbD as an opaque window, that is, you can't see through it. It forces teachers to follow the rigid backward design model with ends preceding the means. This is similar to what Scott Sander (2013) in *Curriculum Windows 1960s* volume refers to in his chapter, "A Window Toward Expanded Experiences: Exposing Today's Limited Menu of Classroom Offerings and Asking for More Variety." Sander talks about how the curriculum today with instructional objectives and goals is so confined with boundaries and is limited. Sander argues that irrespective of the diversity of student, teacher, subject, or location we tend to offer the same "best practice" and this "view is simply too simple" (p. 23). There is not any opportunity for the students, as well as the teachers, to engage in conversations and question the schooling system itself. I see this design serving the standardization movement worldwide. The standards are the objectives/ends to achieve and UbD proposes this backward design to plan with the ends first. This has in turn commercialized the educational field. Hirsch, Kett, and Trefil (1993) explicitly argue for core standards that a student in each grade needs to know. I believe it is the rhetoric again that is inhibiting teachers' freedom to plan and design curriculum. Moreover, this leads to a "recipe" style design that favors the marketing of books and commercial publishers who propose predefined objectives and assessments for each unit (Eisner, 2002). However, I believe that teachers have not bought into this narrative, yet the hegemonic influences force them to follow the standardization movement.

To me, UbD and similar opaque windows have created a massive impact on teaching and learning that has stagnated the education system globally. These opaque windows are *no longer* windows, rather they have changed to *tough, strong, and rigid walls* feeding into the demands of a hegemonic educational system. But that does not mean it is the end of the story. Instead, the key is to maneuver possibilities and transform this *opacity to transparency*. Eisner (2002) and Pinar et al.'s (2006) texts help me as an educator to see the possibilities in designing curriculum aesthetically and in moving away from the traditional curriculum design approach. The first two sections of this chapter connected the concepts from UbD with my past teaching experiences. But, I would like to stop here for a moment and see how I can weave what I have learned from my past experiences into my present teaching.

FROM OPACITY TO TRANSPARENCY: A TEACHER'S EFFORT

Teaching sociocultural studies in education to undergraduate students in the United States has given me a great opportunity to transform my teaching practices. The following scenario is a very different one than what you read at the beginning of this chapter.

The classroom is bright and lively with 18 students. They are seated in small groups of fours and fives. Informally, the class begins with greetings and clarifying any concepts and concerns from the previous class. Students are prepared with the readings for the class. They respond to each other's questions, and I further clarify their understanding when needed. I facilitate students' learning with the help of videos and other pedagogical methods. Then, I engage students with questions to begin small group conversations. I take turns talking to students in each of the groups who share their thoughts. Then, we collaboratively dig deeply into the ideas as we come together in large group discussions.

So, what is different in this vignette from the one I narrated before? Some of the obvious thoughts would be, the first one was an elementary classroom and this is an undergraduate classroom, so age of students is a key factor in designing a lesson, along with the geographic location, and so forth. I do agree that the classrooms are different in these terms, but now, as a teaching associate, neither am I handed a set of standards to meet nor do I have to assess students on standardized tests. At least, in the higher education field I am not having to do that. One must be wondering if that means I do not have any objectives and goals to teach or if I do not evaluate students learning at all! Of course, I do walk into the class with a lesson plan, but that is not rigid and not an end in itself. As the lesson moves forward, my questions change depending on the needs of the students. I evaluate and assess students' learning through a variety of assessments. They assessed on their performance on written quizzes, their contribution in class participation that is assessed as I walk around listening to their small group discussions, how they can apply the concepts learned in the outside contexts, and the writing of academic papers. Depending on the students' needs I modify my lesson plan, and this is what Eisner (2002) proposes in his five step artistic way of educational evaluation. Eisner and Pinar et al. (2006) have helped me ground my thoughts theoretically. Given my varied responses to UbD over time, I argue that teachers and educators need to be exposed to and reflect on a variety of scholarly literature.

This is just one snippet I thought to share, and I believe progressive teachers may have many similar experiences. Moreover, the concept of this experience as a journey from *opacity to transparency* is something worthwhile to share. First, the way the lessons are designed is not a "backward design." We do have the broad goals and objectives of the course in mind, but there is no one fixed way to achieve those, in contrast to what UbD has proposed in three sequential steps. Second, learning is happening in the process, and this is what Eisner (2002) calls as "expressive outcomes" (p. 118). Third, evaluation is not dreadful to students. They are continuously evaluated throughout the semester by a variety of assessments. Finally, there is lot of room for creativity on part of teachers and students. I am not bounded to cover n number of standards in a particular class for a particular term to assess students for end of term tests. There are plenty of opportunities that the curriculum offers students to think of their learning experiences in other contexts.

When I look back into my K–12 teaching experience in view of my current doctoral classroom discussions with other PhD students who serve as school administrators, teachers, and also parents, I hear their cry of being trapped into the standardization movement that forces them to unintentionally follow the "backward design," as it meshes well with this educational system where teachers are accountable for everything. The famous narrative "blame the teacher" aptly corresponds to the current education scenarios. Teachers are sandwiched between the school's management system and parents. At all levels of the educational system, there is one person who is to be blamed for student achievement, and it is the teachers. But why are we running behind this student achievement, when students are just programmatically tested on exams? The learning is fake when students are just assessed on the standards they ought to learn. To me, this is clear hegemony. Quantz (2015) explains hegemony as the process in which the institutions such as the legal system, the media, the churches, the health care system, the economic system, and the schools are harnessed by the powerful to work in their own interests, rather than in the public's interest. (p. 103)

It is evident that there are some people of power who act upon teachers to follow the rigid curriculum without leaving any room for creativity. Quantz (2015) further argues that, even though the education system seems to call itself progressive, the reality is that it is leaning more towards an essentialist style. Critical pedagogues like Paulo Freire call this banking education where students are just fed the knowledge and skills that they can store and retrieve in their adulthood to feed into the job marketplace (as cited in Quantz, 2015). I believe this is exactly what is happening. Despite the teachers adopting a variety of teaching methods, the end goal is turning out to be the same. My undergraduate students ask me, "Okay! So, what can we as educators do? Is there a way to bring about any change? How can we change this whole system?" I certainly believe that educators can be one of the greatest forces that can bring some change. It may be a small drop in a mighty ocean, but still it does have impact. Therefore, the rest of the chapter expresses a hope for a teacher's dream that will come true. The UbD criticism has paved an obvious way to see it as an opaque window. However, there are some great thoughts in UbD that teachers can use in their teaching. The main idea is to reflect on these scholarly recommendations and explore what is there in UbD that can best serve to educate students creatively.

THE TRANSPARENT WINDOW: A TEACHER'S DREAM

Wiggins and McTighe (1998) had one common theme throughout their book, the concept of *understanding*. I believe that the six facets of understanding: explanation, interpretation, application, perspective, empathy, and self-knowledge, can really make a big change in the teaching and learning of students. However, the key is that these facets need not be applied in the backward design model. Wiggins and McTighe laid out remarkable ideas to play with these facets while exploring enduring understanding, with the teacher as an assessor, and even while planning the curriculum and instruction. But, the issue is that these facets need to fit and work within that rigid backward design model. Having the end in mind and working towards those finite ends without any creativity is very disturbing to me as a teacher. However, I also see that Wiggins and McTighe have given us a window, "a blessing in disguise" for teachers in the form of these six facets. I call this as a blessing in disguise since the main takeaway from the book is the "backward design" model, and I do not advocate for that. Yet, the hidden idea within that model is the "blessing" in the form of these six facets.

Though one may argue that these six facets emphasize individualism and neglect the community and the social aspect on the whole, I, as a teacher, see that when the last two facets, empathy and self-knowledge, are presented creatively to students, many opportunities will arise for students to explore the social aspect as responsible citizens. I further argue that only when teachers are given that freedom to aesthetically plan the curriculum and instruction for their students will there be an opportunity for true learning. There needs to be a way to get rid of this top-down hierarchical method of handing the curriculum to teachers and forcing them to follow it. Teachers are the only ones who spend most of the time with the students, and they know better what the students need. Eisner (2002) argues that in the process of teaching and meeting the standards, one must not neglect the needs of the teachers themselves. Just as in other professions a person looks for job satisfaction, so it should be the case with teachers as well. There needs to be a way where teachers' voices will be heard, and they will be a part of the curriculum. And, there needs to be a way where the diversity of students will be embraced and their learning interests are taken into consideration. And this is what will give shape to my dream. A dream of an artistic teaching career! I hope the readers will be a part of the dream. Imagine....

A teacher walks into a third grade classroom with a vibrant and energetic smile and greets the students. Responding to the teacher's greetings, students on the other hand are excitedly waiting for the teacher to arrive. Students comment, "Yea, we have Ms. XXX class now!" and settle down to explore what the teacher has for them today. The teacher starts the class by presenting the ideas they will learn today. It is a class on discussing the hazards of pollution. The teacher groups the students with some prompts to engage in group research in class, and the students report back their ideas to all students. The teacher facilitates students' learning and researching the hazards caused by pollution. All these junior scientists begin their research. The students are extremely engaged in research, in dialogues, brainstorming ideas to present their understanding to their peers. They are imagining a real pollution scenario and interpreting it from different lenses from their own perspectives. Every student contributes valuable thoughts that lead to more engaging dialogues. The teacher assesses the students in many ways, such as their participation while doing the research, the content of the research ideas, the interaction among the peers, the presentation to the whole class, and so forth. The class comes to an end, and students are still engaged. The teacher encourages students to explore further with homework activity.

Wow, what a great satisfaction a teacher will get from such a class. I wish to dream further. But for all this to happen, teachers need to be given freedom to design the curriculum and not be held accountable for teaching to tests or to narrowly predetermined standards. For Eisner (2002), the curriculum and teaching cannot be separated at all. One can argue that this type of teaching and learning happens even in today's classrooms. I do agree that this may happen in progressive teachers' classrooms; however, even a progressive teacher is forced to feed into the standardization system serving to the end goals. Their pedagogical methods may be progressive, but they philosophically fit into an essentialist category! For instance, in this dream scenario, as an artistic teacher, I see that the broad goal was to learn about the pollution hazards. However, I see that students may have learned infinite knowledge and skills during this research process. In the backward design, a teacher may not credit the other means of learning and may focus solely on achieving the end goal as they have to prove it on the tests.

Let me elaborate on what I am advocating for, *artistic teaching* as Eisner (2002) has described it. Eisner posits that there are four senses in the art of teaching. First, a teacher hones his/her craft and then presents it to the students, and this in itself is an "aesthetic experience" (p. 155). Second, the teachers make decisions throughout the process and keep "tempo, tone, climate, pace of discussion, and forward movement" (p. 155). Third, a teacher's activity cannot be confined and dominated by the ideas that are predefined when they are not aware of the real classroom scenarios. Therefore, a teacher needs to automatically adapt to the needs of the students and the particular situation. Fourth, the unimagined ends are sometimes great. Pinar et al. (2006) argue that the aesthetic experience will not only lead to the "material experience" but rather to the "lived experience" as well (p. 580). However, this calls for curriculum reforms within the educational system itself.

Can a teacher amidst these massive standardization, accountability, and reform movements imagine artistic teaching? I believe that Wiggins and McTighe's (1998) six facets can be at least be *one* means toward artistically developing and teaching a curriculum. It basically needs to come out of the cage of backward design so that the teachers can use the six facets at any point of their curriculum plan to enhance learning. It need not be glued to the first step of the backward design and then followed throughout the whole process. Instead, teachers must be able to implement it any point of their teaching to add an artistic edge to it. Furthermore, the teachers need to be creative in executing a plan and maneuver possibilities to maximize students' learning. When that is done, I see a transparent window that I can see through, when these six facets are embedded in the aesthetic curriculum. This is a challenging dream, but not an impossible one!

My teaching of undergraduate students is going well, but I am curious to explore how I will adapt myself in a K–12 teaching system. I believe that being reflective is a good start for transformation, but I also believe that learning from best practices is an addition that will help me navigate my path easily. I wanted to utilize this scholarly learning opportunity of writing a book chapter and decided to talk to some of my professors in the College of Education, Health, and Society (EHS) at Miami University about UbD.

My Journey Continues ...

I spoke with some professors and understand their thoughts on UbD and the strategies they use to plan their teaching and curriculum. I met three professors, and the moment I reiterated that UbD is advocating for a backward design curriculum in which the ends precede the means, all I heard was a big NO to this design template. They all echoed similar thoughts:

Are the teachers empowered in this design?

How far do we teach in terms of social justice to students with this backward design model?

We have narrowed down the role of the teacher to just technicality!

There is unquestioned hegemony in this whole process.

Having a rigid model is problematic.

Not ALL learning is measureable!

With all these questions in mind, I shared their experiences of curriculum designing and teaching. One professor commented that s/he has broad goals of the course for each semester, but then s/he does not have a clear weekly plan of what students will be learning. I was amazed when I heard this. I wondered how this could be happening because I felt disturbed, and from a student's perspective, I believed in having a roadmap well ahead of time. The response to this was stunning that learning happens due to this disturbance, and to me, this was an aesthetic way of teaching. I could sense that teaching was happening in the process and that the professor was altering and modifying the plans based on students' needs. This professor further emphasized on ways teachers can use UbD as a transparent window. The note below motivated me to think of UbD in a different way.

What's stopping the teachers from using UbD in a more flexible, humanistic, or artistic manner? What will it take for teachers to "see" UbD as a loose, not rigid framework? I use it all the time, mentally, but my "ends" are "growth," "engagement," "understanding," and "independence." I just don't pretend that they reach that by a single lesson, but I make sure my pedagogical decisions are pointing my students and me in that direction.

Ritchhart's (2015) *Creating Cultures of Thinking: The 8 Forces We Must Master to Truly Transform Our Schools* is inspiring; this professor believes in creating opportunities for students to enhance thinking skills. Ritchhart mainly emphasizes developing and giving students the opportunities to think and explore their learning, rather than any particular fixed curriculum. Ritchhart calls for eight cultural forces that a teacher and students can utilize to create a platform for thinking: expectations, language, time, modeling, opportunities, routines, interactions, and environment.

Another professor commented that s/he has used this UbD planning template in the preservice teacher programs to design lessons. But s/he emphasized that though they had the end goals laid out, it was not fixed and rigid. There was plenty of room for creativity. The plans were amended based on the requirements of the students. To this professor, embracing the diversity of students was very essential, and UbD had not many options for that. In addition to this, the professor also remarked that forcing teachers to follow the backward design model is clear hegemony. Though planning lessons based on "essential questions" is important, there needs to be freedom for teachers to modify them as needed, s/he added. During this dialogue, it was also emphasized that the inclusion of students and teachers in the curriculum and designing is a key factor that can cause some change in the educational system.

For another professor, the education system on the whole today has become a mere technical, engineering process. There is hardly any creativity, s/he commented. This was further elaborated by distinguishing between outcomes-based instruction and value-based instruction (Quantz, 2011). Outcomes-based instruction narrows down the teaching process so drastically that if a teacher knows the ends to achieve before even starting, then the teachers' sole focus is only to achieve those goals. And this is just referred to as a "technical exercise" (Quantz, 2011, p. 152). But with value-based instruction, where the core idea is to plan our teaching around values and not just on the measurable objectives as we do in UbD, the emphasis is not the "efficacy and efficiency," but rather on the "ethics" (Quantz, 2011, p. 168). It is worth noting that when I see UbD as a transparent window, there are lot of opportunities for me to transform these measurable objectives into value-based objectives by adopting an aesthetic curriculum and pedagogical methods.

Ultimately, through these discussions and my curiosity to explore the best practices I learned that there are many professors who look for opportunities to navigate their paths, yet teach aesthetically. Hence, for UbD to transform from opacity to transparency, I argue that educators need to teach aesthetically. Basically, one has to utilize UbD's core idea on the need of understanding and its six facets in an artistic way that uncovers UbD from its routine cage of "backward design." It is evident that many curriculum scholars, especially Eisner (2002) and Pinar (2006), argue that evaluation must take place within the learning process, rather than just at the end. Finally, I believe that educators can be one of the greatest forces of change and certainly have the power to transform UbD to a transparent window by Eisner's and Pinar's artistic teaching. Theoretically, the Eisner (2002) and Pinar et al. (2006) texts paved my way to understand the aesthetic curriculum through planning and teaching, but practical knowledge I gained from my colleagues is even more remarkable. My journey does not end here. I am looking forward to implementing aesthetic curricula rigorously into my teaching career!

ACKNOWLEDGMENTS

I would like to thank Dr. Richard Quantz, Dr. Scott Sander, and Dr. Brittany Aronson for their valuable time and thoughts shared that helped me reflect more on UbD. I also want to thank Dr. Thomas Poetter, who has helped me shape this chapter by facilitating my learning as a doctoral student and providing rich feedback

REFERENCES

Brewer, D., Augustine, C., Zellman, G., Ryan, G., Goldman, C., Stasz, C., & Constant, Lo. (2007). *Education for a new era: Design and implementation of K–12 education reform in Qatar*. Rand Corporation. Retrieved February, 17th, 2015, from http://www.rand.org/pubs/monographs/2007/RAND_MG548.pdf

Eisner, E. (1985). *The educational imagination: On the design and evaluation of school programs* (2nd ed.). New York, NY: Macmillan.

Eisner, E. (2002). *The educational imagination* (3rd ed). Upper Saddle River, NJ: Prentice Hall.

Hirsch, E. D., Kett, J. F., & Trefil, J. (Eds.). (1993). *The dictionary of cultural literacy: What every American needs to know* (2nd ed.). Boston, MA: Houghton Mifflin.

Pinar, W. F., Reynolds, W. M., Slattery, P., & Taubman, P. M. (2006). *Understanding curriculum: An introduction to the study of historical and contemporary curriculum discourses*. New York, NY: Peter Lang.

Quantz, R. A. (2011). *Rituals and student identity in education: Ritual critique for a new pedagogy*. New York, NY: Palgrave Macmillan.

Quantz, R. A. (2015). *Sociocultural studies in education: Critical thinking for democracy*. Boulder, CO: Paradigm.

Ritchhart. R. (2015). *Creating cultures of thinking: The 8 forces we must master to truly transform our schools*. San Francisco, CA: Josey-Bass.

Rolling, J. J. (2010). A paradigm analysis of arts-based research and implications for education. *Studies in Art Education, 51*, 102–114.

Sander, S. (2013). A window toward expanded experiences: Exposing today's limited menu of classroom offerings and asking for more variety. In T. S. Poetter et al. (Eds.), *Curriculum windows: What curriculum theorists of the 1960s can teach us about schools and society today* (pp. 17–33). Charlotte, NC: Information Age Publishing.

Wiggins, G., & McTighe, J. (1998). *Understanding by design*. Alexandria, VA: Association for Supervision and Curriculum Development.

CHAPTER 7

CENTRAL PARK EAST

The Power of Their Ideas and the Possibilities of School Change

Jody C. Googins

I can imagine the energy inside the walls of Central Park East (CPE) School in Harlem, New York, in the early 1990s. I can imagine the energy from the students, from the teachers, and from CPE's fearless leader, Deborah Meier. I imagine it would be *almost* overwhelming—working in an environment that demanded so much, an environment that didn't allow issues to go unsettled, an environment that commanded accountability from each and every stakeholder. I can imagine that there were days that were struggles, days when it didn't seem that things could go right. Perhaps issues beyond the walls and windows of the school came creeping into its protected core. Perhaps a student or several students were causing teachers to question their purpose, to question their choices both curricularly and pedagogically, to question their very mission. Perhaps there were days when teaching at CPE was just really hard. I can imagine that the demands of giving of one's *whole* self, day in and day out, must have been taxing. And to work under a leader who seemed to never tire, who never lowered

Curriculum Windows: What Curriculum Theorists of the 1990s Can Teach Us About Schools and Society Today, pp. 99–113
Copyright © 2017 by Information Age Publishing

her standards, who never cut corners, who never said "never mind"—some days must have just felt... tiring.

Alice Seletsky, one of the original teachers at CPE describes her experiences as she wades through boxes and boxes of her saved materials from the years:

> So much time and thought, effort and anguish—mine *and* theirs; so much wondering and worrying; so much tracking and backtracking; so many unanswered, perhaps unanswerable, questions. They tumble around in my mind, still troubling after all these years. Some are about everyday teaching matters—what else can I do about fractions, punctuation, times tables, map symbols? Some are the large, haunting ones, the stuff of bad dreams: Did I do the right things? Did I teach them well? Are they prepared? Will they succeed? (Bensman, 2000, pp. 129–130)

Alice talks about the tough times of tackling issues of personal and communal needs that come to light in a place like CPE. They used "a let's-try-it-and-see-what-happens-because-we-don't-know-what-else-to-do approach" (p. 132), which often left issues "fuzzy, unresolved, messy, and open, which left everyone a bit dissatisfied, but also left room for more improvisation" (p. 132). Working at CPE demanded much more from its teachers than closing a door, teaching to a test, and interpreting data. And I can imagine that forging those uncharted waters was tough.

But then I imagine the days that were full of the goodness of that place—the days when their visions came to fruition. I am sure that the days when students returned to CPE as college graduates or professionals, or as moms and dads, were some of the most rewarding. I imagine that after a 2-hour, heated faculty meeting that happened once a week at CPE when they just-try-it-and-see-what-happens, concluded, after a troubling issue had been dissected, examined, diagnosed, and a solution was proposed and accepted by the entire faculty. I imagine they felt that those days were good and that their faith was restored. Those days probably carried them through the tough days. I imagine that every teacher at CPE felt the satisfaction of delivering a true child-centered education, of allowing children a space to thrive and grow and choose and develop at their own pace, guided by their own interests. And that they flourished in the community that was built, brick by brick, day by day, with the parents, with the students, with each other, and with the extensions of all of those stakeholders.

> Alice Seletsky expresses her pleasure when reading recollections from CPE graduates: The graduates echo one another in acknowledging that their early schooling, at Central Park East School, *made a difference*. Some describe, in detail, the effect of their school experiences on their later lives. I love reading the stories even as I recognize that the testimony is biased. It is colored

by nostalgia and sentiment, and the absence of other school experiences with which to compare their own. (Bensman, 2000, p. 130)

She discusses the community that is built when teachers are open and accountable with and to their colleagues. When teachers needed guidance, materials, inspiration, they just shared:

Inevitably, a sense of community grew from these informal comings and go-ings. Popping in to borrow a ball of twine meant spending a few minutes observing and catching glimpses of the work going on in a colleague's room; asking for help with a youngster or advice about curriculum invited reciproc-ity. (Bensman, 2000, p. 132)

Community, improvisation, accountability to others, and passion created an environment where students thrived, teachers could take risks, and learning truly occurred.

CENTRAL PARK EAST

What a place Central Park East must have been! As an educator who has spent my career at enormous, corporate high schools, under the ever-changing conditions and mandates of the public education system, I can only imagine what it must have felt like to work at a place like CPE. Deborah Meier (1995) allowed me to peek through the windows of CPE and learn about it in her work *The Power of Their Ideas*. The first CPE opened its doors in 1974 amid crisis in New York City's school system. As the school system was laying off more than 15,000 teachers and closing elementary school libraries and music and art programs, and communities were still suffering from the teacher strikes of 1967 and 1968 which pitted the "mostly white teaching force against minority communities and one set of parents against another" (p. 18), Central Park East opened its doors. It was a tumultuous time, but a visionary superintendent, Anthony Alvarado, decided to ask Deborah Meier to open this small elementary school in one wing of another elementary school and to try and make it a go in one of the city's poorest, lowest performing communities. There were a distinct set of problems, and CPE served as response to those problems. Meier could not refuse.

Central Park East was opened with a small staff of six teachers and one paraprofessional, a large vision, and an unwavering commitment to child-centered, progressive ideals. The teachers of Central Park East, under the leadership of Deborah Meier, sought all that could be good and just in a school setting and that had been slowly drained away in traditional schools by policies and mandates that turned schools into factories, neglecting students of color and their often low socioeconomic status. The teachers yearned for autonomy and a break from the constraints of the bureaucracy that had become the New York City's public school system. They wanted an environment where the entire staff could sit at a table and make decisions, take action, and sort out complications; where they could "know their students as learners well ... [something that] takes time and trust" (Meier, 1995, p. 49); and where they could be held accountable and hold their peers accountable. So Meier created CPE—a school that didn't follow traditional curriculum, pedagogical methods, or an administrative top-down approach. CPE became a community of students, parents, and teachers; and it was successful.

Deborah Meier (1995) chronicles CPE, which is actually "four public schools working in close collaboration with each other under all the constraints of the public school system, but without all the problems that plague many others" (pp. 15–16), in her 1995 work *The Power of Their Ideas*. She takes the reader through the creation of CPE, along with all the trials and tribulations that went into such an endeavor. She works from a progressive, democratic, child-centered philosophy and addresses the benefits of building a school on progressive principles, as well the obstacles, head-on.

CPE was built from the ground up with the influence of Meier (1995) and her colleagues, who say that a good school should be

> a little like kindergarten and a little like a post-graduate program—the two ends of the educational spectrum, at which we understand we cannot treat any two human beings identically, but must take into account their special interests and styles even as we hold all to high and rigorous standards. (pp. 48–49)

Meier claims that teachers need a framework that is centered on trust built through relationships and community. And she stresses that these needs cannot be mandated—choice is the basis for mutual trust. At CPE, it is important to have an entire staff at one table for a conversation. This way, decisions can be made with the voices of all and do not need to go through a hierarchy before changes can be enacted. This also increases accountability among staff members. In order to allow for this type of atmosphere, the structure of CPE and its offspring, was created with these ideals in mind. There is a flexibility of scheduling, small class sizes, common plan time, as well as built-in staff collaboration time. This structure demands deliberate decision-making by the teachers. In Central Park East Secondary School (CPESS) that was produced in the years following the establishment of CPE, in order "to create a unity across disciplines and a focus on the essential that hadn't seemed so critical in the younger grades" (p. 49), Meier and her colleagues created the "Habits of Mind" that are so important to CPESS.

The "CPESS Habits of Mind" are at the center of CPESS, for students and staff alike, and are a part of all that happens at CPESS. The habits help students and teachers to be caring and compassionate by working to make them habitual—by demanding in-depth practice and immersing young people in their use. The Habits of Mind stress "The acceptance of increasing levels of responsibility, the increasing capacity to communicate appropriately to others, a willingness to take a stand as well as a willingness to change one's mind, and being someone who can be counted on to meet deadlines as well as keep one's word" (Meier, 1995, p. 49), instead of the students' capacity to collect trivia. Teachers and students alike practiced the Habits of Mind; by practicing these habits, teachers were able to foster a "buy-in" by all parties to the central ideals of CPE and CPESS.

The Habits of Mind are:

- The question of evidence, or "How do we know what we know?"
- The question of viewpoint in all its multiplicity, or "Who's speaking?"
- The search for connections and patterns, or "Who causes what?"
- Supposition, or "How might things have been different?"
- And finally, why any of it matters, or "Who cares?" (Meier, 1995, p. 50)

Meier (1995) says that these habits are "at the heart of each curriculum as well as being the basis for judging student performance" (p. 50). The curricular significance of these Habits is immense. They are practiced in-depth and woven through all phases of the students' lives. In order to accomplish this, the teachers will cover less content, but will dig deeper. This approach is in stark contrast to the attempt by typical schools to cover an enormous breadth of curricular goals. This approach makes a small school even smaller. Students are given time, resources, and support to explore topics that are relevant and of interest. Instead of racing through an American literature class that starts in the 1600s and desperately tries to make it to the post-modern period of the mid-1900s, reading hundreds of pieces with little analysis and depth, teachers and students can dig into literature and genres that speak to them. What a gift—time to explore, appreciate, and *learn*.

Meier (1995) sought to deliver the highest quality education to each and every child that attended CPE, regardless of class, race, or ability level. By providing this high quality schooling experience for every child, she was essentially opening the window to justice, with education as the conduit. Providing one level of education to some students, while providing a different level of education to other students, could not and would not serve

Meier's purpose—giving students a future in a social and political democracy in which the Habits of Mind matter.

THE ANTIBLUEPRINT APPROACH

When I think about CPE, my perspective is from that of a teacher. This is my lens, one from which I cannot divorce myself. The creation of CPE was a direct response to a troubled school system. This response united a group of like-minded teachers. Deborah Meier (1995) discusses her disillusionment with teaching in a system that did not reach students and her desire to work in a community of teachers with the same goals and ideals as hers. She was frustrated in her early years of teaching by the silencing of "playground intellectuals" (p. 3) in schools and schools' inability to "loosen rather than tighten" the "constraints that poverty and racism impose on the lives of children" (p. 3). These concerns kept her close to the classroom for 30 years, and she knew early on that there were problems with the way many schools were structured and operating. The creation of CPE, though, was not a hasty, thrown-together decision. Alvarado and Meier didn't decide to start a school and then open the doors a few short weeks later; sans supplies, the appropriate staff, and facilities. They did not create a system using a preexisting blueprint and then resist changing that system if it was imperfect. They did not open the next two buildings in haste, either. Meier and her colleagues made it a priority to work through all the problems that they encountered, and then to enact an appropriate response. They were not afraid to take risks and they were not afraid to fail. They began "small and carefully" (p. 20), putting democratic ideals at the forefront.

What is astounding is that CPE *worked*. The curricular and pedagogical structure, the community of teachers and learners, and the leadership that guided CPE and its offspring affected change. David Bensman (2000) shows this with his longitudinal study of CPE's graduates in his book *Central Park East and its Graduates*. He gathers both quantitative and qualitative data in his research and shares the successes of CPE and its graduates. Through his interpretation of data and personal stories, he comes to a conclusion about CPE:

> I realized that much of what had made CPE successful was not part of the original blueprint, but instead was created by teachers as they identified problems and searched for solutions. Suddenly, what stood out was less CPE's grounding in progressive theory, and more the organization's ability to learn and grow. (p. 7)

Bensman subtly reminds us that it is often not a "blueprint" that makes a school work or not work; it is the people, the attitudes, and the relationships that do.

Bensman (2000) recognizes that a place like CPE cannot be replicated. Keri Rodgers (2014) contends that the success of CPE and of Meier's other experiment—the Mission Hill School in Boston—caused school reformers to believe that Meier's small schools could cure the ills of our urban schools, that they could raise graduation rates and student achievement. But these "school reformers attempted to develop a mass model to replicate Meier-type schools, an effort which quickly became much more wide-spread with the aid and support of groups including the Bill and Melinda Gates Foundation and New Visions for Public Schools" (p. 126). I believe that these attempts at replicating places like CPE—using its blueprint—failed because they are top-down approaches. What made CPE unique and special is the work that was done on the inside, by the teachers, students, and community, not by a set structure, administrative teams, and governing bodies. Bensman (2000) talks about CPE's ability to constantly learn and grow. This learning and growing occurred on a daily basis, through deliberate thought and action, and with all the teachers' knowledge that "the values and attitudes that the CPE staff brought to their job were equally important" (p. 122).

Implementing change—sometimes a minor change and sometimes a complete restructuring of a school—cannot be executed by replication. It can be achieved only from the inside and only when all stakeholders are "in." Because a certain model is effective in one setting does not mean it will be successful in another setting. In this era of reform, it is tempting to school leaders to simply *restructure*; however, "Restructuring offer(s) no panacea" (Newman & Wehlage, 1995, p. 4). Newman and Wehlage (1995) say that at the core of all school change is student learning. Restructuring has advanced "student learning when it concentrated on the intellectual quality of student work, when it built schoolwide organizational capacity to deliver authentic pedagogy, and when it received support from the external environment that was consistent with these challenges" (p. 4). Just making a change, modeling a school restructuring project on another school, putting puzzle pieces together methodically, cannot and does not work when there are teachers and students and administrators and parents and communities who vary. The window to change cannot be mass-produced.

MAKING BIG SCHOOLS SMALL

Deborah Meier and the Small Schools Movement represent a stark contrast to my path as an educator thus far. I am a veteran high school teacher who has spent 14 years in large, public high schools. As Deborah Meier has allowed me to peek through the window of CPE, I would like to open a window to show you the inside of a large, public high school in 2015. All three schools in which I have taught have similar blueprints; there are very few differences. I have taught hundreds of students and have passed thousands more in the hallways of these schools. I often worry about the sheer *bigness* of it all, the lack of community. I currently teach at a school of about 1,600 students and 150 teachers. I think I know about 100 kids, just a small fraction of the total enrollment. I pass adults in the hall daily that I have never seen before, but apparently we work together. I remember once attempting to go see my principal about an issue I was having in my class and him telling me to make an appointment with his secretary, even when I said I only needed 5 minutes. I have learned to beg forgiveness instead of ask for permission when I want to do something different, because going through the endless chain of the bureaucracy is an exhausting process; plus no one will probably notice any way.

I think there are problems that can be identified in the high school where I currently teach, and in the high schools I worked previous. Specifically in my current school, there has been a persistent problem in our staff culture and professional community. In the last several years, leadership did not work to create a cohesive professional community. Teachers here have been free from interference in the classroom for many years. This is an interesting "problem" to have because autonomy is often many teachers' biggest desire.

In this case, though, it is not autonomy that is the primary activity practiced by teachers, instead, it is often a lack of trust and accountability to and between other teachers that leads to many closed doors. Departments do have common plan time, and there certainly is coordination within disciplines, as teachers of the same subject do discuss curricular choices and creating a cohesive school experience for students within the discipline. This is a common blueprint for large high schools; they are divided nicely into departments who work independently of each other. In some ways, many would argue that this freedom has been good. And when a high school is churning out 20+ National Merit Finalists a year, and performing very well on state and national measurements, there was not always the need for interference from an administrative force.

That being said, a large staff of 150 teachers, divided into subsections, working independently of each other, does not create a cohesive experience for the students. So while my lens is that of a teacher, I cannot help but consider what it must be like as a student who may pass from class to class, teacher to teacher, and year to year, with disconnections and breaks. A staff that does not get the opportunity to become familiar with what is happening in other classrooms cannot possibly complement nor reinforce other teachers' curriculum and pedagogy.

In addition to staff culture, there is the problem of the aforementioned *bigness* of it all. It is this bigness that is most concerning to me in some of today's large schools. One illustration of the problems with the large size is a story about a student I taught named Amy...

As I look out over the crowded gym filled with anxious seniors, it's hard to believe how many I do not know. There are over 700 in this room; I have taught probably 200 of them, but would struggle to recall each name. It's the annual graduation practice—one of only 2 days when one can guarantee that all 700+ seniors will sit in one room, the second day being the actual graduation. My eyes come to rest on one particular student—Amy. As I look at her, I become concerned. She looks so different from the Amy I knew. As a junior, Amy was energetic, fit, motivated, with-it. She was an excellent student—conscientious, curious. Looking at Amy now, I could see she was not the same. She was slouched over in her seat, not even bothering to pretend to be engaged. She was dressed sloppily, and had clearly stopped the workout regiment that I knew her to be so committed to as a junior. It created a panic in me. What was going on? Had anyone noticed? I walked over to one of the senior English teachers and asked if she had taught Amy this year. The teacher immediately talked about how lazy she was, how she slept practically every day, how she came late often and was never engaged. She said, "What a waste of a great mind." In my mind, I panicked. I thought—when did we lose Amy? Did anyone notice? Did the anonymity of this 700+ class of seniors mask her struggles? When she left my class the previous year, I assumed she was fine and that she had continued to be a strong, engaged student. Apparently, when she entered her senior year, she was changed. But no one knew because no one connected it. What had happened to Amy and how could we have missed it?

What would Deborah Meier do if faced with a large, high-performing high school that lacks a camaraderie and mutual trust within its faculty, and that houses thousands of students in an environment that does not engage each and every learner, but that still produces excellent results for the top-tier students as measured by mandated tests and outcomes? What would a school reformer say? How would different stakeholders address the closed doors and the loss of Amy? Deborah Meier says that small schools work and big schools do not. Gregory and Smith (1987) argue against arbitrarily splitting up large schools into small ones because large public high schools are often the hub of a community, and contend that people do not want to divide them into smaller, separate schools because high schools are "often far more than just places of learning" (pp. 77–78). So what is the answer?

Maybe high achieving students who have access to cultural capital are thriving in this environment, but what about the students in the "middle" or students who are "lower" performing? There is a population of students who are not National Merit Scholars, not on an honors track, not high-performing athletes, not a part of something/anything that makes them feel like they belong. While one can argue that big schools serve as a community hub, one can also argue that big schools are not providing an environment where all learners can thrive. Teachers and students can be disconnected—within their own population and from each other.

One might suggest a school restructuring that makes a big school small as the answer to these ills. Taking a large, faceless student population, and providing students with a smaller space that has connectivity and purpose is one possible answer. This would also give teachers a natural community in which they could collaborate, mentor, and be mentored with and by other teachers, not just teachers in their own departments. So—does one just *restructure* a school by changing the blueprint? Newman and Wehlage (1995) say that when restructuring a school or reforming a school,

> The quality of education for children depends ultimately not on specific techniques, practices or structures, but on more basic human and social re-sources in a school, especially on the commitment and competence (the will and skill) of educators, and on students' efforts to learn. (p. 1)

Deborah Meier and her colleagues were at the heart of CPE and its struc-ture, and all the other stakeholders were valued and on board—from the superintendent to the students to their parents. So making a big school a small school cannot be executed by just implementing a new blueprint. The *people*—the students and teachers should be at the heart of this change. If the issues are a lack of professional community and a school size that causes students to become "lost," then the changes need to be a result of painstaking deliberation by teachers, administration, the community, *and* the students that address those pointed issues.

FEDERAL HOCKING HIGH SCHOOL

If we were to change or restructure a large, corporate, public high school, it would be very important for all stakeholders to know *why* that change is necessary. Change should be implemented as a means for accomplishing desired objectives—in the case of the high schools I have been a part of, lack of a professional community and a large, impersonal enrollment. I can see this clearly; many can see this clearly. But unless all stakeholders, including the teachers and students, see this as an issue worth trying to fix, any school change will certainly fail. I believe this is the first misstep in many attempts at school restructuring. Fullan (1991) says that when there is implementation of a major change, "people involved must perceive both that the needs being addressed are significant *and* that they are making at least some progress toward meeting them" (p. 69). Without participation and deliberate action by teachers, students, and community alike, change cannot be authentic. Additionally, *clarity* is essential. Teachers need to know what they should do differently as a result of this change. Further, Fullan says that

> The more complex the reform, the greater the problem of clarity... lack of clarity—diffuse goals and unspecified means of implementation—represents a major problem at the implementation stage; teachers and others find that the change is simply not very clear as to what it means in practice. (p. 70)

Deborah Meier and her colleagues were all very aware of the objectives of creating CPE. They worked hard to have a constant dialogue about what was happening, why it was happening, and providing ownership for the teachers during implementation.

While Deborah Meier created a school from scratch, there are other examples of school restructuring that are in the spirit of CPE and its demo- cratic ideals. In the early 1990s, a case study was performed chronicling the transformation of Federal Hocking High School (FHHS) outside Athens, Ohio. The study examines the high school as it reaches a sort of boiling point and the actions taken by the teachers and community to address this "school in turmoil" (Murray & Wood, 1999, p. 3). At FHHS in south- east Ohio in 1990, one first-year teacher described her experience in the environment that was isolated, cold, and miserable: "School had taken my energy and my enthusiasm and squashed it" (Murray & Wood, 1999, p. 3). Federal Hocking High School, in the early 90s, had a distinct set of problems in the way it operated and in its culture.

The case study of FHHS followed teachers and the principal through the varying situations faced in the fledgling school environment. "When the situations that these individuals encountered on a daily basis are analyzed, five major problems emerge: the problems of size, time, discipline, study halls, and misery" (Murray & Wood, 1999, p. 3). At the beginning of the study, teachers at FHHS averaged around 140–200 students a day, which reduced the teachers' ability to demand high-quality work. They had little time for prep and no collaboration time or time to form relationships. Discipline was not supported by the administration, and teachers spent more time disciplining than focusing on pedagogy. Large study halls with little supervision created an environment that cheapened the learning of the academic classes. Most students and teachers were miserable, with little to no sense of pride or regard for the community of FHHS.

FHHS spent several school years methodically implementing change. Each year brought a milestone in the nearly decade-long progression that was led primarily by staff. By developing a plan, focusing on staff development and support, building on successes, changing school structures with the guidance of the stakeholders, surviving crises, involving students and community, and consistently working to create a democratic learning community, FHHS was transformed into a community where teachers and students feel they belong, and the problems they faced in the early 1990s were remedied. FHHS has become a school where the entire staff is "committed to the realization of its vision" (Murray & Wood, 1999, p. 62)—a true staff community. Teachers are on teaching teams in which they can collaborate and form relationships. Teachers are mentors and leaders for other teachers, passing along pedagogical strategies. Students exhibit learning with new graduation requirements through portfolios and exhibitions. They also participate in the democratic environment, feel valued, and can make a difference. Size, time, discipline, study halls, and misery were no longer the items that plagued FHHS. All those involved addressed these problems through thoughtful and painstaking consideration. "Federal Hocking High School is a democratic learning community, and the transformation that occurred there has created a nurturing, yet challenging environment for teachers and students" (Murray & Wood, 1999, p. 62).

The story of FHHS is important in relationship to CPE and to other schools today. Again—with the support of a school board and superintendent and the unwavering commitment of a progressive-minded principal, George Wood, teachers who were willing to invest their own blood, sweat, and tears, and students who bought into new ideas, change was affected and a place that once caused misery is now a place of learning. It was again *the people* who made the difference. Like Meier and her colleagues, Wood started small and carefully, building on the efforts that were started by teachers. It took almost a decade, but, like CPE, it *worked*.

Learning Communities as an Answer?

After gazing through the windows of CPE and FHHS, I again returned to my current school—the large, high-performing, public high school that lacks a professional community. Would everyone in this environment recognize the problems as I do? Or would high test scores and success stories be enough to mask any need for change? Fortunately, there is a new principal in my school who is not afraid of change, and not afraid of addressing perceived issues head-on. He began this school year with efforts to build rapport between administration and teachers, teachers and students, and administration and students. He is visible and engaged. He would give me 20 minutes if I asked, and would never send me to "make an appointment." He cares what students and teachers think, and I believe that others' ideas and desires are often at the root of his decision-making.

The new principal began talking with the staff in the winter months about changes that would be coming to our school. He intends to launch a new initiative in the coming school year, just a few short months away. We are moving to a structure that includes *Learning Communities*. When I questioned the principal about this new initiative, he provided me with the following definition: "A learning community is one in which all members acquire new ideas and accept responsibility for making the organization work" (Hiatt-Michael, 2001, p. 113). To expand, in the Hiatt-Michael Learning Community model, students, parents, faculty and staff all work together to achieve the mission of a school, and do not just fulfill mandates passed down from leaders without critically assessing the need and usefulness of the mandates. She says there are "four essential elements to a learning community: a servant leader who performs as a guide and nurturer, a shared moral purpose, a sense of trust and respect among all members, and an open environment for collaborative decision-making" (Hiatt-Michael, 2001, p. 117). To me, this sounded pretty great, and reminiscent of what a Deb Meier or a George Wood would do. But I was skeptical because the definition provided was certainly a *restructuring*. I learned from Meier that change takes time and buy-in, and that it cannot follow a prescribed model, that every situation demands a unique approach.

When I asked why we were moving to this model, trying to probe if he recognized some of our issues as I had, my principal expressed concern that we are sending students off to college or post-high school employment without helping them develop their future career goals and paths. He stated that students needed to begin that career path in high school, with a prescribed course plan and opportunities for real-life experiences. His explanation broke from the definition of learning communities as it was presented to me. I thought learning communities were going to mean that we were going to make our big school smaller, provide students with continuity between teachers and classes, and give students a "home" and a chance at authentic student learning that is directed by their interests, all while building a professional community among teachers that provided collaboration and mentoring beyond the current departmental work. Instead, these proposed learning communities are to help students become more "career and college-ready," an often used term in the current accountability movement, and does not truly change our school at all.

I am not sure what will come of the learning communities next year; because of the extremely short time to create, plan and implement, I am not sure if it will come together. As Newman and Wehlage (1995) say, "the quality of education for children depends on basic human and social resources in a school, especially on the commitment and competence (the will and skill) of educators, and on students' efforts to learn" (p. 1). With the introduction of the learning communities, I am not sure all teachers are committed to the same goals, and I am not sure there is clarity about what exactly the teachers should be doing to achieve these goals. I do not know if our staff will grow as a community with this change. I do not know if there will be full "buy-in" of the change. I *do* know that my principal is a strong leader who truly cares about students and teachers. But I am not sure that is enough if the initiatives do not align with the needs and desires of all involved. I can hope that with this new structure, "Teachers pursue a clear shared purpose for all students' learning, teachers engage in collaborative activity to achieve the purpose, and teachers take collective responsibility for student learning" (Newman & Wehlage, 1995, p. 30), but without careful and deliberate planning by all, and the construction of our own blueprint, I am not hopeful. Perhaps knowing what I know now, the window has already closed on this attempt at "restructuring" in my school. The approaching demise may simply be inevitable.

WHAT CAN BE LEARNED FROM DEBORAH MEIER

If I have learned anything from Deborah Meier, it is that this small effort cannot possibly be enough. Before anything meaningful can occur at any school, my school included, there needs to be a body of people committed to something different—and this something must be tied to a shared purpose, like providing a high-quality, child-centered education for all students, or building a professional learning community and valuing the worth and opinions of educators who have so much to offer the students and each other. This kind of change would require time, a commitment to shared values, democratic decision-making, perseverance, and *hard work*. It would also require the opportunity to fail, the willingness to try something new, and the opening of one's classroom door in order to share the curricular and pedagogical happenings within that classroom. Deborah Meier created a place like this—the place I can imagine pouring my blood, sweat, and tears into, and receiving fulfillment in return.

Deborah Meier opened a new window for me—a window to what *could be*, if only we are willing to take the risk, and the necessary steps for making true change, and see it through.

REFERENCES

Bensman, D. (2000). *Central Park East and its graduates: "Learning by heart."* New York, NY: Teachers College Press.

Fullan, M. G. (1991). *The new meaning of educational change.* New York, NY: Teachers College Press.

Gregory, T. B., & G. R. Smith. (1987). *High Schools as Communities: The Small School Reconsidered*. Bloomington, IN: Phi Delta Kappa.

Hiatt-Michael, D. B. (2001). Schools as learning communities: A vision for organic school reform. *The School Community Journal, 11*(2), 113–127.

Meier, D. (1995). *The power of their ideas: Lessons for America from a small school in Harlem*. Boston, MA: Beacon Press.

Murray, S. R., & Wood, G .H. (1999). *Creating a democratic learning community: The case study of Federal Hocking High School*. Columbus, OH: Ohio Department of Education.

Newman, F. M., & Wehlage, G. G. (1995). *Successful school restructuring: A report to the public and educators by the Center on Organization and Restructuring of Schools*. Madison, WI: Board of Regents of the University of Wisconsin System.

Rodgers, K. (2014). With liberty and justice for some: A philosophical argument in opposition to the small schools movement in New York City. *Philosophical Studies in Education, 45*, 125–135.

CHAPTER 8

MAY I HAVE COFFEE WITH YOU?

What I Learned About Teaching From My Time Sitting in bell hooks' Kitchen

Vanessa G. Winn

In 15 essays on a diverse array of topics, bell hooks (1994) writes *Teaching to Transgress: Education as the Practice of Freedom* to share her insights, strategies, and joy in teaching (p. 10). This book came to me feeling like a gift of wisdom and hope about teaching in higher education. It is the first book that has spoken to me directly about how to teach in higher education. This may be surprising, since many of the theories and philosophies that I learned about in my own teacher education program, teaching life in early childhood classrooms, and current work with preservice teachers can be universalized to education, in general. Yet, this text feels different to me and my personal connection to it takes precedence over the generalizations that are available from hooks' book. When I realized this was the case and began drafting an essay for this book chapter, I struggled with how to regeneralize my response for a wider audience. But, under guidance from friends and colleagues, my treatment of this book will be personal.

Curriculum Windows: What Curriculum Theorists of the 1990s Can Teach Us About Schools and Society Today, pp. 115–130
Copyright © 2017 by Information Age Publishing
All rights of reproduction in any form reserved.

Readers who desire an overview of the book need not abandon me yet; I will summarize hooks' (1994) main themes, her scholarly lenses, and styles of writing she uses in the book. I will suggest other potential lenses for using the essays in contemporary work as well. However, I will spend most of the time writing about three major parts of the book that stood out for me: one particular essay on theory as liberatory practice, the concept of fully embodied teaching, and grappling with what teaching to transgress and teaching for freedom looks like in higher education. These elements of the text are central to my personal theorizing about continuing to teach in higher education.

I suspect that like most rich texts, a reread of this book in time will highlight different aspects of my teaching practice, suggest new strategies, and bring to light different joys of teaching. I will not assume that I am an unchanging reader or that this essay is a final judgment of the important aspects of this book. I also will not assert that the most relevant parts of this text, as evaluated by me, are universalized for fellow scholars who read her book. However, what I do offer is an essay that is closely tethered to my own practice and myself. I have always been most successful with academic work in which I incorporate my personal response and I hope that the excitement that hooks (1994) elicits for me carries you along with me in this chapter.

Before discussing the essays in the book in depth, I want to first position myself within the work. This positionality is not intended to discount me from doing the work of drawing hooks (1994) into 2015, it is intended to make *me* visible in the same way that hooks makes herself visible in her work. In qualitative research, positionality is used to describe the sociocultural context of the researcher. I am extending the assumption that a writer's cultural background, gender, race, class, socioeconomic status, and educational background constitute important variables that may affect the writing process, much like the qualitative research process (Bourke, 2014, p. 2).

I am a cisgender, monolingual, White female who currently lives in the upper socioeconomic class. However, I experienced my childhood and early adulthood in a low socioeconomic position. I am a PhD student, like my colleagues producing this text, and have attended and taught in both public and private educational institutions. I grew up in rural Appalachian Pennsylvania in a racially and linguistically homogenous and privileged, although not materially privileged, background.

I am a White, shall we say, "budding" scholar. My experience as a White woman from Western Pennsylvania is different than hooks' (1994) experience as a Black feminist, critical scholar from the American South. I can read about, write about, and make my own connections to hooks' experience, but her experience in the world is different than my own because of race and racism in the United States. As a writer, hooks draws on her racial experience in many of the essays of this book. I, too, am raced but my experience of racial privilege frames a different understanding than her experience in the world with race does.

As an author reinterpreting her text, I feel the tension and complexity of a white woman being the one to draw hooks' (1994) curriculum text into 2015. What I pull through, highlight, and claim as important parts of hooks' text may be very different than that of a contemporary Black scholar. In addition, contemporary critical, feminist, and anticolonial scholars may draw more nuanced understandings through each of these lenses. While I intend to treat the text with as much integrity and consideration as possible, it is possible that I may unintentionally reinforce my own racist, sexist, and colonized view of the world. I work as hard as I can, however, not to do this.

TEACHING TO TRANSGRESS: AN OVERVIEW

As a series of essays, this book can be consumed in parts or as a whole. Her essays generally begin with a vignette about a personal challenge, an experience in her past, or a current concern in teaching. She then picks up her pedagogical lenses to investigate the problem and resolve it in context. hooks (1994) states, "The engaged voice must never be fixed and absolute but always changing, always evolving" (p. 11). Therefore, she uses a variety of voices and styles to write her essays. By using an essay structure, hooks (models the importance of dialogue and personal narrative and embeds every essay in a unique context. And because her recommendations are made in context, this book is not a set of blueprints and it is important that the reader not take it as such because, "To do so would undermine the insistence that engaged pedagogy recognizes each classroom as different, that strategies must constantly be changed, invented, reconceptualized to address each new teaching experience" (p. 11).

Throughout the essays, bell hooks (1994) uses three primary lenses for her curricular work: anticolonial, critical, and feminist pedagogies (p. 10). Anticolonial pedagogy draws from postcolonial theory. Postcolonial studies address both the legacy of colonial rule and contemporary imperialism in ways that challenge universal rationality and objective truth. Postcolonialism engages the world textually and discursively and examines the influences and operation of power (McLeod, 2010, pp. 45–46). Critical pedagogy draws from critical theory. For hooks (1994), her model of critical pedagogy is based on the work of Paulo Friere. Freire (1993) describes a humanist educator as one that partners with students to think critically and pursue a mutual quest for humanization (p. 56). hooks draws a deep connection between her childhood education and Friere's critical pedagogy. Her early childhood education in segregated schools was steeped in the politics of resisting the oppression of racism and White supremacy led by black, women teachers which I will discuss further in later parts of this chapter. In *Feminism is for EVERYBODY: Passionate Politics*, hooks (2000) writes, "Feminism is a movement to end sexism, sexist exploitation, and oppression" (p. viii). Feminism also examines and challenges the power of patriarchal systems.

hooks (1994) engages these three lenses flexibly in her work. Each of her essays utilizes the different theories to greater degrees than others. For example, "A Revolution of Values" and "Paulo Freire," mutually emphasize her colonial, critical, and feminist lenses to analyze multicultural education and the work of Paulo Freire. Other essays, such as "Feminist Thinking in the Classroom Right Now" heavily emphasize her feminist and critical lenses while the anticolonial lens is less prominent.

hooks (1994) does not ever write exclusively from one lens in these essays. For example, there is evidence of an anticolonial lens even in "Feminist Thinking in the Classroom Right Now." However, the essays do not share the same level of emphasis throughout. In other words, hooks uses all three but does not use each of them with equal weight for unequal tasks. hooks explains her work with multiple theories from the beginning of the book in this way: "This complex and unique blending of multiple perspectives has been an engaging and powerful standpoint from which to work" (p. 10). From this standpoint, hooks utilizes theories that not only allow her to interrogate biases but also to teach in ways that do not reify those biases and systems of domination that include imperialism, racism, and sexism, with which her essays are primarily concerned (p. 10).

If I were to take on the book as parts, each essay is rich with a topic to pursue for further research and a window from 1994 to 2015. In "Language: Teaching New Words/New Worlds," hooks (1994) describes how transgressing the barriers of Standard American English allows individuals to practice freedom. This would be a strong starting point for discussing the dominance of Standard American English in schools from preschool through university settings in the United States and abroad.

hooks' (1994) engagement with practicing freedom through production of knowledge that diverges from traditional canons of knowledge and language, using anticolonial pedagogy, is a rich window into teaching pedagogies that use popular youth cultural productions. This brings to mind the poetry of Nikki Giovanni's (2008) *Hip Hop Speaks to Children* and scholarship of Jeffrey Duncan-Andrade (2004) on teaching with popular culture.

"Holding My Sister's Hand: Feminist Solidarity" is about the historical relationship between Black women and White women. Historically, White women's dominance over Black women in slave and servant roles has a history that hooks (1994) asserts is still felt today in relationships between Black and White women. Recently, romanticized visions of that history in novels such as Kathryn Stockett's (2011) *The Help* and Sue Monk Kidd's (2014) *The Invention of Wings* have revived this tension in popular culture. This essay might help illuminate new aspects of conversations and conflicts that arise when novels produced by White women, which emphasize the cooperation between White women and Black women in the antebellum south, are facets of popular culture for a primarily White female audience.

However, to take just one essay as only a part of this whole text is to ignore the overarching purpose of the book. That is, as hooks (1994) tells the reader:

> I intend these essays to be an intervention – countering the devaluation of teaching even as they address the urgent need for changes in teaching practice. They are meant to serve as constructive commentary... to emphasize that the pleasure of teaching is an act of resistance countering the overwhelming boredom, uninterest, and apathy that so often characterize the way professors and students feel about teaching and learning, [and] about the classroom experience. (p. 10)

hooks (1994) also continually addresses what it means to teach as a practice of freedom. As a young girl, her first schooling experiences were in segregated Black schools. Through fond recollections of this educational experience, she describes the excitement, danger, and freedom of engaging ideas that ran counter to her parents' values and beliefs at home (hooks, 1994, p. 3). She describes her early education as fundamentally political and rooted in antiracist struggles (p. 2). This stands in contrast to when she was bussed to all white schools, after legal desegregation, she experienced a racist education that relied on what Freire (1993) calls the banking method of education. She was a vessel to be filled up. Her consumption and memorization of the "official" knowledge of White men was valued over her mind, her ideas, her politics, and experience.

Freire's (1993) banking system of education is the metaphor that she uses consistently to describe her school experience in a racially integrated high school through graduate school at Stanford University. As a university teacher, hooks (1994) works against the banking method by constructing her own pedagogy (p. 10). hooks writes about the excitement that can enliven classrooms (p. 7), engaged pedagogy that values student participation and expression, including students' voices (pp. 20, 40–41), and self-actualized teachers who reject the notion that the mind can be separated from the body (pp. 15, 22, 139). These are just some of the ways that she constructs her own radical pedagogy as a practice of freedom (p. 10).

WHY I HAVE TOLD EVERYONE ABOUT THIS BOOK

Since March of this semester, I have been reading, taking notes, and contemplating how to construct this book chapter. One part of the creative process for organizing my writing is drawing the authors into conversations with friends. I try to take on the ideas of authors and use them in different contexts. I often use a phrase that sounds something like, "I think that hooks (1994) might think or say" in conversations to take on the voice of the author and better understand his or her ideas more thoroughly.

For example, a good friend of mine from college has a new teaching position in a Texas high school. In her school, she is teaching a course on short stories in English literature in addition to math classes. In her work, she is doing some critical pedagogy with her students. This includes reexamining favorite childhood stories, advertising, and other popular culture artifacts with critical lenses that highlight the racist, classist, and sexist messages. Her response from students has been mixed. My friend's concern is that her students are sad, and resistant in turn, when their beliefs are challenged by the dynamics of oppression. She believes in the power of critical pedagogy, even if she doesn't call it that by name, but she struggles with the student response that usually follows.

Students' negative and frustrated responses to critical pedagogy, in other words, the challenge of not being able to "unsee" the power of institutionalized oppression, can be discouraging and difficult for students whose privilege allows them to be unaware of these dynamics previous to engaging with critical pedagogy. hooks (1994) speaks to this in her essay "Embracing Change." hooks writes about the conflict and tension that arises when she uses feminist critical pedagogy. She talks about how some of the students in her classes are not receptive to the information and are hurt by new realizations.

Then, she writes about how most of her students eventually come to see the importance of the material, even if it is not immediate. She also shares lessons learned about the compassion that is needed in these new and untraditional learning settings and the importance of processing the experience with students in her course. hooks (1994) writes, "This gives them both the opportunity to know that difficult experiences may be common and practice at integrating theory and practice: ways of knowing and habits of being... through this process we build community" (p. 43). I read this portion of hooks' essay aloud to my Texas friend and she was grateful to hear her tensions affirmed and the hope of appreciation to come. In response to this conversation, with hooks and myself, she is planning to process these feelings in her classroom more explicit.

This is one of the examples of how I have picked up this title again and again to talk with my colleagues and friends. A singular definition of what it means to teach to transgress or teach towards a practice of freedom is not offered to the reader. hooks' (1994) does not address each of these themes explicitly in every essay, but much like literature, one can find the themes running throughout the book as a whole. Therefore, I cannot reveal the definitions for you to memorize and bank into a scholastic repertoire. hooks encourages us to walk with her through her essays, make connections, draw from what speaks to us, and contemplate how we can teach to transgress and educate as a practice of freedom.

I like to think of this process using the metaphor of joining hooks (1994) for coffee in her kitchen. In the essay "Engaged Pedagogy," one of hooks' students talks about what it is like to learn from Gloria. He writes about learning from her in her yellow kitchen, "where she used to share her lunch with students in need of various forms of sustenance" (Dauphin, as cited in hooks, 1994, p. 20). In the remainder of this essay, I plan to pull up a chair to hooks' kitchen table, pour an ample cup of coffee, and share with you what has stuck to me during my time with her.

THEORY AS LIBERATORY PRACTICE

This is why I love graduate school. Theory has been a liberatory practice for as long as I can remember and graduate school steeps me in theory. As a young girl, I began journaling in order to better understand my world and myself. I used to sit down frustrated, angry, upset, or confused and write and write until I was able to get behind my feelings and work out what it was that drove my feelings. I used writing as a way of working toward understanding. The conclusions that I came to were often that I was jealous, not angry, or that my sister and I were misunderstanding each other, not transitioning into sworn enemies. This is not high theory or official knowledge. It is probably, not even terribly difficult to arrive at. But this was the way that I made sense of my world. Like hooks (1994), "I found a place of sanctuary in 'theorizing,' in making sense out of what happened" (p. 61).

Then, when I reached my undergraduate university, theory gave me so many more tools to open up my understanding of the world. I grasped onto Annette Lareau (2003) who put into words my feelings about the complexity of living and identifying with two different socioeconomic classes. I yearned for the theory of Robert Jensen (2005) to help me talk about my white racial identity after an urban immersion program in Philadelphia. The power of wrangling feelings and experiences with theory is just what hooks (1994) describes as liberating and communal as well.

Many other women authors that I have encountered in academia share this liberatory space. Andreotti (2011) writes this in her text on postcolonialism in education, "when I encountered postcolonial theory, I found a language to articulate the issues that had always driven and haunted my life. Spivak (2004), in particular, helped me 'language' the pedagogical questions at the heart of my work" (p. 176). hooks (2000), in her book on feminism mentioned above, writes, "I needed feminism to give me a foundation of equality and justice to stand on" (p. x). hooks (1994) also writes about how critical theory helped her in her graduate studies:

> I came to Friere thirsty, dying of thirst (in that way that the colonized, marginalized subject who is still unsure of how to break the hold of the status quo, who longs for change, is needy, is thirsty), and I found in his work (and the work of Malcolm X, Fanon, etc.) a way to quench that thirst. (p. 50)

Then, in her essay "Theory as Liberatory Practice," hooks (1994) writes about a non-academic woman who approached her after a lunch were she was informally talking about feminism with a small group of folks who lived in a small town in the American South. The woman expressed her gratification for, "enabl[ing] her to give voice to feelings and ideas that [she] had always 'kept' to herself, [and] that by saying it she had created a space for her and her partner to change thought and action" (p. 73).

By finding this essay and the evidence of similar need and excitement for theory from other scholars, I have found good company. It feels good to be in the company of other women who have been theorizing alone and eventually come together in a community that feels scholarly as well as personal. This is an integral part of my graduate studies. Sometimes I commune with cohort members who have seen the same things in schools and share my concerns that were previously "too nitpicky" for other colleagues. More often, I find myself wanting to pull up a symbolic kitchen chair to folks like Marilyn-Cochran Smith (2004) or Geneva Gay (2010) to think about working with preservice teachers.

This way of thinking about theory has changed the way I conceptualize and talk with others about research as well. In a course on "teacher leadership" that I teach for preservice teachers as a graduate teaching assistant, my students write a research essay on a topic of their choice. In the past, I had trouble situating and explaining this assignment to my students because I had not fully conceptualized the idea. Like most young graduate students, I inherited this course from talented professors before me and it takes time to make others' work my own. So, when my students asked, "What kind of topics do you mean? What can I write about? Does this subject count as a topic for this research paper?" I responded with guidance but my responses felt flat and reflected the same questions that I pondered.

After reading hooks' (1994) essay on theory as liberatory practice and considering how research and theory have helped me find academic friends, I decided to change the prompt for the assignment. I suggested that they ask questions about what they *think* they know or what they have some opinions about but cannot justify alone. This framework for the assignment was far more successful than last semester's prompt and these kinds of questions led my students to deeper places in their research.

Rather than researching the policies of standardized assessments, my students began asking question about the effects of the standardized testing regime that made them uneasy. They began asking questions about the implicit assumptions that hide behind the standardization movement, such as, "Why do we think that students don't know anything before they get to school? and Why do we have to always start at the beginning with 'basic skills?'" From there, I could suggest doing some research on deficit thinking and, from this research, my students were able to connect with research that answered more meaningful questions. But the source of their questions was their own theorizing. This led them to finding their academic giants to "stand on the shoulders of" in order to make judgments, driven by research, about the state of schools and children. This was using theory to liberate a hidden concern.

The Fully Embodied, Self-Actualized Teacher

Recently I was in class with my preservice teachers when groups were wrapping up their work for the day and their conversations transitioned into casual chatting. As I listened in to the din, I heard something that caught my attention: "Just tell me, do you have a dog?" To which another student responded, "I know! Sometimes I see his screen saver on the projector and it has cute pictures of his kids, maybe his family? I can't tell because he jumps to turn it off so fast." "I am so curious about him," the first concluded. My students were referring to another instructor that they have this semester.

Just yesterday, I heard another group talking about seeing this same professor wearing a baseball cap and walking with two small children who were speculated to be his children. I am not overly familiar with the individual in question, despite having professional meetings with him myself, so I cannot confirm their suspicions about his family or if he has a dog or not. But I took note of their conversation because it made me think more about what hooks (1994) describes as a fully embodied, self-actualized teacher and the potential disembodiment of the academic persona.

The banking system that Freire (1993) describes is the model for unembodied, unactualized teaching. According to Freire the banking system of education is an education in which the teacher, the one assumed to have the authority, fills up students —those assumed to be empty—with knowledge (p. 53). When hooks (1994) talks about her experience with the banking system of education, she describes how professors are pre-sumably emptied out the moment that they cross through the academic doorway, as if the professors are suddenly objective in that space, and the information that came from them is impartial to themselves (p. 17). The disembodied professor has no connection to his or her physical body or his or her personal life in an academic space. This disconnect is portrayed as an important aspect of professors' impartiality in the classroom.

hooks (1994) discusses how the mind/body split in the institutionalized academy, cloaked in neutrality, is not neutral at all. The curricular choices that are made and the attempt at disembodied teaching methods of univer-sities continue to reproduce a privileged class of values and elitism (p. 140). This is uncovered by exposing neutrality as, more accurately, uninterro-gated Western canons of knowledge with anticolonial studies. Postcolonial /anticolonial studies challenge the assumption that any information is neutral and can be disconnected from the individual who is disseminat-ing knowledge. In some sense, to an anticolonialist the positionality of an educator, whether being a pet owner or parent is immediately relevant or not, is part of the discourse through which knowledge flows.

In contrast, a humanist, revolutionary educator engages in critical thinking with students for mutual humanization; educators and students must be partners (Freire, 1993, p. 56). In an essay written in dialogue with a colleague about choosing radical pedagogy, hooks (1994) and Ron Scapp (1994) come to the mutual conclusion that, "again and again, [we] are saying that different, more radical subject matter does not create a liberatory pedagogy, [but] that a simple practice like including personal experience may be more constructively challenging than simply changing the curriculum" (p. 148). hooks says,

> Along with them, I grow intellectually, developing sharper understandings of how to share knowledge and what to do in my participatory role with stu-dents. This is one of the primary differences between education as a practice of freedom and the conservative banking system which encourages profes-sors to believe deep down in the core of their beings that they have nothing to learn from their students. (p. 152)

Is it necessary that academic instructors share pictures and stories about their children and pets in classroom settings? No. Showing pictures of one's family on the first day of class as an act of embodying oneself is not a recipe or blueprint for being self-actualized with students. What Scapp (as cited in hooks, 1994) and hooks (1994) are discussing is a process of learning with students, students whose experiences have value, and how sharing one's own experiences shape the world as we understand it.

Pictures of my family are wonderful but when working with preservice teachers, my family is mostly irrelevant. What is relevant are stories that share my personal regrets and accomplishments when working with early childhood students in the classroom. For example, I talk with my students in "teacher leadership" about the ways in which I was underprepared to teach in an urban school district straight out of my undergraduate degree program. I share with them how I failed to make early contact with parents that might have built more rich relationships that could benefit my students. I also shared with them how finding an older, African American teacher and listening to her advice helped guide my classroom practices and interactions with parents in more culturally responsive ways. I shared with them how humbling it was to learn from a veteran teacher whose life in schools and the same community as our students informed her work with more nuance than the theory of my undergraduate work could have ever done.

I also listened as students told stories about the things they observed in their field assignments. We talked together about how they processed their observations within the frameworks of their preexisting biases and how they might need new frameworks to understand the life of schools and students whose experiences were unlike their own in schools. These rich exchanges, sometimes in classroom dialogue and sometimes in school hallways during field visits, were some of the most educative moments in our classroom together. The texts in the course supported and illuminated important facets of these conversations, just as theory has the power to do, but they were rooted in our own experiences, not the neutrality of an official lecture unconnected to our lives. This exchange required my presence and the presence of students. The disembodied instructor who makes every effort to erase his or her personal self from the classroom is less likely to present him or herself as open for these types of interactions.

Sitting in bell hooks' (1994) Kitchen: Making Sense of Teaching to Transgress and Education as a Practice of Freedom

Throughout my life, I have needed mentors. This is not an uncommon need or acquisition; many share my need. But in my experience, mentors are difficult to find and I am not inspired very often. Slogans, catch phrases, and "leadership" figures are never my targets. So my new devotion to bell hooks (1994) feels incongruent with past mentors, considering the academic stardom that hooks has achieved in her career, but I find myself wanting to be one of the many students that hooks allows into her yellow kitchen. I am attracted to bell hooks the teacher. She writes that "long before a public ever recognized me as a thinker or writer, I was recognized by a classroom of students—seen by them as a teacher who worked hard to create a dynamic learning experience for all of us" (p. 11). It is this teacher that I want to learn from and it is this example of teaching for freedom that models what her pedagogy looks like that speaks directly to why teaching to transgress is worth my time and effort.

In this last section, I will use the time to gather together the vision for teaching to transgress that hooks (1994) provides. In my brief time at her kitchen table, these are the aspects of my teaching that I think hooks (1994) might look for in my classroom with preservice teachers. I sometimes imagine that my teaching mentors are watching me. This kind of pretend accountability often takes the form of the personal question, "What would hooks (1994) think about what I am doing today?"

Additive Multiculturalism Is Not Teaching to Transgress

First, hooks (1994) points to my syllabus and teaches me that content does not translate directly to teaching to transgress. As mentioned above, "more radical subject matter does not create a liberatory pedagogy" (p. 458). According to Scapp (1994 as cited in hooks, 1994), work on race, ethnicity, and gender can be used to superficially update the curriculum in classes without meaningfully engaging or subverting the systems of power that maintain the systemic privileges of race, ethnicity, and gender (p. 142). Whereas there are occasionally changes in the information presented in classrooms, it is infrequently presented in new or transformative ways (hooks, 1994, p. 143). For example, in literature courses, Toni Morrison's work is frequently included in the reading lists. This is an addition of an African American author in the course curriculum. However, hooks points out that rarely are a reading of Toni Morrison's books embedded in a racial context. Some professors even teach Toni Morrison in their courses without mentioning race (hooks, 1994). Teaching for freedom requires more than shallow representations of inclusion.

This is a lesson that I am learning and working to improve upon. My students who take "teacher leadership" are in a preservice education program. Throughout their 4 years in the program, they are grouped together into several blocks for shared coursework and field experiences. At the point at which preservice teachers take my course, they are in block 3 and finishing up their coursework before student teaching. In our block, I have a shared commitment with other instructors to discuss what it means to teach for social justice. Social justice has enjoyed a recent upwelling of popularity in educational research (North, 2008). However, this increase in popularity does not necessarily bring clarity to what it means to teach for social justice. There are a myriad of competing definitions and conceptions of what it means to teach for social justice (North, 2008). hooks (1994) and

Scapp (1994 as cited in hooks, 1994) highlight the importance of changing pedagogical styles that challenge oppression in education as opposed to simply including a smattering of social justice related readings and authors from diverse racial backgrounds.

VOICE: HEARING FROM TEACHERS AND STUDENTS TO ENHANCE ACADEMIC KNOWLEDGE

Next, hooks (1994) listens to who is speaking in my classes. The issue of voice, who speaks and who listens, is highlighted in hooks' focus on anticolonial pedagogy. The person whose voice and ways of knowing are heard is a powerful role that teachers are not traditionally compelled to share. However, engaged pedagogy necessarily values student voice (p. 20). hooks emphasizes that students should be allowed to share their voices, not simply to feel safe or feel included because when students share their voice, more ways of thinking and knowing are introduced to the learning community.

A multivoiced community can be difficult to manage. No one's experience in the world prepares him or her for a full array of understanding and knowing the world in increasingly multicultural settings. hooks (1994) herself writes about this challenge at the beginning of her career. It required her to learn much more about new ontologies and epistemologies. Encouraging the use of voice can also be difficult because it changes the traditional classroom dynamics. Students have been trained that they are not the ones with authority in traditional classrooms. So, teaching to transform must encourage students to see themselves with legitimacy previously denied them in the traditional banking method of education (p. 144).

Students are not the only ones who are asked to share (hooks, 1994, p. 21). Teachers must also share their voice, make their own confessions, and share of their experience. This concept of sharing oneself with a class, not presenting information from a "neutral" teacher is an important aspect of being a fully embodied teacher, as mentioned above. Sharing voices, however, can be risky. "One of the ways you can be written off quickly as a professor by colleagues who are suspicious of your progressive pedagogy is to allow your students, or yourself, to talk about experience" (Scapp, 1994, as cited in hooks, 1994, p. 148).

However, sharing one's voice is not just telling one's story or experience. Experience is a way to deepen discussion (hooks, 1994, p. 86). Personal narratives can be linked with academic information in order to enhance one's capacity to know (Scapp, 1994, as cited in hooks, 1994, p. 148). hooks states that this is often a misunderstood aspect of using voice in the classroom. Dialogue about academic issues, which include voice, requires orchestration so that using one's voice doesn't become a class session that is dominated by people who love to hear themselves talk or discuss unrelated experiences (hooks, 1994, p. 151). When there is a purpose and direction for the class dialogue, there can be respectful interruptions to redirect individuals who have gone off course (Scapp, 1994, as cited in hooks, 1994, p. 151).

> This pedagogical strategy is rooted in the assumption that we all bring to the classroom experiential knowledge that is knowledge that can indeed enhance our learning experience. If experience is already invoked in the classroom as a way of knowing that coexists in a non hierarchical way with other ways of knowing, then it lessens the possibility that it can be used to silence. (hooks, 1994, p. 84)

The pedagogical choice to use students' experiences to bolster and enhance academic understanding also aligns with the importance of theory as liberatory pedagogy. As discussed above, a reconceptualization of the importance of voice for research and theory has already been playing out in my classroom with preservice teachers.

Teaching to Transgress is Important Teaching and Can Be Radical

When I first thought about how I was going to transition from early childhood settings, with students who are just 5- and 6-years-old, to teaching a class for undergraduate pre-service teachers, I sought advice rather openly from a variety of friends, family, and acquaintances. The most common response was generally: "I don't think it will be very different than kindergarten." This comment did not imply the advice giver's confidence in the fluidity of my skills. Rather, this flippant comment implied that kindergarten students and undergraduates are basically the same teaching audience. The underlying assumption is that, like 5-year-olds, undergraduates require "hand holding," carefully directed activities, and need the same kind of control measures that the media generated stereotype of the animalistic kindergarten class needs.

I have significant issues with these control measures at the kindergarten level and I continued to be disappointed when I find that this commonly held assumption reaches all the way into the undergraduate community. I was saddened by the common assumption and it elicits a personal dissonance between this assumption and my beliefs about students. In fact, this dissonance in august sent me to revisit my own connection with Freire (1993). Upon my own first reading of Freire last summer, I found this quote and have had it on a digital sticky note on my desktop for over a year:

> They talk about people, but they do not trust them; and trusting people is the indispensable precondition for revolutionary change. A real humanist can be identified more with his trust in the people, which engages him in their struggle, than by a thousand actions in their favor without that trust. (Freire, 1993, p. 42)

The essence of trusting people, in my interpretation, has to extend to students. If we want unjust schools to be more just spaces, we have to trust those with whom we are engaging. When I decided to save this quote, I was still thinking mostly of P–12 school students, particularly my kindergarteners who need to be seen as more capable and trustworthy. But I have now begun to think more and more about my new teaching audience, and hopefully the new teaching partners that I will continue with in an academic position, that is, undergraduate, preservice teachers.

When I transitioned from teaching early childhood to college students, I found also that I initially fed into the assumption that I was leaving the difficult work of "real teaching" in public schools to escape into the leisure of academy teaching. However, what hooks (1994) has done for me is called my attention back to the fact that I am *still teaching*. I have an audience of students who need me to teach them in multicultural ways. I need to consider how the explicit, implicit, hidden, and null curriculum (Eisner, 2002) of my class creates spaces that do not reinforce existing systems of racism, imperialism, and sexism. I am continually called to think about why I face classes of primarily White, heterosexual, gender conforming, upper socioeconomic class women. In my doctoral coursework throughout this semester, I have heard from the women of color in my cohort how pre-service teacher education programs are not welcoming spaces for women of color. What is it about my class and the overall program that reifies the dominance of the hegemonic teaching force?

These questions have not been wholly answered in this essay, but hooks (1994) illuminates ways that my teaching can be more multivoiced and engaging. And it is here that I will leave you, my reader, with hooks' parting words

> The classroom, with all its limitation, remains a location of possibility. In that field of possibility we have the opportunity to labor for freedom, to demand of ourselves and our comrades, an openness of mind and heart that allows us to face reality even as we collectively imagine ways to move beyond boundaries, to transgress. This is education as the practice of freedom. (p. 207)

I am eager to join hooks as a comrade in this possibility as preservice teachers and I transgress beyond the banking system of education towards progressive and critical pedagogies with students so that we all have a chance to be more free as a result of our public education. I also plan to take pleasure from teaching in higher education—the pleasure that comes from a genuine engagement with the students in my class, to not treat our classroom sessions as obligatory but joyful—and cherish time spend with preservice teachers who I trust are eager to learn.

REFERENCES

Andreotti, V. (2011). *Actionable postcolonial theory in education.* New York, NY: Palgrave Macmillan.

Bourke, B. (2014). Positionality: Reflecting on the research process. *Qualitative Report, 19*(33), 1–9.

Cochran-Smith, M. (2004). *Walking the road: Race, diversity, and social justice in teacher education.* New York, NY: Teachers College Press.

Duncan-Andrade, J. M. (2004). Your best friend or your worst enemy: Youth popular culture, pedagogy, and curriculum in urban classrooms. *The Review of Eduacation, Pedagogy, and Cultural Studies , 26,* 313–337.

Eisner, E. W. (2002). *The educational imagination: On the design and evaluation of school programs* (3rd ed.). Columbus, OH: Merrill Prentice Hall.

Freire, P. (1993). *Pedagogy of the oppressed.* London, England: Penguin Books.

Gay, G. (2010). *Culturally responsive teaching: Theory, research, and practice [Kindle Cloud Reader]* (2nd ed.). New York, NY: Teachers College Press.

Giovanni, N. (2008). *Hip hop speaks to children: A celebration of poetry with a beat (A poetry speaks experience).* Naperville, IL: Sourcebooks Jabberwocky.

hooks, b. (2000). *Feminism is for everybody: Passionate politics.* Cambridge, MA: South End Press.

hooks, b. (1994). *Teaching to transgress: Education as the practice of freedom.* New York, NY: Routledge.

Jensen, R. (2005). *The Heart of whiteness: Confronting race, racism, and white privilege.* San Francisco, CA: City Lights.

Kidd, S. M. (2014). *The invention of wings: A novel.* New York, NY: The Penguin Group.

Lareau, A. (2003). *Unequal childhoods: Class, race, and family life.* Berkeley, CA: University of California Press.

McLeod, J. (2010). *Beginning postcolonialism* (2nd ed.). New York, NY: Palgrave Macmillan.

North, C. E. (2008). What is all this talk about "social justice"? Mapping the terrian of education's latest catchphrase. *Teacher's College Record , 110* (6), 1182–1206.

Stockett, K. (2009). *The help.* New York, NY: The Penguin Group.

CHAPTER 9

FRAMING DROPOUTS OR FRAMING URBAN SCHOOLS? ARE WE THE PROBLEM OR SOLUTION!

Framing All My School Experiences

Crystal Phillips

Dear Teacher,

Please help my son learn his ABC's and 123's.
I am not rich so he is a treasure to me.
He is not perfect so he may get a little out of line.
Don't hesitate to correct him God knows I'll whoop his behind.
Remember he is a child and look deep into his eyes.
He is a reminder of his ancestor's soulful cries.
Teach him to love reading and writing too.
His future depends on you!

~ Crystal L. Phillips

Curriculum Windows: What Curriculum Theorists of the 1990s Can Teach Us About Schools and Society Today, pp. 131–143
Copyright © 2017 by Information Age Publishing

As I sit at my desk and glance over at my high school diploma in my windowsill, my mind begins to travel to the fall of 1987. The year I started high school! I was totally blind to the barriers facing me, and my 399 freshman classmates. I remember my principal saying on the first day of school, "Look to your left and look to your right; the people sitting beside you won't be there on graduation day." I didn't understand what he meant and how true this statement is for students in urban schools. High school for me meant an opportunity to join the club of family members that graduated from my high school before me. My high school is the only high school that was built for African American Students. The school has a legacy of rich tradition that is still alive. I joined the Marching Band the summer before 9th grade and had made several new friends but still felt anxiety about the teachers, students, and the need to fit in with my peers. My elementary school experience left me feeling incapable of school success; however, middle school gave me the boost of confidence necessary to believe high school would be my chance to show that I was a smart and competent student.

By the time I reached my senior year I was holding on by a thread! I was trying to break a generational curse and become a graduate without being a teenage mother. My high school boyfriend had dropped out after our freshman year but I was committed to finding a way to draw him back into school. Unfortunately, the opposite was happening; he was drawing me away from school. In my senior year I had several friends who were succeeding in high school with exceptional grades and several scholarship offers. There were also those who had fallen behind, became parents, or who were incarcerated. My four years of high school were filled with highs and lows.

I had no idea at this exact same time as I was suffering from the uncertainty of who I was and what I hoped one day to become that a sociologist and author by the name of Michelle Fine was "framing dropouts" in an urban public high school in upper Manhattan, and in so many ways she was framing me! I went from an overzealous freshman to a student who began to feel that high school may not be the place for me and graduation just may not happen!

In my life now, based on my past experiences and my understanding of what now looks like in schools for my students, I work to open windows in the lives of all the students that feel as though high school graduation won't happen for them. I am fueled by the opening poem because each child I serve is depending on my school to give them the support to become future leaders within our community. Remarkably, I returned years later to become the principal of my own high school. This chapter is in part the story of my journey to now.

EQUITY VERSUS ACCESS

Michelle Fine suggest that our concern for urban education should not focus on "educational access but on educational outcomes." This thought has followed years of legislation for equal opportunities for all students while losing the real battle over unequal outcomes. One may wonder why the idea of opportunity should even be a topic of discussion today. Children across the U.S. can go to school wherever their parents choose and in 13 years they walk away with their high school diploma. History has shaped our thoughts to believe that one court case changed education for Black children for the better. *Brown v. Board of Education* was filed against the Topeka school board by representative-plaintiff Oliver Brown, parent of one of the children denied access to Topeka's White schools. Brown claimed that Topeka's racial segregation violated the Constitution's Equal Protection Clause because the city's Black and White schools were not equal to each other and never could be. The federal district court dismissed his claim, ruling that the segregated public schools were "substantially" equal enough to be constitutional under the *Plessey vs. Ferguson* case. Brown appealed to the Supreme Court, which consolidated and then reviewed all the school segregation actions together. The Supreme Court ruled in favor of Brown and thus began the desegregation of schools.

But if we stop and look beyond the accessibility of education, we begin to see a problem within schools that is deeper than access. In fact, Ladson Billings (2004) suggests that the *Brown* decision is not the result of America as good and altruistic but rather the result of the decision's historical and political context. President Eisenhower was counting on the power of the states' rights to hold school segregation in check so the federal government could point to the ruling as an example to its commitment to equality (p. 4). From the *Brown* ruling all the way to now, equality for all students has not been achieved. President Obama stated in his second Inaugural Address, "We are true to our creed when a little girl born into the bleakest poverty knows that she has the same chance to succeed as anybody else, because she is an American; she is free, and she is equal, not just in the eyes of God but also in our own land." He makes this statement as an attempt to reassure us that the idea of the American Dream is still alive and well!

Unfortunately, I am not sure that urban high school students are afforded the opportunity nor the resources needed to acquire the land of milk and honey once promised to those who "work hard." In 1991 when I graduated from high school, there were only 212 graduates; this number is a far cry from the 400 that started there four years earlier. I am not saying that the rest of my classmates never received their high school diploma—some finished that summer, some finished that following year, and others may have gotten their GED. The tragic truth is that I'm not sure what happened!

I just know that some of these students I am speaking of were bright. In fact, a few of them were in my freshman honors English course. How did we lose them? Did we push them out, or were they unable to navigate the complexities of social consciousness? This question draws me to W. E. B. Dubois (1903) who wrote about the dual consciousness in The Souls of Black Folk, which Fine also mentions in her book:

> The Negro is a seventh son, born with a vile gift with second sight in this American world, in a world which yields him no true self—consciousness; but only lets him see himself through the revelation of the other world. It is a peculiar sensation this double-consciousness, this sense of also looking at one's soul by the tape of a world that looks on in amused contempt and pity. (p. 8)

I can remember my ninth grade honors English teacher making us feel unsure of ourselves and our level of intelligence; she had a cold demeanor. When called upon to answer questions that I knew I could answer, I put my head down hoping she overlooked me. We were never given the opportunity to express ourselves and feel a sense of a positive student–teacher relationship. I dropped out of the course at the end of the first semester, even though I received a B. I didn't like the uneasy, inept feeling I got every day in her classroom. She had an opportunity to open my eyes to great literature and build my educational confidence. Instead she let me walk away and I never enrolled in higher-level courses the remainder of my high school career. She never even stopped me in the hallway to see why I was no longer in her class, leaving me feeling as though I had made the right decision. Fine would call this classroom experience "institutionalized silencing." This event didn't make me quit school immediately. However, it made me begin to feel the need to separate myself from school because perhaps I wasn't smart enough. When Michelle Fine went to Comprehensive High School (CHS) she had no idea the number of students who were systematically being dismissed from high school. The moment she saw a glimpse of this tragedy she decided to chronicle the urban high school experience.

An Apple for the Teacher!

I brought an apple for the teacher it's sitting in my bag.

I tried to give it to her but she made me pull my tag.

On my way to circle I tripped on the rug

She yelled at me to sit but I was just trying to give her a hug.

During circle time she placed me in the hall.

I'm starting to feel as though she doesn't care at all.

I raised my hand in class to show to her I was smart

She never called on me and that broke my heart.

I put the apple in my lunch box hoping for the perfect time.

On the way I bumped into Amanda, so Mrs. Miller stood me on the line.

The whole afternoon I felt so all alone but when I started talking she put me out the room.

Finally it's over I see my mother's smiling face.

I ask her for a snack but that comes only after grace.

Dear God, Please speak to Mrs. Henry she doesn't like me at all. Even during recess she stood me on the wall.

Mom spies the apple and asked why it is still here I dropped my head and a few tears!

She sees my sad face and realizes it's going to be a long school year.

I told her I didn't get a chance to give it to the teacher. It seemed like such an easy task but I just couldn't reach her.

.

This poem is written to express the silencing that students experience in school, which creates a distance from school that often grows with students throughout their school careers. This leads to student disengagement that causes students to drop out or walk away from a place that has not given them a voice, success, or acceptance. In this work I will be looking out of the window by reviewing Fine's frame of dropouts, while looking in the window as well, recalling my own urban school experiences, and reflecting on the urban school experience today.

REVIEWING

Michelle Fine (1991) in her book *Framing Dropouts: Notes on the Politics of an Urban Public High School* brilliantly links her narrative with heartfelt stories that can be linked to the politics of public schooling. This helps the reader to hear the voices of those involved in the dropout situation as well as to have the opportunity to reflect on the role of society in public education. The inquiry into urban schools continues to plague cities across the country. Fine sheds light on race, class, and gender and utilizes Black theorists to make her work more relatable for those who attended or work in urban public education. I chose this book for several reasons, since it helps me frame my own agenda as a principal serving an urban public high school. First, I understand the struggle of the urban school student and the barriers they face. Second, I am committed to transforming the urban school experience for African American Students. Last, I believe that altering the lives of students that have been disregarded is My Life's Work.

Dr. Fine (1991) begins her story with her findings that only about 20% of the ninth-graders entering CHS, a typical New York City comprehensive neighborhood high school, would graduate. These findings lead her to clear evidence that the school is failing the students or framing them to join the growing population of high school dropouts. The school attempts to divert attention away from its policies and practices, in some cases blaming students for their failure to navigate through high school. The "appearance" of providing access and opportunity within inner-city schools systematically muzzles the voices of the students who enter the school door. Ignoring the contradiction between curriculum and social reality widens the gap between urban schools and their students. This gap continues to show its face in the form of the low academic achievement of students of color as measured by tests as compared to their White counterparts. Cameron McCarthy (1990) makes the argument that "the relationship between schooling and inequality has been looked at almost exclusively towards understanding the dynamics of class not race" (p. 73). Stepping away from solely looking at class allows me to ask the question:

- How do the struggles that Black students face counteract with an educational system built on "Whiteness?"

"If youths who drop out are portrayed as unreasonable or academically inferior, then the structures, ideologies, and practices that exile them systematically are rendered invisible, and the critique they voice is institutionally silenced" (Fine, 1991, p. 5). African American children score lower on standardized tests, graduate from high school at lower rates, and are considered more likely to be suspended or expelled than the general population. The achievement gaps are still large between African American and White students. The systematic federal evaluations conducted under the No Child Left Behind law have given districts and states powerful incentives to move lower-achieving students out of their general populations to special education placements, alternative schools, or just allow them to become high school dropouts. I have seen transcripts in which a student has been allowed to fail and retake the same class three times without providing any remediation, intervention, or other academic support. This pattern is simple: If you do what you have been doing you will get the exact same result.

When speaking to students throughout my career about their struggles in urban schools, their answers range from boredom to not feeling valued by teachers and the school community. Students have stated that school was boring because they felt teachers didn't do enough to engage them in their lessons. They felt teachers delivered curriculums in a boring fashion; some students described it as monotone. Due to the delivery of the lessons, students stated it was hard to pay attention and keep interested. Other students felt that teachers should utilize more classroom time for group work, rather than merely lecturing. Students recommended that teachers use incentives to keep students motivated and engaged. They also thought that a teacher's attitude makes a big difference in how much they are engaged in class. In some cases their engagement in the classroom is greatly affected by the teacher's ability to build a positive rapport with their students. Students are less likely to be engaged and do well in a class if the teacher is unfriendly, unwilling to provide extra help, unable to deliver information in multiple ways to accommodate different learning styles, or has a negative attitude toward students. Students need to understand the connection between what they are learning in high school and what they hope to do in the future. Without providing a connection for students, the work appears meaningless.

Fine (1991) speaks of an African American teacher, Pat Reed, who chose not to eat in the teacher's lounge because she couldn't stand to hear the negative comments made by her colleagues. I had a similar experience during my first year of teaching. I heard a teacher speaking negatively about a student and I addressed my concerns to the teacher immediately. The failure by teachers to address inappropriate assaults on students can become a negative part of the school culture when teachers allow it to take place.

I recently had the opportunity to discuss the "teacher lounge" with a group of teachers who were among the faculty at the high school in which I attended. I wanted to know what the culture was like at the school in 1991. The staff was 75% Black and the enrollment was around 1,300. Their memories of the teacher's lounge revolved around smoking (which is now illegal on school property) and making copies. One teacher stated that negative comments about students were not made in an open forum but students may have been mentioned from time to time as a way to solicit ideas on how to reach a student. Another teacher recalled disagreeing privately with an administrator for what she felt was an unjust suspension. The suspension was not rescinded but the teacher felt a responsibility to voice her concerns. Most teachers felt as though the school maintained a nurturing environment but also recalled repeated suspensions and poor grades as the main reasons students dropped out. Mrs. Strong recollected that some students at 16 years of age felt like they no longer wanted to come to school and the compulsory school age at that time ended at 16, so they got a work permit and that was the end of high school for them. One math teacher felt that requiring Algebra for all students became a gatekeeper that left some students unable to pass, therefore leading to failure and in some cases the student deciding to leave school. As the conversation ensued I was amazed by some of the issues discussed that still plague our schools.

Compulsory schooling is now required for students aged 6–18 so the law keeps students and parents from "discharging" at 16 and holds them accountable for attending school. The term "discharge" is the official term Fine (1991) indicates was used by the New York City Board of Education to describe a student who is no longer in attendance at a particular school. I worked as a student services advisor for 10 years where my primary duties were to locate truant students and support them back into a school setting. The alarming concern for me was the number of students who were allowed to stay home from school. Fine mentions, "A dean warned students, we're going to get rid of anybody we think is capable of making trouble, so you better watch your rear end" (p. 16). These kinds of comments are what have led to some students deciding to just stay home. I believe that everybody wants to be good at something. When students are spoken to negatively or ridiculed by the people hired to teach them and make them feel good about themselves, we are causing the discharge to happen. I once asked a teacher, "Would you keep coming to work here every day if I came to your room every day and critiqued you or your work?" He replied, "NO!" And I rebutted, "So why are you doing that to children?"

I sometimes believe that we forget that our students are people, too, and they require the same level of nurturing and support that we would like to receive from our boss. Fine (1991) found that many students remembered a teacher who cared, gave special time, and poured commitment into school, but most dropouts questioned at least some teachers' general level of concern (p. 73).

RECALLING

As I attempt to recall my urban high school experience I am reminded of incidents that may have derailed my peers from graduating. Fine (1991) implores us to look at the silencing of students that occurs in high school by looking at policies, practices, and ideologies that exist within the high school culture (p. 32). Silencing of students does not support building an environment that can meet the needs of all students, just a select few. In order to graduate from high school, all students must take and pass American government. One teacher who taught the government course could have used the class to motivate us; instead his practice was filled with 100 question packets given on Monday and collected on Friday. A test over the same questions that were on the worksheets would be administered on Friday. This process was repeated throughout the entire school year. There were never opportunities given for self-expression or questions, no individuality or differing views that may exist within our society. These types of schooling practices silence student creativity and negate any opportunity to utilize problem solving or real world applications.

Zero tolerance policies create an environment that silences students through punishments that mostly exclude students from the classroom. Zero tolerance policies strive to reduce violence in schools and make schools a safer place for staff and students. The start of no tolerance policies within schools brought attention to school safety, changed the mindset of school officials, and raised the number of students suspended and expelled. Exclusion from school does not only take place in a physical sense but students also feel an emotional exclusion from school. The negative interactions between teachers and administrators leave students feeling like outsiders. They are not included in extracurricular activities or enrichment programs that may help to increase their level of academic achievement. Inside public schools there persists a systematic commitment to not name the aspects of social life or of schooling that activate social anxieties (Fine, 1991, p. 33). In the book *Other People's Children*, Lisa Delpit (1995/2006) argues that the classroom and academic problems found in minority students' experiences are often caused by miscommunication between students and teachers of different races and cultural backgrounds. The author uses professional research and her own experiences from schools to discuss ways in which educators can build on students' backgrounds and cultural experiences to prepare them for life outside of school. Delpit proposes that we conceptualize teaching as a profession that actively labors to "recognize and overcome the power differential, stereotypes, and the other barriers which prevent us from seeing each other. Those efforts must drive our teacher education, our curriculum development, our instructional strategies, and every aspect of the educational enterprise" (p. 36).

Those most likely to leave high school prior to graduation carry with them the most critical commentary on schooling. High school students who leave school before graduation have wounds that are directly caused by the socialization of schooling. Socialization refers to "our systematic training into the norms of our culture" (Sensoy & DiAngelo, 2012, p. 15). When I bump into my former classmates who did not graduate they always have a story to tell me that contains high school hurts that still have not healed. The irony is that 25 years later the push out of school or dropping out of school still traumatizes former students; dropping out affects them for the rest of their lives. All at the same time, the top 20% of students view their high school experience completely differently. Fine calls this difference a view from "the Top" (p. 126).

REFLECTING

The opportunity to become principal at the high school I attended has been a blessing and a curse at the same time. When I enrolled my son in school, I believed in the "American Dream." I thought if he attended the best schools he would have the same opportunities as every other American. My hopes deteriorated with time; I couldn't figure out the tools needed to break down the barriers that he faced. I didn't realize at the time that my liberal thinking was perpetuating the same social order that my son was being excluded from. Racism that exists in the United States is "a normal fact of daily life in U.S. society" (Taylor, 2009, p. 5). This ideology and assumptions of White supremacy are ingrained in the political, legal, and educational structures in ways that make them hard to recognize. The structure of White supremacy has a profound effect on the world and is an "all-encompassing and omnipresent" (Taylor, 2009, p. 4) system of privilege, power and opportunities that are often invisible to its own beneficiaries.

Fine (1991) speaks of working in a system that speaks of equal opportunities and guarantees unequal outcomes (p. 154). She mentions five belief systems that exist among educators within the school community that play a major role in students' failures within our schools. Unfortunately, I have witnessed them all while still attempting to encourage my staff, my community, and my family not to give up on our public schools and our children. She says that "Many adolescents are shut out of their high schools, psychologically if not bodily" (p. 161). Those are the students that are allowed to sleep in class or are chronically absent and never have a call home or the teacher never takes a moment to inquire about how often the student misses class and would love to see them there more often. I know that in the hustle and bustle of the school day we all get caught up in forgetting to do the little things that may keep a student coming to school. The reason that I make it my mission to learn every students' name in the school before Thanksgiving is so that I can address each of them by name and work to build a relationship that may keep them in school.

Fine (1991) includes a chapter titled "Burning at Both Ends: Low-Income Mothers, Their Public Schools, and Their Adolescents" (p. 161). I relate to this chapter even though I have been fortunate enough to have a job to provide for my family. But trying to juggle motherhood with everything else and ensure that my son was educated has not been an easy task. In fact, I failed at making sure my son walked across the stage to receive his diploma. "One might turn to parents and guardians and ask, why aren't you on the scene? Why aren't parents disrupting, challenging, demanding, that their children not be driven from the one institution which promises a better life?" (p. 161). My response to those that present this question: How do you know that we are not advocating for our children. The author uses Langston Hughes' 1931 "The Negro Mother" to speak to the struggle of the African American women trying to protect her children. I have written a piece that opens a window to my feelings and the feelings of mothers like me that are raising African American male children.

See My Son!

I want the teacher to see a child when she looks at my son. She watched the news last night and a Black boy murdered someone. The next day when my innocent boy walks in her room she sees not his face but the man from the news. The images form prejudices within her mind that are continually criminalizing him in her mind throughout the school day.

I'm not asking for special treatment I'm just asking you to allow yourself to see my son!

In the teachers' lounge she begins to read a magazine with the faces of all the criminals convicted of violent crimes in America. When she returns from lunch she begins to make sure through her power as the teacher my son conforms to the hegemonic order of the classroom. The moment he appears to be disobedient or non-compliant a punishment is given instead of an opportunity for learning. Unfortunately, she doesn't see my son anymore; she sees the rapist, robber, or drug dealer from the magazine she read earlier. My son has begun to see the difference in the way she interacts with him in comparison to other students in the class. He doesn't understand the subtlety, all he feels is rejection and disappointment.

I'm not asking for special treatment I'm just asking you to allow yourself to see my son!

A dinner party of middle class teachers attended on the weekend brings up the subject of rap music and how it is making Black boys so violent. So on Monday you hear my son singing a lyric with no profanity but yet he is told to quiet down and sit because, the teacher says, his actions are chaotic and distracting to the other students. However, other students come in singing quite often. The pressures to break the stereotypical thoughts placed on music through media are unclear to boys in third grade.

I'm not asking for special treatment I'm just asking you to allow yourself to see my son!

Black boys receive constant messages that they are not good enough, smart enough, or privileged enough to be among the best and the brightest. Teacher expectations create an environment in which a teacher will assign easier work to the Black male student because it is clear he lacks the capability to compete with his peers. By creating a lower level of self-worth and no capacity for higher level learning, he is unprepared for college. The teacher believes that his lack of motivation is due to his low academic skills rather than the teaching strategies being employed within the classroom.

I'm not asking for special treatment I'm just asking you to allow yourself to see my son!

I need teachers to see my son not as a group or statistic but as a single individual with the potential to achieve as well as any other student in his classroom. He is full of hope and promise just waiting on an opportunity to shine. See My Son! Due to the way that our society sees a Black man as this destructive, dangerous, and uneducated human being, he struggles to exist as his best self. As I seek to help my son rebuild his self-image and establish his own identity, I uncover a boy that sees himself through a lens of incapability. Through rejection, lack of acceptance, and fear, he attempts to grasp the mirror to see something other than what he has seen through the eyes of someone else. So that he can begin to see himself as the king he was born to be, he drops the mirror feeling that it is way too heavy to hoist. The struggle is not only with him, but also with the oppression heaped on him through historical, social, and institutional power.

CONCLUSION

As a principal within an urban high school, the same one I attended as a student, I recognize some of the practices and policies that prevent students from graduation that in many cases I am charged to uphold. So many urban high schools have been called dropout factories. These policies and practices can be broken down into categories structural and cultural challenges. Michelle Fine's research at CHS in New York City provided an in-depth look into the causes of students learning or being discharged from high school. I have personally and professionally dealt with the realities of students dropping out of high school. The barriers that exist within schools begin when children enter school. The social stratification within schools point out the differences that divide teachers and students within our school communities these differences push students out. Social stratification is the concept that social groups are relationally positioned and ranked into a hierarchy of unequal value (Sensoy & DiAngelo, 2012, p. 4). Unfortunately, adults in schools walk through the doors with their own biases that are woven into the fibers of how they see themselves and others. John Ogbu and Herbert Simons (1998) argue that the differences in minority education and their low level performance is caused by the treatment they receive in schools and the perceptions in society that are embedded in the minds of their teachers, administrators, and the community. Black students are considered involuntary immigrants that were brought over from Africa to be slaves. Involuntary immigrants are those who have been incorporated into society against their will. These groups have been systematically exploited throughout centuries; therefore their culture has been depreciated from slavery and colonization. Today's Black students do not subscribe to the idea that they must conform to the normal practices that provide them with what Lisa Delpit (1995/2006) would call "the code" (p. 36). It is imperative for the survival of public education that we continue to address the number of students that are being discharged or discharging themselves from school. I don't know if it will happen in my lifetime but as I look out my office window I know I will do everything in my power to be a school leader that continues to work and build a school culture that keeps students in school.

REFERENCES

Delpit, L. (2006). *Other people's children* (2nd ed.). New York, NY: The New Press. (Originally work published 1995)

Dubois, W. E. B. (1903). *The souls of black folk.* New York, NY: Gramercy Books.

Fine, M. (1991). *Framing dropouts.* Albany, NY: SUNY Press.

Ladson-Billings, G. (2004). Landing on the wrong note: The price we paid for brown. *Educational Researcher, 33*(7), 3–13.

McCarthy, C. (1990). *Race and curriculum: Social inequality and the theories and politics of difference in contemporary research on schooling.* London, England: Falmer Press.

Ogbu, J., & Simons, H. (1998). Voluntary and involuntary minorities: a cultural ecological theory of school performance with some implications for education. *Anthropology & Education, 29*(2), 155–188.

Sensoy, O., & Diangelo, R. (2012). *Is everyone really equal?* New York, NY: Teachers College, Columbia University.

Taylor, E., Gillborn, D., & Ladson-Billings, G. (Eds.). (2009). *Foundations of critical race theory in education.* New York, NY: Routledge.

CHAPTER 10

RETHINKING MULTICULTURAL EDUCATION FOR AUTHENTIC EMANCIPATION

Loveness Ngorosha

The 1990s saw a new breed of educational writers who not only advocated for school reform, but who also shared a critical reconstructionist perspective regarding education. These scholars fought against the repressive social aspects of schooling and advocated for social justice in education. These critical reconstructionist scholars argued that schooling in the United States perpetuated economic and class inequalities in service to the dominant power elite, yet true education can and should be emancipating (Schubert, Schubert, Thomas, & Carroll, 2002). One among these scholars is Cameron McCarthy, whose scholarship reconceptualizes education through exploring race and difference issues in education. McCarthy's (1990) book titled *Race and Curriculum: Social Inequality and the Theories and Politics of Differences in Contemporary Research on Schooling* provides unique perspectives on race, its concomitant consequences, and the shortfalls of multicultural education.

Prior to reading McCarthy's (1990) book, I had not read any books by him except for a few of his quotations that were cited in the chapter titled *Understanding Curriculum as a Racial Text* in Pinar, Reynolds, Slattery, and

Curriculum Windows: What Curriculum Theorists of the 1990s Can Teach Us About Schools and Society Today, pp. 145–156

Taubman's (2006) book, *Understanding Curriculum*. After reading the first few pages of the book, *Race and Curriculum*, I became convinced that I needed to contact the author in order to pick his brain about the issues he raised in his book. This was necessitated by two reasons. First, I am an international student from a country whose school curriculum does not expose students to issues of race, either in county or internationally. The history curriculum I experienced mostly focused on Zimbabwean, African, and European history. Although initially naïve to his scholarship, I intuitively recognized that McCarthy's work was important and could simultaneously expand and alter my perception of education. Second, when reading the introduction of the book and trying to make sense of it, I realized a gap existed between my experiences and the nuances and intricacies of race-relations. His text introduced a sensitive and controversial conversation—a subject that many scholars, given an option, would not dare explore, but only the courageous are willing to tackle! Reading the introduction to *Race and Curriculum* helped me to identify more with Hall's (as cited in McCarthy, 1990) assertion that, "Race is a phenomenon which one only begins to fully comprehend when one sees it working within different institutions, processes, systems, and practices of whole societies in their full complexity" (p. ix).

Although race and racism appear to be conflated in Hall's (as cited in McCarthy, 1990) observation above, situating these concepts in complex social practices made a lot of sense to me. As a phenomenon, race is not a biological manifestation of humankind, but a result of sociocultural constructions that assign people into different racial groupings. Racism is the oppression of people based on social creations via arbitrary rules and codes (Quantz, 2015). Both race and racism are more fully understood when institutions and social practices are interrogated in ways that reveal how the social constructions of race and the application of rules and codes favor some racial groupings over others. The upshot is that racism leads to the mistreatment and domination of members of certain racial groups. With this understanding, the claim with how race can be fully comprehended truly resonated with my own personal experiences with race. Like other international students, before I came to the United States, issues of race and racism did not directly confront me on a daily basis. Being Black was not something I thought about, and neither did I recognize that I spoke with a so-called accent. McCarthy's (1990) work served as a guide for me in understanding how race and racism interconnect to affect my experience as an educator, and how issues of race and racism are integrated into the curriculum of our schools. Join me as I take a walk through McCarthy's work and examine the intricacies of multiculturalism and curriculum.

CAMERON McCARTHY: TEACHER AND SCHOLAR

Cameron McCarthy is an African American scholar and instructor, and serves as the divisional coordinator of global studies for the University of Illinois. Professor McCarthy has published widely on topics related to globalization, educational policy, postcolonialism, school ritual, and adolescent identity in various reputable journals. He has written extensively on the issue of race and multiculturalism including *Contradictions of Identity: Education and the Problem of Racial Absolutism* (1995) and *The Uses of Culture: Education and the Limits of Ethnic Affiliation* (1998). McCarthy also coauthored a book with Dimitriadis (2001) titled, *Reading and Teaching the Postcolonial: from Baldwin to Basquiat and Beyond.* This portrait of McCarthy's scholarship gives us an understanding of his commitment to issues of race and multicultural education he discusses in his book, *Race and Curriculum* (1990). In the next section of this chapter I will summarize the issues raised in the book, and explore McCarthy's examination of those issues.

An Overview of *Race and Curriculum*

As an international student, I had a hard time harmonizing my perception of racism in the United States with the reality that McCarthy (1990) painted. I could not fathom how deeply race and racism were entrenched within the fabric of the United States and its schools. Although written over 25 years ago, McCarthy's book still speaks to us today about racial disparities and hostilities prevalent in the American society. These disparities persist in numerous arenas, but the achievement gap between Black and White students is the most galvanizing. Although McCarthy's book was written almost three decades ago, it continues to find a contemporary footing in the discussion of social inequalities resulting from conceptualizations of race and racism; a battle in education that still rages today.

Pinar et al. (2006) acknowledged that throughout the 1970s and the early 1980s, racial issues were virtually absent from curriculum theory. Racial discourses were not considered essential, so they were intentionally excluded from educational conversations. It was not until the late 1980s and the 1990s that scholars such as McCarthy emerged to evoke thoughtful conversations about race and curriculum; reframing education as a racial text. This reframing prompted an examination of the role race plays in informing the organization and selection of school knowledge, and the production and reproduction of subcultures among school youth. This purposeful selection occurs through inclusion and exclusion of particular social and cultural norms on behalf of the privileged majority. The result is that particular social inequalities are perpetuated, marginalizing cultures of nondominant groups.

Through his book, McCarthy (1990) provides a narrative for understanding the relationship of race and curriculum as it is reflected in research on schooling. As pointed out earlier, it is important to keep in mind that the concept of race is a complex, dynamic, and changing construct; that is, racial identities are specific historical and social constructions (Pinar et al., 2006). As McCarthy (1990) puts it, racial differences are not natural, but a result of ever changing human work, activity, and interaction. Throughout his book, McCarthy explores race issues in curriculum and provides a narrative for understanding the relationship between race and curriculum as it is reflected in research on schooling (Schubert et al., 2002). McCarthy focuses on the theoretical and political perspectives surrounding the issues of racial inequality and the academic underachievement of African American students, and other groups such as Latino and Asian American students.

In the beginning of his book, McCarthy (1990) explores the following questions:

- How have mainstream and radical American educators, curriculum theorists and sociologists of education sought to explain racial inequality in schooling?
- What is the relationship of race to the modern school curriculum and how should this relationship be theorized in order to give us greater explanatory purchase on the nature and effects of racial inequality?
- What type of principles should guide current and future approaches to the reform of race relations in education?

In response to the questions, contrasting explanations for the persistence of racial inequality in schooling are given. On the one hand mainstream educators saw students of color through the cultural deficiency lens. They explained the underachievement of students of color as situated within their "uneducable" mental faculties, and tended to blame the victim as they perceived Black cultural values as unnurturing due to lack of solid family structures and poor parenting practices. Mainstream theorists also believed that curriculum interventions on variables such as, placement, counseling, methods of teaching or testing, and teacher behavior could have positive impact on underrepresented students' performance. On the other hand, radical theorists reduced the complexities associated with racial inequality to a general rubric of working-class oppression. Thus, mainstream and radical theorists confined their explanations to cultural values and economic structures as the only sources of racial inequalities in school.

McCarthy (1990) challenges these theorists who emphasized linear, single-cause explanations of educational difference. He argues that both mainstream and radical conceptual frameworks do not effectively capture the heterogeneous and variable nature of race relations in either the school setting or society because their "explanations depart from the exploration of political, cultural, and economic contexts in which racial groups encounter each other in the school and social life" (p. 6). Thus, McCarthy, in disagreement with most theorists, chose to use a relational method to analyze formulations on race and education. He uses this perspective in order to indicate that relations of class and gender are integral to shaping the racial character of contemporary schooling. McCarthy perceives the relational approach as providing the basic method for reformulating the relationship of race to schooling while simultaneously affirming the autonomous effectivity of racial antagonism; subsequently theorizing racial disconnections as the catalysts to gender and class oppression.

McCarthy (1990) describes the theory and practice of multiculturalism as a contradictory and problematic "solution" to racial inequalities in schools. Banks (1991) commented that the multicultural solution was implemented during the period when the discourse over schools had become increasingly racialized as a response to minorities' curriculum demands. Black and other minority groups insisted that educational policy should address issues of racial inequality, minority cultural identities, and the distribution of power within institutions such as schools to change the curriculum that emphasized Anglo-Saxon values. Through this tension, McCarthy posited the conceptual and practical claims of three approaches to multicultural educational. These approaches include cultural understanding, cultural competence, and cultural emancipation. McCarthy acknowledged that each of the three approaches to multicultural education represented a "subtly different inflection on the question of what is to be done about racial inequality in schools" (p. 55). McCarthy noted that these responses all seem to deflect attention from confronting the issue of racism in American schools. At that time, multicultural proponents were optimistic that their multicultural education curriculum would solve the racial issues in schools. However, McCarthy maintained that "these multicultural approaches to curriculum reform really do not offer viable explanations or solutions to the problem of racial inequality in schools" (p. 56). McCarthy claimed that the failure was largely because "multicultural education as a new form disarticulated elements of black radical demands for the restructuring of school knowledge and rearticulated these elements into more reformist professional discourses around issues of minority failure, cultural characteristics and language proficiency" (p. 41). He further argued that proponents of multiculturalism failed to realize and acknowledge the differential structures of power, resources, and opportunities that help to define students of color and their relationship to a dominant White group. His focus was on the effect of differential structures of power, inhibited access to resources and opportunities for the marginalized, and exposes how codes and programs embedded in social institutions such as schools lead to the domination of those assigned a disregarded racial identity (Quantz, 2015). Therefore, it is not only an attitudinal change or sensitivity and appreciation of cultural differences that closes the achievement gap, but also attending to "structural and material relations in which racial antagonism is embedded" (p. 54). In other words, the Black radical pluralism was misappropriated and tweaked to remain friendly to the original Eurocentric foundations of the American school curriculum. Thus, the new multiculturalism tended to "undertheorize race—racial antagonism is seen as a kind of disease that is triggered by some deeper flaw of character or society" (McCarthy, 1995, p. 298). Although potential solutions are offered elsewhere in the literature, McCarthy (1990) critiques the limitations of mainstream liberal and multicultural educators' explanatory variables of culture and values as they are seen through the lens of neo-Marxist theories and the sociology of education. He critically analyzes the radical approaches of the structuralists, cultural reproductionists, and critical theorists to help the reader understand "the variation that exists in radical theories of racial inequality in education" (p. 68).

In chapter five, *Nonsynchrony and Social Difference: An Alternative to Current Radical Accounts of Race and Schooling*, we find the core ideas of the book. McCarthy (1990) analyzed the tensions between and among radical approaches to racial inequality in the curriculum and educational literature. He then proposed his alternative approach to racial inequality. McCarthy identified his theory as *nonsynchronous theory* of race relations in schooling and society. McCarthy argued, "against the essentialist or single-cause explanations of the persistence of racial inequality in education" (p. 71), and as such, he redirected "attention to the complex and contradictory nature of race relations in institutional life of social organization such as schools" (p. 71). He shed light on the connection between race, class, and gender and how these variables play out in the encounter between members of marginalized groups and those of the dominant culture.

McCarthy's (1990) proposal of a nonsynchronous theory seeks to close the gap that has been created by theorists who ignore the prevalence of racial inequalities in America's communities and schools through overlooking the dynamics of tension, contradiction, and discontinuity in the institutional life of the school. McCarthy's nonsynchronous theory is aligned to Hick's (as cited in Pinar et al., 2006) thesis of nonsynchrony. Hicks argues that "race, class, and gender function in contradictory fashion in daily life; they do not reproduce themselves in any simple manner" (p. 319). McCarthy argues that in the nonsynchronous approach to race relations, "class and gender are integral to the shaping of racial character of contemporary schooling" (p. 7). Further, he argues that:

> The articulation of a nonsynchronous perspective entails a more positive conceptual and practical task—that is to stake out a field within contemporary debates on schooling for a more inclusive, affirmative politics that takes seriously the differential needs, interests, and desires of minority men and women and urban working-class youth. (p. 119)

Thus, the concept of nonsynchrony is perceived as a type of panacea that attempts to address the vast differences in interests, needs, desires, and identities that separate diverse groups from each other and from the White majority in educational settings. The synchronous approach to race recognizes that minorities are not a homogeneous group and acknowledges that African Americans, Asian Americans, and the Hispanic-Latino, have different and unique experiences with race, racism and racial inequalities— a reality that the "essentialist approach to race ignores or flattens out" (McCarthy, 1990, p. 118). For this reason, McCarthy suggests that through the process of nonsynchrony, we need to pay attention to contradiction, discontinuity, and nuance within and between embattled groups expressed in the long history of tension and hostility between the Black and White working classes in the United States.

In his final chapter, McCarthy (1990) spells out his theory's effects for policy, including implications for state, societal, institutional, and curricular initiatives. McCarthy suggests an educational reform that takes into account the nonsynchronous nature of race in school (Carter, 1991). Furthermore, he calls for a broad-based "alliance across different interests, and different groups of activist educators, oppressed minorities, working-class women and men, and teachers and students" (p. 134) to collaborate in challenging the Eurocentric status quo and eliminate racial inequalities in school. When these groups come together and have an honest conversation about race and racism, they can reconstruct race and unearth the injurious institutionalized racism that many commit by simply following rules and codes established in their institutions (Quantz, 2015).

REFLECTIONS ON McCARTHY

Given that the focus of the text was race issues and the curriculum, I anticipated that McCarthy's (1990) book would interrogate the sensitive but courageous conversations about race in our society in a manner that was more accessible to the reader. On the contrary, I found the book quite dense to connect with on a personal and professional level. In some sense, books like McCarthy's can be isolating, as one cannot interact with just anyone about the ideas presented. It took me a great deal of time to comprehend what McCarthy's *nonsynchronous theory* was about and how to practically make sense of it in curriculum work. I have read difficult academic books before —yes, they were hard reads, but I almost gave up while attempting to make sense of the McCarthy text. There were times when some of the historical and analytical descriptive content of the book was winding and in such "thick language" that I lost the line of argumentation. I eventually consoled myself by realizing that interpreting scholarly work in not always a "happily ever after" story, but should be thought provoking, challenging, and disturbing, for doctoral students and scholars alike. There are also moments of clarity, where the author's ideas suddenly take shape and emerge from the text. These moments are like the early morning, when darkness dissipates, paving the way for morning sunlight. Although I found the book a hard read, that did not prevent me from having that experience of "Yes, now I understand!" Indeed, reading McCarthy allowed me to envision a new pathway and direction to take on issues of race and curriculum. McCarthy conveyed ideas that 21st century educators and curriculum theorists can utilize today to make schooling equitable, accessible, and meaningful for all American children regardless of race. Below, I discuss the window of an authentic multicultural education curriculum for the American society using some of the big ideas I learned from McCarthy.

AUTHENTIC MULTICULTURAL EDUCATION

Is there a curriculum that can be described as authentic? Where did the idea of an authentic curriculum come from? Throughout *Race and Curriculum*, McCarthy (1990) asserted that the "multicultural solution" to racial inequalities was in fact no solution at all. McCarthy expressed disappointment and discomfort over the tendency of mainstream educators to overlook the problems of race and racism in education. I was disheartened by how previous iterations of multicultural education were misappropriated and implemented as a curriculum that stressed the sociocultural liabilities of minorities. The differentiated, compensatory curriculum, and educational enrichment programs that were put in place in the name of multicultural education were not a solution as they constituted the core process of racial marginalization and subordination of students in the institutional culture of the school. The manipulated programs implemented only superficially resembled multicultural education, remaining far from an authentic form.

McCarthy's (1990) critical analysis of the multicultural solution removes the heavy curtain covering the window to authentic multicultural education and multiculturalism. His analysis opens the readers' eyes to authentic multicultural education that recognizes and embraces cultural diversity as a fact of life in American society; whereas students of different cultural identities are affirmed and preserved through the educational process. It is an implied possibility that a radical curriculum reform toward authentic multicultural education might bring hope for students of color in America's White dominated school systems. To bring racial sanity in America's troubled schooling system, McCarthy argues that, "Any discussion of curriculum reform must address issues of representation as well as issues of unequal distribution of material resources and power outside the school door" (as cited in Pinar et al., 2006, p. 346).

Now that our eyes have been opened to see race-relations in curriculum through McCarthy's (1990) nonsynchronous lens, what would an authentic multicultural curriculum look like? Similar to McCarthy's idea of an empowering curriculum, Scott (as cited in Pinar et al., 2006, p. 346) calls for a "curriculum that teaches people to think about difference—not as a biological essence but as a historically created and changeable identity—is a democratic curriculum". To build on the idea of an authentic and culturally affirming curriculum, I thought it would a good idea to revisit some of the "radical possibilitarian themes" (McCarthy, 1990, p. 38) embedded in the multicultural education that Banks and other proponents of multiculturalism put forward.

MULTICULTURAL EDUCATION

Although Banks (1995) asserts that multiculturalism and multicultural education have different meanings, in the following discussion I use the concepts interchangeably. In addition to the two concepts, a third term "multicultural literacy" will be used synonymously with the first two. Banks conceptualized multicultural education to mean, "an idea, or concept, educational reform movement, and a process ... that maintains that all students should have equal opportunities to learn regardless of racial, ethnic, social class, or gender group to which they belong" (p. 391). Taylor and Hoechsmann (2011) conceptualized multicultural literacy to describe an approach focused on developing a means of measuring openness to contestatory knowledges, intercultural awareness, and respect as lived relations and processes. From the definitions above, I conceptualize multicultural education to be an approach in education that promotes the recognition, inclusion, and integration of diverse cultures in the curriculum to promote cultural pluralism that allows students to be their true selves with an identity, a voice of their own, and above all, an equal access to resources and opportunities. An education that is multicultural will thwart attempts to diminish cultural values. This possibility expressed by Boateng (as cited in Pinar et al., 2006, p. 347) who argues that one of the most injurious of factors contributing to poor academic achievement of African American children, and the one that seems to have the most damaging impact, is the continuous deculturalization of Black cultural values in the curriculum. To improve race relations in school, we have to go beyond simply validating cultural values in the curriculum, and must proceed with a deep understanding of the multiplicities of life found in all cultures. Students of color (Asians, Latinos, Blacks, etc.) are not a homogenous body possessing uniform, discernible traits, and schools need to recognize this reality. McCarthy (1995) proposed that:

> A relational and nonessentialist approach to the discussion of racial identities allows for a more complex understanding of the educational and political behavior of minority groups. Such a complex understanding of racial inequality, focusing on the contradictory nature of racial subjectivity, identity, and the dynamic intersection of race with class, gender, and nation, must be taken into account in strategies for improving race relations in schools. (p. 299)

With a deep understanding of minority and majority groups in our schools, we are likely to make informed multicultural decisions to cater to the best interest of learners because we can understand them better.

Envisioning the possibility of authentic emancipation from the problems of racial inequalities in our schools requires a profound and clear understanding of authentic multicultural curriculum and what it entails. Huynh (2013) acknowledges that real multicultural education is not superficial, but it involves a deep understanding of cultures and interdisciplinary ways of analyzing the roots of racism. Curriculum needs to move beyond White dominance, and move into the realm of integrating historical information. Taylor and Hoechsmann (2011) maintain that authentic multiculturalism is based:

> Not on the just-in-time recall of significant facts, but on a growing repertoire of knowledge, an appreciation for the global intellectual heritage of different cultures and disciplines, a balanced learning regime (family, community, media, and school), and an apparent willingness or respectful desire to learn more. (p. 221)

Professional educators and preservice teachers alike should continue to press forward to understand the cultural nuances and identities of students and their families.

Multicultural education needs to be understood as an ongoing process of affirming diversity. The goal of the continuing process of multiculturalism is to create within schools and society the democratic ideals that are stated in the Declaration of Independence, the Constitution, and the Bill of Rights (Banks, 1991). These ideals of social justice, equality, and freedom should continue to be expanded on and understood. Huynh (2013) goes further to suggest that a democratic curriculum based on authentic multiculturalism should interrogate textbooks, the media, and the curriculum, and should equitably utilize educational technology, and engage counter-narratives as a way to move towards an antibias approach to history. Furthermore, an authentic multicultural educative experience should emphasize both the constructive and deconstructive power of words, names, and labels. Cultural heroes, both famous and ordinary, should be acknowledged and celebrated.

McCarthy (1990) suggests that there be content-addition models of multiculturalism that should be interdisciplinary and emphasize heterogeneity of perspectives, intellectual challenge, debate, and vigorous interrogation of received knowledge and traditions. In other words, authentic multicultural education should provide all students with multiple lenses for analyzing existing knowledge as well as greater opportunities for the creation of knowledge. Therefore, a multicultural curriculum should empower students with the autonomy to interact with multiple sources of information rather than having to accept corrective bits of knowledge presented as already settled truth.

To sum up the discussion on what an authentic multicultural curriculum would involve, Erickson (1992) argues that true multiculturalism entails the disruption of the status quo. He claims that a strong version of multiculturalism is not reducible to pluralism structured in dominance or a master tradition that defines, organizes, and categorizes others. In fact, strong multiculturalism is a process that does not "envision immediate, total, clear-cut victory but helps to identify problems worth struggling against even when it cannot completely eliminate them" (p. 113).

CONCLUSION

Now that the window to authentic multiculturalism has been opened, what remains is to challenge all education stakeholders to go back to the drawing board to redesign curricula based on the characteristics of authentic multicultural education discussed above. Following McCarthy's (1990) suggestions, I propose that we commit ourselves to working towards eliminating racial inequalities and antagonism in American society from a grassroots level, through collaboration among the various groups of education theorists and educators in the field. Mainstream, liberal and radical theorists, minority scholars, university departments of education, school administrators, teachers, and staff, the community, minority and majority students and their parents who possess funds of diverse knowledge should come together and consult one another in developing multicultural strategies that address the existing racial problems prevalent in American society. We need a shared vision as a nation regarding the importance of multicultural curriculum and instructional initiatives. These initiatives must equitably prioritize the educational needs of not only the marginalized youth, but all students regardless of race, gender, class, religion, and sexual orientation. Otherwise, our hope for reimagining authentic multicultural education for every learner's emancipation will remain a dream that never becomes a reality.

REFERENCES

Banks, J. A. (1991). *Teaching strategies for ethnic studies.* Needham Heights, MA: Allyn and Bacon.

Banks, J. A. (1995). Multicultural education and curriculum transformation. *The Journal of Negro Education, 64*(4), 390–400.

Carter, B. (1991). [Review of the book Race and Curriculum: Social Inequality and the Theories and Politics of Difference in Contemporary Research on Schooling by Cameron McCarthy]. *Contemporary Sociology, 20*(5), 689–690.

Erickson, P. (1992). What multiculturalism means. *Transition 55,* 105–114.

Dimitriadis, G., & McCarthy, C. (2001). *Reading and teaching the postcolonial: from Baldwin to Basquiat and beyond.* New York, NY: Teachers College Press.

Huynh, A. (2013). Courageous conversations about race: Exploring counter-narratives on Black Heritage day. *Schools: Studies in Education, 10*(2), 274–280.

McCarthy, C. (1990). *Race and curriculum: Social inequality and the theories and politics of difference in contemporary research on schooling.* New York, NY: The Falmer Press.

McCarthy, C. (1995). Contradictions of identity: Education and the problem of racial absolutism. *The Clearing House, 68*(5), 297–300.

McCarthy, C. (1998). *The uses of culture: Education and the limits of ethnic affiliation.* New York, NY: Routledge.

Pinar W. F., Reynolds, W. M., Slattery, P., & Taubman, P. M. (2006). *Understanding curriculum: An introduction to the study of historical and contemporary curriculum discourses.* New York, NY: Peter Lang.

Quantz, R. A. (2015). *Sociocultural studies in education: Critical thinking for democracy.* Boulder, CO: Paradigm.

Schubert, W. H., Schubert, A. A. L., Thomas, T. P., & Carroll, W. M. (2002). *Curriculum books: The first hundred years.* New York, NY: Peter Lang.

Taylor, L. K., &, Hoechsmann, M. (2011). Beyond intellectual insularity: Multicultural literacy as a measure of respect. *Canadian Journal of Education, 34*(2), 219–238.

CHAPTER 11

REFLECTION ON MULTICULTURAL EDUCATION

From Nationalism to Existential Aesthetics

Shaobing Li

Every form of beauty has its own uniqueness.
Precious is to appreciate beauties of the others with openness.
If one beauty appreciates and interacts the other with diversity and
integrity;
The world will be blessed with harmony and unity.

—Xiaotong Fei, 1990

James Banks was born in 1941 in Marianna, Arkansas. Growing up as an African American during the Jim Crow years, Banks had noticed the tremendous differences between happy images of slaves in his social studies textbooks and severe situations of racial segregation in his own lived reality. Accordingly, he wondered how the curriculum narratives of happy slaves were developed and who made them. His viewpoint was certainly framed by his early experience and education. As an African American who grew

Curriculum Windows: What Curriculum Theorists of the 1990s Can Teach Us About Schools and Society Today, pp. 157–171

up in the South, young Banks wondered who had made those happy slave images and how school curriculums were produced. These initial racial, social, political, economic, and cultural issues may have provoked him to engage in social justice research across black, ethnic, multiethnic, multicultural, and intergroup studies. He has a strong educational background in elementary education and social science. He got his Master's and PhD degrees from Michigan State University, and a Bachelor's degree from Chicago State University.

WHAT DOES CURRICULUM WINDOW MEAN TO ME?

As Dr. Thomas Poetter said in our seminar class, the curriculum window as a metaphor reveals many different and rich meanings, either literally or metaphorically, running across inside and outside, known and unknown, ego and nonego, dead and alive, the past, the present, and the future. I like the window metaphor, which occurs to me as a living mirror. The mirror always has two sides. One side of the mirror represents the places, peoples, things, stories, or theories with which we are familiar. The other side refers to the new and mysterious landscape of unknown, unseen, unexperienced, or uncultivated. How do we make sense of the inside arena of a window? How can we respond to the verbal or nonverbal calling from outside of a window? And what are the joint points we can count on to connect and fill the gap between inside and outside, known and unknown?

When I read *Understanding Curriculum* (Pinar, Reynolds, Slattery, & Taubman, 1995) during the semester when we undertook the project of reading curriculum books from the 1990s, I sometimes felt overwhelmed and frustrated. It is a heavy book, both in terms of physical weight and spiritual depth. I felt frustrated because all the special, interesting, and original educational ideas I had in my head had already been examined systematically or sporadically in deep in this book. They were already there! What could I do for the meaning making process of understanding my curriculum window? Later, I felt at ease when I realized that I still could make contributions through "taking into account how complex the project of reading historical curriculum texts can be" and "offering a contemporary, hopeful, honest interpretation of what it all means and what might be possible" (Poetter, 2013, p. xxxviii). Even though my curriculum knowledge is to Pinar et al.'s (1995) genius book as a drop of water to the sea, I also recognize theories and books cannot have real living effect until they are engaged and interacted with our genuine living lives in educational processes, and they cannot fully grasp and predict distinct conditions and problems facing our contemporary educational environment. Given that the meaning of the window metaphor is epitomized in the three aspects (the inside facet, the outside facet, and the joint point which connects both of the sides), multicultural education (MCE) as the curriculum window in this chapter is accordingly expressed as the following three narratives: nationalism, existential aesthetics, and self-reflection.

The first narrative of MCE is nationalism, which is the existing facet of the curriculum window metaphor. The nationalism narrative window was opened by James Banks. Later I will explain the reason why Banks' multicultural education is ascribed to a nationalism narrative. In *An Introduction to Multicultural Education*, Banks (1994) investigated the purpose, dimensions, pedagogies, paradigms, essential knowledge, and skills required by or implied in multicultural education.

The second narrative of multicultural education is existential aesthetics. Based on the analysis of the strength and shortcomings implied in the nationalism narrative, the new and mysterious window was haunting me and emerged as the existential aesthetics narrative. The ideas haunting me were as follows: What was missing from and what were the limitations of the nationalism narrative? What were the differences and similarities in terms of social conditions facing multicultural education in 1990s and the present time? Was there any alternative narrative to moving forward towards the just, diverse, and inclusive school culture?

Self-reflection is the third narrative, which connects the existing window of the nationalism narrative with the emerging window of the existential aesthetics narrative. Curriculum as real life experience means not only the acquisition of the given knowledge and skills, but putting them into daily life experiences. What were we struggling, hoping, and imaging during the process of experiential learning? What perspectives were we making? How will we make sense of the dynamic interplaying process of multicultural education? Curriculum design should become a continuous moral growth internalized in our life experiences. If a theory, however advanced it is, does not get put into practice, it will become hallow. Likewise, the mission of social transformation will not be realized until each member in our society is empowered and has the will and strength to achieve that goal.

OVERVIEW OF BANK'S MULTICULTURAL EDUCATION

Banks' research interests focus on multicultural education, citizenship, diversity, and teaching strategies. He has written multiple books, including *Teaching Strategies for Ethnic Studies; Multicultural Education: Issues and Perspectives* (1991); *Cultural Diversity and Education: Foundations, Curriculum and Teaching* (2015); and *Multicultural Education, Transformative Knowledge, and Action* (1996), among others. Because of his influential work, he has won multiple awards from the education field and held multiple social positions in associations such as the American Educational Research Association (AERA) and the National Educational Association (NEA). He has been nick-named the "father of multicultural education," in which field he has made significant contribution. James Banks is a prestigious professor of Diversity Studies at the University of Washington, Seattle. He is also the director of the Center for Multicultural Education at the University.

Banks approaches multicultural education by examining the issues and challenges facing the educational and societal systems in the United States. He displays the struggling and severe racial divide intertwined with economic and societal polarization caused by repudiating multiethnic and multicultural education. At the same time, he notes the progress that has been made and possible opportunities and expectations that can be achieved if multicultural education can be valued, institutionalized, and implemented into educational practices in schools, classrooms, and communities. His two assumptions underlying multicultural education are: (1) race, ethnicity, culture, and social class have become salient parts of the U.S. educational and social systems; (2) ethnic and cultural diversity enriches the whole nation, its school system, and all individuals in the United States.

Banks (1994) outlines five dimensions of multicultural education, consisting of content integration; the knowledge construction process; prejudice reduction; equity pedagogy; and an empowering school and social culture. He further details four approaches adopted by educators to forge multicultural education into the existing curriculum framework: the contributions approach, the additive approach, the transformation approach, and the social action approach. Banks advocates the use of the transformative approach.

NARRATIVE INQUIRY OF MULTICULTURAL EDUCATION

Narrative as a method is different from narrative as a phenomenon. Narrative inquiry as a methodological approach relies on "life experience as narrative by those who live them" (Chase, 2011, p. 421). A person's lived experiences, at the same time, reflect the social nature endowed by the society wherein he or she lives. Different from narrative as a method reflecting a dynamic and ongoing construction and reconstruction of the lived social experience, narrative as a phenomenon is a static exhibition of a given story (Boje, 1991, 1995; Bruner, 1986; Gergen, 2009). Narrating our lived experiences and their social character in an educational environment reflects different world views, values, and philosophies (Gergen, 2009), and thus, the narrative process, as a method, epitomizes a redescription, recreation, and reframing process of the actual world (Kearney, 2002).

Following a nationalism narrative, MCE is designed to provide students with the democratic beliefs, values, knowledge, and skills necessary to function effectively as both human citizens and human capital in a cross-cultural country. Given the standpoint and purpose of national survival underlying Banks' MCE, I argue that Banks (1994) addressed his MCE curriculum mainly by engaging in this type of narrative. The limitations of the nationalism narrative of MCE lie in that: (1) The essential dimensions of people as human beings, such as humanity, cultural identity, aesthetic judgment, and emotional character, have been neglected; (2) U.S.-centric nationalist discourse cannot address the needs and concerns proposed by international and cross-national students, who may encounter institutional discrimination because of the differences of their ethnicity, culture, language, and customs and not know how to safeguard their equal, safe, and creative learning opportunity if they; and (3) Minority group rights cannot easily be protected based on nationalism, since the states always reinforce allegiance by excluding certain minority groups and promoting the interests of the dominant races and castes (Marx, 1998).

Thus, I advocate existential aesthetics, which situates students in international and cross-cultural educational environments, as the alternative narrative to recount and broaden the MCE curriculum. Following an existential aesthetics narrative, students are humane, aesthetic, and emotionally acting agents capable of pursuing and fulfilling their life meanings through building relations to others, the world, and themselves in which differences are appreciated (Greene, 1973).

I will start by examining the meaning of MCE through the nationalism narrative implied in Banks' (1994) book, then explore MCE in terms of the narrative of existential aesthetics, and finally, present the sense making process of connecting the first two facets of the MCE window through the jointure of an introspection narrative.

PART 1: NATIONALISM NARRATIVE WINDOW

The country's ultimate test as a nation will be not how it treats its citizens who are successful but how it responds to the desperate plight of those who are poor and undereducated.

—Banks (1994, p. 43)

In this section I will examine the nationalism narrative window opened by Banks (1994) from his four perspectives of the aim of multicultural education, transformative curriculum, political identity, and caring education.

THE AIM OF MULTICULTURAL EDUCATION

Banks (1994) analyzes the three main purposes of implementing MCE. Initially, MCE helps to provide all students with democratic beliefs, values, knowledge, and skills needed to function effectively in the cross-cultural, social, and educational environment in the present day. All students need to be educated through multicultural curricula to survive effectively "in a culturally diverse future society and world" (Banks, 1994, p. 23). MCE reduces the pain and discrimination that the students and racial groups of color may experience because of their differences from the dominant group. In addition, MCE helps students to better grasp essential reading, writing, mathematics, and science knowledge and skills.

The urgency of furthering MCE first lies in the demographic imperative. Banks (1994) suggests that by 2030, 22% of the nation's population will be retiring. Back then, he noted that during 1980 to 2000, "about 83 percent of the new entrants to the labor force will be women, people of color, or immigrants" (p. 36). The second urgency lies in the fact that the economic process is becoming increasingly global. Transnational corporations will have transnational identities and demand future workers to exhibit cross-cultural competency across the world, instead of being restricted to the domestic market. Third, the deepening social-class schism within and across racial lines will be pernicious to the whole society. Last, MCE is needed for restructuring schools and for societal reform. The major goal of education to help low-income students, linguistic minority students, and students of color to develop knowledge, attitudes, and skills cannot be achieved but by "restructuring educational institutions and institutionalizing new goals and ideals within them" (p. 40).

TRANSFORMATIVE CURRICULUM

Consistent with Dewey's civic education tradition, Banks (1994) advocates that MCE curriculum and educational reform should be the catalytic agent to bolster social transformation. Students should not be educated merely to maintain the status quo, to fit into the work force and societal structure, but also to help reform and reconstruct the educational and social systems. Conservative school reform advocates suggest returning to a mythical past, "when American exceptionalism was rarely questioned within mainstream society, when there was more national clarity and consensus, when authorities often spoke without challenge, and when issues related to race, class, and gender were silenced in mainstream discourse" (p. 98). In contrast, transformative reforms emphasize recognition of the diversity, equal opportunities, and transformation of the American identity.

Banks (1994) thinks curricula should be designed to rejuvenate the lives of students and their locations in the political, economic, and social institutions of society, instead of merely teaching and transferring the passive knowledge from the textbook to students. Corresponding with this, mainstream scholars adopting a conservative curriculum insist that knowledge is objective, value-neutral, and independent of action; whereas, transformative scholars advocate that our knowledge is value-laden, positional, and involves in action. In terms of multicultural education, while a curriculum infusion approach means some ethnic and gender content is added into a curriculum, the experiences of the people of color and women are still judged from the traditional, White, male dominated, Western canon. Furthermore, curriculum transformation involves paradigm shifts in which the American and world experience is viewed "from the perspective of different racial, ethnic, cultural, and gender groups" (p. 21).

While Dewey and other pragmatic philosophers say that education is a fundamental avenue for social reconstruction, the educational issues and transformation cannot only be discussed and solved from and within the education arena. Rather, they are embedded and constructed in the social background and conditions of today's technological era.

PLURIBUS UNUM OF POLITICAL IDENTITY

How can the national identity in the U.S. be reconstructed according to the multicultural perspective? Banks (1994) adopts the philosophical term "pluribus unum" to explain the dynamic and ongoing process between the "one," a national identity, and the "many," different, distinct, and diverse races, ethnicities, voices, and social classes. Banks asserts that "Unum" means the one and "pluribus" means the people. Historically, the unum was Anglo-Saxon, Protestant, male value imposed upon the pluribus. Banks (1994) thinks of the unum as moral authority that "people will feel they bought into, feel there's a need for them to respect it, feel that there's need for them to use it as a guide for their own moral and civic behavior" (p. 95). The unum is not static, absolute, and an ultimate "one," but involves reflecting our own struggles, dreams, hopes, and possibilities, and constructing or transforming the status quo.

CARING EDUCATION

Education not only means educating the mind, but educating the heart. The mind education mainly teaches students to know what they should learn, and the heart education teaches students to care, to love, and to act.

Being or becoming a fully educated person mean in a pluralistic demo-cratic society means more than the mastery of basic knowledge and skills required in a competitive job market. It also means educators need to be sensitive and take care of students' struggles, feelings, hopes, dreams, and even the shadows of their life experiences in a diverse racial, ethnic, and cultural society. Banks (1994) argues, "The mastery of basic skills will be essential but not sufficient as the diversity within our society deepens and our nation faces new challenges and possibilities" (p. 99).

How can we promote and build the caring, sharing, and flourishing classroom learning environment? Adopting the terms of ordinate catego-rized group and superordinate group developed by British psychologist Henry Tajfel, Banks (1994) holds that it is necessary to create a superordi-nate group in the classroom. Ordinate group means people will naturally categorize in-group and out-group based on the most trivial differences. Superordinate group is defined as building a sense of community, wherein people accept their differences between each other and also value equality, cooperation, oneness, and general interests. In order to overcome ordi-nate categorization and build up a sense of community, Banks introduced superordinate group practices in classrooms. Superordinate group identity accepts the differences among members, and at the same time, values the common life experience. Banks introduced Allport's (1954) group contact theory to explain the ways that we can achieve community or social char-acter. The first principle is to create cooperation, not competition, within the group. The second demands the equal-status situations for members. Equal status does not mean all members have the same social economic or intelligence status, but they are equal agents in social dialogical conditions or platforms.

PART 2: EXISTENTIAL AESTHETICS WINDOW

The ultimate criterion of education is an aesthetic criterion rather than a product criterion. It may be that the most important goal of education is to enable people to think in such a way that the kind of experience they undergo is a feelingful experience, is an aesthetic experience. If we enable them to have that kind of experience in school, then maybe they would be more likely to derive that experience subsequently.

—Elliot Eisner, 1969

I feel there is a tension in terms of the standpoint Banks (1994) holds in his book between White Anglo Saxon culture and non-White minority culture, the institutional change and the individual agent. While he tries to go beyond the Black or minority radicals and advocates MCE for all students, the challenges or problems facing multicultural curricula are unilaterally ascribed to the mainstream Anglo, White, and male hegemony. Since MCE is for all students, regardless of race, each person from any ethnicity needs to reflect on the underlying cultural background and mindset he or she has. While Banks argues the challenges facing school restructuring are derived from the social and institutional hierarchy of demographic imperative, poverty, and disproportionate share of future work force among different races, at the same time, he holds teachers should be accountable for, and have "an enormous responsibility" for, MCE (McCarthy, 1993).

Given the contradictory tensions implicated in the nationalism narrative approach, existential aesthetics aims to address multicultural education relying on the concrete, individual perspective of living and studying in a concrete environment, instead of in the nationalism's abstract and grand narrative. Existential meaning is to "relate the attainment of meaning to an individual's particular project and standpoint, to conceive it in terms of concrete, human relations to others and to the world" (Greene, 1973, p. 173). The aesthetic approach is supposed "to confront the individual with himself; to stimulate a personal search for patterning and meaning; to open perspectives beyond the everyday" (Greene, 1973, Preface). Viewed from existential aesthetics, the subject or agent is not restricted in breaking down barriers of racial, political, economic, or gender differences in a nation, but is extended to breaking down the virtual barriers facing a person in a broader cross-national and technological era. Next, I will exhibit the new emerging window from the similar four aspects analyzed in the nationalism narrative: the aim, the agent, identity, and caring education

THE AIM OF MULTICULTURAL EDUCATION

Greene (1973) extends the aim of MCE in two aspects. Different from Banks' (1994) orientation of MCE as domestic-nation-centered, Greene understands the aim through initially reflecting the condition of our age. She introduced Hannah Arendt's view on the distinctive feature of this age as "heedless recklessness or hopeless confusion or complacent repetition of 'truths' which have become trivial and empty" (cited in Greene, 1973, p. 6). Emile Durkheim called the disease of modern age—the feeling of hollowness and disbelief in nobleness—"anomic suicide" (cited in Greene, 1973, p. 61). Facing the mechanization and controls of modern society and education systems, teachers and students should create themselves as human beings, freeing other human beings to choose themselves.

The significance of considering a concrete person in the broad condition of our modern and technological time lies in MCE, not a constraint in the traditional rhetoric of race, ethnicity, class, or politics, but in realizing cultural and social justice issues are complicated and intertwined with the whole modern production and technological system. Greene's consideration that teachers and students should create themselves as human beings is absolutely not an easy enterprise. Human being is always in the danger of being ordered, manipulated, paralyzed, colonized, or seduced into a human resources, human machines, and human capital by the tangible or intangible technological system. The real danger is people not being aware of this danger and having their being degenerated by modern propaganda, social media, and popular culture.

CULTIVATING THE PASSIVE ACTIVE AGENT

There are many agent images throughout the history of philosophy, ancient Greek philosophy's rational and contemplative man, medieval philosophy's religious moral image, the modern enlightenment philosophy's analytic reasoner, and so on. The following influential images include Freud's libido-driven human being, Jung's collective unconscious definition, Buber's "I and Thou" encountering, Marx's class analysis, and Dewey's problem-solving and good habits of thought. Greene (1973) argues that there is no a scientific criteria determining which agent image is the best. She prefers the perspective of existential philosophy of education, viewing the word man as "an existing person, subjectively aware of himself and his possibilities, free to create himself in the situations of his life, free to choose" (p. 77).

Active agent means a person who is aroused or awakened to action, either by other persons or by herself. A teacher as an active agent may reflect the role of gadfly in Socrates' sense, enabling students to feel the teacher was "always fastening upon you, arousing and persuading and reproaching you" (cited in Greene, 1973, p. 72). The similar meaning holds with the reflective agent, "to be reflective and to act responsibly in that reflective practice by challenging assumptions, engaging new ideas, and helping students and colleagues to learn in a just, safe, open, and democratic setting" (Poetter & Badiali, 2001, p. 37). The role of gadfly stimulating and developing students' potential consists of the two tensional processes: teachers need take initiative action to stimulate students' learning processes; at the same time, this deliberation is based on students' autonomy and initial learning.

Passive agent means the suspension of the conscious control, submitting oneself to the inexpressible mystery or aesthetic richness of our living experience (Greene, 1973). Just image when you are surfing in the sea. The active agent may mean you need to control the board and adjust the directions and strengths, but you also need to learn how to be submissive and take advantage of the strong power of the movement of seawater.

SELF-IDENTITY AND NATIONAL IDENTITY

The essential questions of "Pluribus Unum" can be presented as the relationship between self-identity and national identity. This philosophical term "Pluribus Unum" was first developed by German philosopher Leibniz (1714/1945) to deal with the relationship among self, others, and the world. For Leibniz, the "one" means a monad or soul, which is the simplest unit of composites; the "many" is the composite consisting of the monad and its corresponding material appearance. Leibniz thinks soul is a perpetual living mirror of the universe (Leibniz, 1714/1945).

Given the contemporary social and educational environment, the "one" can be defined as self-consciousness, self-encounter, or finding oneself. Greene (1973) defines the self-encounter as a person appropriating "what he learned into his life; he must use this knowledge in making choices and in determining his future actions; he must constantly decide on the appropriate techniques for particular explorations" (p. 137). She thinks it is existentialism instead of natural science that can serve this purpose, because scientific thinking seeks the objective, excluding the intuitive feeling and self-encounters. For the existential phenomenologist, consciousness is not pure rational thinking but "experienced context" (Gurwitsch, 1970, p. 364). This experienced context is each person's life-world. The life-world is our own biographical practice and perspectives on a complicated world.

The "many" representing the social nature is the prerequisite of the development of self-encounter. For Mead (1934), mind and self-consciousness are defined not by antecedent reflective ego, but the significant responses between organism and environment wherein one and the other organisms are implicated. Joas (1985) holds that "through the theory of the social formation of the self, one of the cornerstones of bourgeois ideology in the strict sense is eliminated, namely possessive individualism" (p. 35). Mead repeatedly stresses this idea, "the whole (society), is prior to the part (the individual), not the part to the whole; and the part is explained in terms of the whole, not the whole in terms of the part or parts" (p. 7).

HEART AND EMOTION EDUCATION

The importance of genuine emotion and heart education to learning, caring, and flourishing has been overlooked for a long time. Existentialism and pragmatism are different from the modern epistemological approach in terms of emotion and heart education. The existentialist thinks rationality is merely one feature of the self, so the self "must not be identified with reason or with mind" (Greene, 1973, p. 136). Mead (1934) thinks that the importance of emotional symbol does not lie in how important it is in itself (intellectual character), but what the emotional symbol is going to reveal (emotional character).

Illich (1971) thinks we should be in favor of Prometheus' brother Epismetheus instead of Prometheus, given that Epismetheus represents the resistance to authoritarian reason and the stirring of our emotional heart. In ancient Greek mythology, there are two different kinds of spirit: Dionysian impulse and Apollonian force. The Apollonian is based on reason and logical thinking. By contrast, the Dionysian is based on chaos and appeals to the emotions and instincts. Greene (1973) argues, "the Dionysian impulse, long suppressed by the public view, was secretly challenging the Apollonian force all the time" (p. 112). Dostoevsky (1945) announced directly that, while reason is excellent, it is only the rational part of man's nature. Our holistic lives include reason and all other impulses.

PART 3: THE AUTOBIOGRAPHICAL WINDOW

Taken socially, autobiography can be understood as creating a space between ego and nonego, as well as expressing their intersections.

—Pinar et al. (1995, p. 548)

As analyzed above, we have explored the two narratives of MCE, the widely accepted version of nationalism and the emerging version of existential aesthetics. The relationship between nationalism and existential aesthetics and how these two narratives may be connected and complement each other resides in the autobiographical narrative. Both educators and students "need to become introspective ethnographers in our own classrooms to decipher the cultural meanings that we and our students bring to the group" (Hidalgo, 1993, p. 105). Hidalgo (1993) recommended three phases to implement the introspection: (1) teachers need to examine the underlying cultural values, and beliefs, both on a societal and individual level; (2) educators must awaken multicultural awareness on an affective level; and (3) teachers' diverse cultural awareness must be put into practice in the classroom.

As an introspective ethnographer, I think the initial introspection should be bilateral and dyadic. Both teachers and students, of dominant race and oppressed race, should reflect on their own cultural inheritance on individual and societal bases. As a first step, both parties of diverse groups need to value their unique cultural inheritance. At the same time, they should reflect on their own possible limitations and unconscious prejudices they may have taken for granted. MCE necessitates a process of mindset transformation, emotional appreciation, and high quality connection with the differentiated others. As Hidalgo (1993) argues, "teachers need to go beyond an intellectual awareness of the influence of culture to an affective understanding" (p. 104). It is meaningful that the purpose and content of MCE are extended from a nationalism narrative focusing on equal political and economic rights to an existential aesthetic narrative involving enlightening aesthetic judgment, encountering self-identity awareness, cultivating active and compliant citizenship, and caring emotional character building.

The subjects in MCE contexts have been broadened from domestic-nation-centered to the global, cross-national, and multi-cultural learning community. With increasing international students recruited in American universities in recent years, studying in cross-cultural classes has become a ubiquitous, challenging phenomenon for teachers and students, whether domestic or international. Because of language, racial, and cultural differences, some international students have met with big challenges when they start their learning in a cross-cultural environment. The globalization process is accelerating concerning economic, cultural, and personnel exchange over the cross-national level. Given the accumulating variety of student diversity in the educational environment, it is timely and significant to re-examine and broaden the meaning of MCE today.

Given the political, economic, and social ladder gaps among different racial and cultural groups in U.S. are still increasing, the nationalism narrative of Banks' (1994) MCE curriculum is still applicable. Yet, under the increasing international and cross-cultural educational environment, the limitations of the nationalism narrative are emerging, since the nationalism narrative mainly focuses on diverse racial, ethnic, and cultural groups with domestic citizenship. International students may not find agency within an MCE curriculum that is exclusively nation-focused, since that focus may only enhance systemic discrimination based on international race, culture, and customs. Also, the essential dimension of students being educated as human beings (humanity, aesthetic judgment, and emotional character), instead of just as human citizens and human capital, may also be neglected in a nationalistic MCE curriculum. The limitations implied in the nationalism narrative are overcome in an existential aesthetic narrative of MCE.

REFERENCES

Allport, G. W. (1954). The nature of prejudice. Reading, MA: Addison-Wesley.

Banks, J. A. (1991). *Teaching strategies for ethnic studies*. Boston, MA: Allyn and Bacon.

Banks, J. A. (1994). *An introduction to multicultural education*. Boston, MA: Allyn and Bacon.

Banks, J. A. (1996). *Multicultural Education, Transformative Knowledge, and Action Historical and Contemporary Perspectives*. New York, NY: Teachers College Press.

Banks, J. A. (2015). *Cultural diversity and education*. New York, NY: Routledge.

Boje, D. M. (1991). The storytelling organization: A study of story performance in an office-supply firm. *Administrative Science Quarterly, 36,* 106–126.

Boje, D. M. (1995). Stories of the storytelling organization: A postmodern analysis of Disney as "Tamara-land." *Academy of Management Journal, 38,* 997–1035.

Bruner, J. (1986). *Actual minds, possible worlds*. Cambridge, MA: Harvard University Press.

Chase, S. E. (2011). Narrative inquiry: Still a field in the making. In N. K. Denzin & Y. S. Lincoln (Eds.), *The Sage handbook of qualitative research* (4th ed.) (pp. 421–434). Washington, D.C.: Sage.

Dewey, J. (1916). *Democracy and education: An introduction to the philosophy of education*. New York, NY: Macmillan.

Dostoevsky, F. (1945). *Notes from the underground*. In *The short novels of Dostoevsky*. New York, NY: Dial Press.

Fei, X. T. (1990, Winter). *The anthropology study in China: A personal experience*. Paper presented at the meeting of the International Conference on social studies in Eastern Asia, Tokyo, Japan.

Gergen, K. J. (2009). *An invitation to social construction* (2nd ed.). London, UK: Sage.

Greene, M. (1973). *Teacher as stranger: Educational philosophy for the modern age*. Belmont, CA: Wadsworth.

Gurwitsch, A. (1970). Some structures of the life-world. *Studies in Phenomenological Philosophy, 30*(3), 116–132

Hidalgo, N. (1993). Multicultural teacher introspection. *Freedom's Plow: Teaching in the multicultural classroom*, 99–106.

Illich, I. (1971). *Deschooling society*. New York, NY: Harper & Row.

Joas, H. (1985). *G.H. Mead: A contemporary re-examination of his thought*. Cambridge, MA: MIT Press.

Kearney, R. (2002). *On stories*. New York, NY: Routledge.

Leibniz, G. W. (1945). *The monadology and other philosophical writings*. London, UK: Oxford University Press. (Original work published 1714)

Marx, A. W. (1998). *Making race and nation: A comparison of South Africa, the United States, and Brazil*. Cambridge, UK: Cambridge University Press.

McCarthy, C. (1993). Multicultural approaches to racial inequality in the United States. In L. Castenell & W. Pinar (Eds.), *Understanding curriculum as racial text: Representations of identity and difference in education* (pp. 225–246). Albany, NY: State University of New York Press.

Mead, G. H. (1934). *Mind, self and society form the standpoint of a social behaviorist*. Chicago, IL: University of Chicago Press.

Pinar, W. F., Reynolds, W. M., Slattery, P., & Taubman, P. M. (1995).*Understanding Curriculum. An Introduction to the Study of Historical and Contemporary Curriculum Discourses*. New York, NY: Peter Lang.

Poetter, T. S. (Ed.). (2013). *Curriculum Windows: What Curriculum Theorists of the 1960s Can Teach Us about Schools and Society Today*. Charlotte, NC: Information Age.

Poetter, T. S., & Badiali, B. J. (2001). *Teacher leader*. Larchmont, NY: Eye On Education.

CHAPTER 12

CULTURALLY RELEVANT CURRICULUM VERSUS CULTURALLY IRRELEVANT CURRICULUM

A Case of Cultures Restricted by Institutionalized Manipulation of Their Ethos(CRIME)

Genesis R. Ross

Gloria Ladson-Billings, an American educator, pedagogue, and critical theorist, has long articulated the need to disrupt the traditional practice of acquiring *knowledge* through schooling as a process of static assimilation. The amalgam of Ladson-Billings' work thematically highlights the problematic and negligent nature of steering all people with different realities of life (i.e., socioeconomic status, racial experiences, gender experiences, etc.) through one set of cultural norms. In *Dream Keepers*, Ladson-Billings (1994) made no exceptions for the steering of Black students through school oriented by the exclusive standards of White cultural norms. One

Curriculum Windows: What Curriculum Theorists of the 1990s Can Teach Us About Schools and Society Today, pp. 173–197
Copyright © 2017 by Information Age Publishing
173

set of standardized cultural norms eliminates the room for norms of other cultures to be regarded as equally relevant or producers of equally usable knowledge.

Normalizing the culture of some students ignores the culturally relevant knowledge of students who have experiences and understandings informed by their own, typically omitted culture. Their lives may have disparate realities that White cultural modes of knowledge cannot explain. White cultural modes of knowledge cannot suffice and those not from this culture should be understood as having lives that are no less real. Ladson-Billings' highlights this in *Dream Keepers* (1994), and her work has proven, so far, to be clarifying and timeless. Her work allows us to glean the past to inform our actions in the present. This is where the Curriculum Window opens, informing us through the types of questions that can be raised out of *Dream Keepers* AND that should always be considered in the process of making decisions about curriculum, such as:

1. Will/should the curriculum function to produce assimilation, to produce relevant culturally inclusive application of knowledge, a combination of both, or something else?
2. Who gets to decide?
3. Who is being decided for?
4. How does this impact such lives?

This curriculum window's chapter entangles these questions together as a way to highlight why a systematic manufacturing approach to curriculum is not just flawed—but ill-paired with culturally DIVERSE human lives. This chapter, best understood as a conceptual analysis of cultural relevance in the curriculum, thinks conceptually with Ladson-Billings' (1994) *Dream Keepers* as a critical framer. Thinking with *Dream Keepers* encouraged what I call a critical conscious reflecting (CCR), an intersectional understanding/ thinking of history and possibility, being critically engaged based on what we know, can now predict, and responses we can take up to retain potentials we have yet to know. I engage CCR metaphorically and literally in this chapter. CCR engaged metaphorically communicates through the aid of stories and symbols the felt/lived realities of Black students who experience chronic cultural omission through the curriculum. The metaphorical story may help minimize the defensive posturing that can occur when trying to discuss issues entangled in racial differences.

With the "emotionally charged subject of Race," Derrick Bell (1995) believes stories can help people "suspend their beliefs, listen to the story, and then compare their views, [...] with those expressed in the story" (p. 43). CCR engaged literally, allows the findings of Ladson-Billings' (1994) research to highlight the relentless criminal-like way the curriculum acts when entrenched in a way of knowing that voids Black student's cultures. In this chapter, *Dream Keepers* provides me an empirical impetus encouraging my use of CCR. CCR inspires my metaphorical use of a trial format for this chapter. This trial is set at the intersection of one culture standardizing curriculum and the materialized realities that embody the answers to the four questions above. These are answers from what history has told us, has taught us to predict, and helps us orient as potential. What the trial format WILL NOT provide is presentations from the Defense. My ultimate focus in this analysis is to understand the impact of omitting culture in the curriculum on those whose cultures are extracted. The goal is to understand, to move towards more holistically considered practices, meaning ones that proceed to inform curriculum through cultural pluralism. The goal is not to reduce solutions to a focus on making a victimizer pay. Holistically considered practices means the next steps should be: collective in thought, design, implementation, and accountable to modes of acquiring knowledge that support the realities in which people live and decide for themselves who and what they would like to be.

The trial is getting ready to begin ...

OPENING STATEMENT

This opening statement sets how the Plaintiffs are placed into a dehumanizing context manifesting out of the American history of dividing people along racial color lines. This dehumanizing context is complicit in the habitual violation of basic human access and rights that becomes negotiated by an inappropriate schooling curriculum for Black students. When Black students' basic human access and rights are negotiated by schooling curriculum, a dehumanizing context about Black people compared to Whites is reiterated. This negotiation further dictates and drives the omission of Black people in other settings throughout the larger society. It perpetuates a struggle to understand Black people and the uniqueness in which their lives are lived in America. This perpetuation creates and continuously inspires ignorance, bigotry, and responses towards Blacks that a "sorry" cannot always correct once actions have been deployed out of the failure to simply understand Black culture, which should not be understood merely as a binary to White culture, but as a different set of cultural characteristics in terms of ways of knowing, communing, being as a nation, aligning to various ideologies, and so forth.

Counsel for the Plaintiff: Opening Statement

Your Honor and People of the Court, this is a case of my clients, though Black, also representing other racially and culturally diverse learners being dehumanized (socially, emotionally, physically, and economically eradicated) by a White Culturally Driven Curriculum. White Culturally Driven Curriculum is what Gloria Ladson-Billings (1994) would call a SOCIAL CURRICULUM OF ASSIMILATION, and it is not fully relevant to my Black clients. It is a curriculum I un-affectionately call Culturally Irrelevant Curriculum (CIC, what I pronounce as SICK). I am speaking to you about a power-imposed handling of the curriculum by Domination that omits the very reality/identity of my Black clients. Their identity, whether the curriculum acknowledges it or not, does not simply detach itself. It does not run and hide nor un-inform the way schema and knowledge exists in my Clients' lives. Their capital "B" Black identity can be observed deeply connected to intelligent productions and human uplift. Their capital "B" Black identity can be observed contending daily with a historically rooted social, political, and racial struggle that challenges their safe and humanizing existence. It is, Your Honor, a capital "B" Black identity SIMPLY, yet COMPLEXLY it holds what Cheryl Harris (1998), who capitalized Black, and W.E.B. DuBois (1971), who capitalized Negro, a socio-political FUNCTION. Encapsulated within its FUNCTIONAL identity is a history of innovations and innovativeness. It encompasses the machine-like capacities of laborious work that helped to build this UNITED (supposedly) STATES of American. This same Black identity nurtured, protected, and aided in the humanization of many lives while their Black lives/identities have been widely degraded, slaughtered, and savagely appropriated for the vast capital gains of many Whites. These Black lives/ These identities cared for the children of the Slave Owners. EVEN while the Slave Owners' ACTS...relentlessly maintained Black identity and reinforced the representation of Black bodies as OBJECTS upon which acts of brutality AND INEQUITY could be applied. This INEQUITY, at minimum, should be understood as the living inhumane battle against V-E-R-Y HUMAN BEINGS – though BLACK BEINGS—I no LESS—HUMAN BEINGS. AND, As SUCH, these BEINGS too should be allowed into their possession EQUITY that David Stovall (2015) would define as an UNCHALLENGED ability to have simply "what they need when they need it." By omitting the culture of my clients' in the curriculum, their Black Identity and any historical, sociopolitical and inhumane state in which it has been or may be lodged, too is omitted—SIMPLY IGNORED—EXTRACTING ITS CURRENT RELEVANCE TO THE WAY THEIR LIVES ARE LIVED. This very act contextualizes them as pure objects/property, existing in no other reality than what HAS ALWAYS been explained, navigated, and made OK in the larger society by WHITENESS. Controversia l ... yes, I know ... but controversy should not be the pass given to dismiss the truth, any impact thereof, and necessary next steps.

And to be CLEAR ... Your Honor and People of THIS court ... my Plaintiffs are NOT interested in this trial SIMPLY producing a PUBLIC record that names the Criminal Acts against them, ACTS dictated by Domination and administered through CIC. My Clients are asking for what Paulo Freire (1998) calls a UNIVERSAL HUMAN ETHIC, a standard way of engaging ethically the human existence of people that does not privilege resources or treatments upon humans of one particular culture over another. It is an ethic within Curriculum that can unquestionably be expected to function. My Clients are asking for a curriculum that produces a critical education—contributing to what Elliot Eisner (1979) calls EDUCATIONAL CONNOISSEURSHIP ... that allows my Clients to develop habits of perceptual exploration they follow to understanding and responding to phenomena, triggering more and more refined thinking and application. Unless we aspire to move beyond CIC to what Ladson-Billings (1994) calls CULTURALLY RELEVANT CURRICULUM (CRC pronounced "Kirk") ... then the inhumanity against the Black identity via Curriculum will be maintained and perpetuate actions that apologies cannot take back. We will find ourselves observing CIC gathered in-line with the same demoralizations that function exclusively as White Property. This means curriculum functions as a power, identity, and possession owned and dictated by White Cultural Norms that is purposed with maintaining domination over all other Cultures. CIC as White Property, of the educational dynamic, is one and the same with socially and legally vetted inhumane practices towards Blacks. It is quite simply attached to the steady historical-to-contemporary acts that maintain and drive White Property through various forms.

Though the face of criminal inhumane practices against Black has changed – it is no longer the pre-1865 face of de facto Black Slavery (the before slave emancipation face)—the discrimination of others by race has not. Never having ceased since it began is the EXISTENCE of some form of dysfunctional inhumane practices against Blacks and the Cultural Relevance in which their lives are attached. The face of CIC is merely a contemporary Botox/ Neoliberal version filling the same existence of negotiating humans' public interest for private gain. CIC is in the same schools of consciousness and dissociative erasure practices that rationalized Black Slavery through a practice of redefining Black reality to assign it a false reality. It has been a reality upon which desensitization builds then socially justifies Whiteness. This removal and reassign practice—power imposed by Whiteness, is a foundation upon which Black Students' dehumanization via education occurs. CIC is justified through THIS very practice. CIC operates within the space of culturally and racially induced de facto crimes—subtly fashioned as "democratic" curriculum ... marketed as though it can be held accountable in the collective efforts aimed at producing a "good" education for all people despite racial and cultural differences. However, Ladson-Billings (1994) detailed this differently through "Dream Keepers" over 22 years ago. In education, Blacks are labeled as being in deficit, "then the school can transform them into people worthy of inclusion in society" (p. 11). "They are identified as CULTURALLY DEPRIVED, DAMAGED, and then removed from such dearth—:

> *their homes, communities, and cultures in order to mitigate against their alleged damaging effect. Educational interventions [then occur] in the form of compensatory education (to compensate for the deprivation and disadvantage assumed to be inherent in [Black] homes and communities, often ... based on a view of [Black] children as deficient White Children. (p. 8)*

This way of identifying leads to characterizing Blacks' Culture as an irrelevant part of what Blacks need or can utilize to obtain what they need from their Education. This identifying works to perpetuate the notion that all they need is CIC via Domination. It does not acknowledge that the knowledge they DO acquire is hegemonic and validated by Whiteness. Your honor, this is a crime. It is how my Clients' **Culture** *is* **Restricted** *by* **Institutionalized** **Manipulation** *of their* **Ethos—***hat is their culture's character that embodies their community, their nation, etc ...*

Culturally Irrelevant Curriculum Versus Culturally Relevant Curriculum

Social Relations and Knowledge Concepts

CIC is a hegemonic social curriculum as much as it is an embodied way of power imposing boundaries and definitions about important and not so important types of knowledge to be determined school appropriate. Through the lens of Ladson-Billings' (1994) research and characterization of CRC, CIC too is defined. CIC, as I named it and in terms of Ladson-Billings' research, embodies what she calls an assimilationist's social relationship and concepts of knowledge. As an assimilationist's social relationship, CIC makes the relationship between teacher and student "hierarchical and limit[s the] formal classroom roles. [Alternatively, CRC makes classroom roles] fluid, humanely equitable [with] exten[sions] to interactions beyond the classroom and into the community" (p. 55). CIC, as a social assimilationist's relation, "encourages competitive achievement [opposed to CRC, which encourages] a community of learners" (p. 55).

Furthermore, CIC's concepts of knowledge are assimilationist in that they are grounded in a "static [process of] pass[ing knowledge] in one direction, from teacher to students [as opposed to the CRC process which is] continuously recreated, recycl[ed] and shared by teachers and students. Knowledge [through CIC is viewed as] infallible [, whereas Knowledge through CRC positions teachers to see] excellence as a complex standard that may involve some postulates but takes student diversity and differences into account" (p. 81).

Empirical Character of Culturally Relevant Curriculum

Ladson-Billings (1994) *DreamKeepers* is an 8-year study focused on 8 female teachers with 12 to 40 years of teaching experience. This study observes their cultural teaching practices connected to how they teach Black students they have in their classes. This study provides examples of how CRC is facilitated via culturally relevant teaching practices. CRC helps appropriately differentiate the instructional process based on students' needs by capitalizing on students' existing knowledge imbued by their culture and cultural experiences. The students' cultural knowledge allows them to cofacilitate their teaching process and evolve their schema by making connections between what they already know and what they are newly being presented. Moreover, having the students' culture as a relevant part of the curriculum and pedagogy processes provides an additional learning platform, what I call the platform of translation.

The platform of translation informs the students about culturally different ways of understanding some of their known phenomena. For example, CRC aids in the clarification of cultural codes. These cultural codes are like the keys to efficient, effective, and increased levels of safe experiences for individuals interacting within or through specific culturally established spaces. For example, a Black person thinking with the communal lens of Black cultural norms takes time beyond a scheduled interview to continue communication as a way to demonstrate flexibility, patience, and a welcoming personality—believing it aids in repeat customers. Alternatively, the individuals interviewing and thinking through a White cultural lens of time is money may read this as someone being unfocused in their thoughts and inattentive, thus wasting time and losing customers, that equals lost money. The Black individual in this scenario employed the wrong code given the context/space. As a result, the intentions and actual behaviors of the Black individual are misread, or mislabeled. Such scenarios can unfairly aid in the manifestation of disparate realities. CRC aiding in the clarification of codes can help communicate what Lisa Delpit (2006) identifies as:

> codes or rules [...] related to linguistic forms, communicative strategies, and presentations of self: that is, ways of talking, ways of writing, ways of dressing, and ways of interacting [... that are driven by the Culture of Power. As result, ...] success in institutions—schools, workplaces, and so on—is predicated upon acquisition of the culture of those who are in power. (p. 25)

Cultural codes or rules provide a different way for students to *know* and therefore acquire more forms of *knowledge*. In this context, students of Black culture can understand how their culture is placed according to codes and power. Understanding such codes and rules helps send a much different message than right knowledge and wrong knowledge and the ways in which Black students may feel empowered by what they know to act, acquire other *knowledge*, and make informed decisions within the realities they live. Ladson-Billings (1994) already informs us that instruction through cultural omission aka CIC can aid in the confusion and frustration of both students and teachers.

When curriculum facilitates a process to knowing that makes cultural codes and power codes clearer, it helps create the conditions for acknowledging cultural differences as not merely oppositional, unintelligible, something needing omission, or some other deficit. It can allow students to prepare for the realities in which types of knowledge are and are not applicable, or are humanizing or grounding functional acts of inequity and domination. Thus, CRC as a pedagogical approach helps minimize students acquiring knowledge as an aid towards domination, ways to perpetuate inequity, or islands of disconnecting information between school, community, homes, and the other areas in which they live their lives.

Empirical Character of Culturally Irrelevant Curriculum

Islands of disconnecting information emerge through CIC in different relationships. For example, it can emerge between the students and their understanding of self, students and the curriculum, the students and home, the students and their community, or others areas in which their lives are lived and certain types of knowledge matter differently. Such disconnections can help construct perceptions in students that the content presented through the school curriculum is simply irrelevant to their lives. Ladson-Billings (1994) explained how a CIC could cause a lesson never to be started by the *educator* when he or she never establishes the initial ability to engage the students in presenting the curriculum. In her study, a student teacher could not get his students "on task" and became so frustrated he sent them back to their seats to figure out how to do their work themselves (p. 125). He never welcomed the students into the lesson and the content he was attempting to communicate to the students never started down the road to being processed by the students, given its' unengaging "drill-kill approach" (p. 125). He did not know what his students knew to establish a starting place to present new content. "[...F]or all of his efforts, his attempts to teach the students were futile. He gave up in frustration, believing the students had relinquished their privilege of being taught" (Ladson-Billings, 1994, p. 126) ...

Plaintiff's Opening Statement (Continued)

... Are my clients TOO not born in America? If so, why do schooling practices work against them function as if they have never arrived? They provided no context from which my Clients can be engaged. This curriculum could have been constructed during slavery when Blacks were legally not allowed to be educated given the way it is exclusively coded through the White Cultural Cannon. What Door does it open

*for my Client and why has a history of how to do things better for all, and not just White, not manifest an OPEN WINDOW? My Clients are still treated like neutered citizens. On many fronts like the applicability of the curriculum they are presented with, their emancipation still goes unsecured. How do we go from a history of NOT acknowledging Blacks as Humans—a history that marked them Property—to then presenting curriculum through the same White Culture as if Black will NOW neatly tuck into it. The very foundation of culture—their Black Culture—that can be used to educate them honestly, fairly, and most of all appropriately are silenced in school, and often omitted through Domination's acts. Such acts insist that the understanding of Blackness, Black People, Black Students, and Black Culture, must be told through the historically flawed and oppressive lens of Whiteness. It has not mattered that the lens of Whiteness has been in charge of counting what a respiration is—like throwing the RITUAL of February out, as the place and time to engage Blackness. Even then, Black History Month is easily made a superficial experience of checking off boxes to say it (BLACKNESS) was done. All the while MANY ... NOT ALL ... but MANY... White Teachers can be heard secretly complaining among themselves about doing, thinking, or having to plan with Black history in mind or silencing certain parts of an ugly history that still informs the way many things operate today. The truth is a large portion of Black History in America is White American's History too even if they were not the negative "objects" being acted upon. Though today's White America is not the direct cause, it inherited the power and privileges/Benefits of the institutional racism in our country. AND its inheritance is still in operation. My Black Students TOO are indeed citizens in this SUPPOSED homeland declared for to be free, though such acts of Domination clearly highlight that this land has never equitably including those from Black Cultures... A **C**ulture being **R**estricted by the **I**nstitutionalized **M**anipulation of its **E**thos!!!*

In Ladson-Billings' (1994) study, students who could be wooed to the curriculum content in a culturally disconnected way struggled to use it. Students could even be observed regarding the curriculum as having no applicable use in their lives based on what they could grasp or foresee. Curriculum content presented in this way essentially acts criminal, particularly when considering that students' education in the United States is compulsory. They have to be in school and are forced into a relationship with CIC in the process. It is almost like Black students presented with the curriculum in this way are victim-inmates needing to be educationally exonerated, or like spouses who have been cheated on by an infidel curriculum. Recognizing some may receive this metaphor as an overstated hyperbole, taken too far, or even as a strike against good teachers, I will rest this statement for the moment and return to it from more details later. Please return with me to the courtroom as the Plaintiff's Council finishes the opening statement...

... This Culturally Driven Domination works contentiously to lead Blacks astray, confiscating their relevance even if curriculum hegemony clearly perpetuates the

notion of White Gems and Blacks' decay. Why are we in a cycle of history simply rewriting itself, premiering the stories already told, where the casts are simply new faces acting out the same disgraces? The script is predictable, and it goes like this ... Cultural Domination of any form relentlessly presses to contend that the Black Cultural ethnicity that Blacks are akin ... surmises to placing them in positions that are less American. Once they have been mislabeled, wrongly identified, attached to a false narrative ... they can then be created into what Cultural Domination wants them to be. What does it mean if Blacks experience life without the manipulation of their education, the acculturation of their narrative? Your Honor and People of the Court, my Clients have asked Cultural Domination to retreat. They are met with denial, their culture of ethnicity life divorced from manipulated normativity, continuously eroded through Dominations' oblique actions justifying their subordination into positions of Peasantry. How has this been allowed to be? ...

Hegemony Made CIC and System Tweaking

Hegemony happens when a particular culture dominates, regulates, and standardizes based on the norms of a certain culture. Hegemony, particularly cultural hegemony, is a familiar practice in American schools. Though cultural hegemony manifests in schools as CIC, school is not where the practice started. Cultural domination has been an inherent function within our legal system. For example, from the colonization of indigenous land, de facto Black slavery, Jim Crow, the Civil Rights Movement, and similar history intermixed within to now, Cultural domination via White culture has not ceased. There is a basic system of White domination in place, and only tweaks to this system are added to it. For example, Blacks went from slaves to freemen, but became freemen hundreds of years after people advantaged by the White culture had accumulated wealth, land, material, and ownerships of the very spaces that make the country operate (banks, stores, materials production, farms, government, etc.). And if I am not mistaken, there is only so much land that can be owned upon which these things operate and can be established. So, unless those always advantaged by this system with a gravely inappropriate head start give up more than a little bit here and there, inequality and inequity will maintain. After all, it would be criminal for the descendants of the indigenous people to just take back the land stolen from their bloodline. The point is simple, adding tweaks to an existing system driven by cultural domination with such a huge head start will not create equity for those who have traditionally been positioned into inhumanness as a result of this system. And education now legalized within the same system for Blacks when it was once a property only for Whites is simply a tweak of the same kind. It is a tweak made more evident by a CIC that easily maintains certain cultures' omission in what is and is not shared as appropriate school Knowledge.

Those whose cultures do not help make-up appropriate school knowledge, must shift, and reorient the different ways in which they exist, understand, and behave to comply with the *right* things/knowledge. Students not of the *contributing* culture for curriculum need to learn certain types of knowledge by ignoring/aborting aspects or the entire existence of their cultures to do so. This abortion dislodges symbolically, intellectually, socially, economically, and so forth, their culture as being able to possess relevant knowledge. At least the culture is seen as not in possession of a *type of knowledge* that makes a difference in the ways non-White cultures live outside of their bodies (i.e., in or outside of poverty, with or without food, shelter, safety, etc.). One of the Plaintiffs is on the stand to testify about who decided the type of curriculum they assumed in schools.

TRIAL

Plaintiff's Testimony About Domination and CIC

Domination has sought every one of us out, under the guise of helping us to prepare for the future. Domination's goal was likened to a Pimp. Domination forced us into a relationship with CIC ... and CIC force-fed us knowledge packaged by the Meritocracy brand. I hear the slogan every time I close my eyes, take a test, or try to recall content from class: "Where Hard Work Focused on the Right Knowledge is the Ladder to the Top!" The knowledge CIC wanted us to have, we could not relate to it though we tried. Day in and day out of school we could not apply outside of school what we learned. It was like learning for a world we would never actually fully be admitted to. Outside of school we still needed to spend time above and beyond our assigned school work, learning and making sense of the realities in which we lived. It was like trying to cram school into our lives twice daily. We did as we had been told to keep the peace in this relationship with CIC ... well, at least that's what we tried to do. As you can see we are in court now. We did not want truancy charges or to be tagged as problems. We saw enough of our friends' lives changed when trying to resist CIC. They were frustrated right out of school, and so many of them still cannot secure a "GOOD" job, at least not the kind of job working hand in hand with helping them to live humanely and freely within the wider society. So you see the alternative was not attractive. We tried to comply with CIC and initially had no manifested personal experience with CIC that would have lead us to seek caution in anticipation of CIC's bias or foul play. As we practiced what we thought was compliance—checking all the required boxes—we achieved levels of success year by year to some degree. Our graduation grew closer and closer. Another year of school would be completed. So you see on the surface, we had no reason to think we were losing in this *curricular set-up/relationship. We had no reason to think our **C**ulture was **R**estricted by **I**nstitutionalized **M**anipulation of our **E**thos or that it was hurting us ...*

Ladson-Billings (1994) discusses the importance of incorporating students' cultures as a regular part of the curriculum pedagogy process. The curriculum is consumed by individuals living in society and individuals are situated in cultures. There are experiences and ways of knowing that already exist in individuals' lives due to their culture that can be taken up in the school curriculum. The curriculum is positioned as a tool to orient the process for students to acquire knowledge, but what good is a fashion of knowing something that likely has delayed application or cannot be used within the lived life of the knower? Moreover ... this type of knowledge becomes a benefit/aid of whose education? How can students be expected to know best about a land that is not home to them, when the land they travel and experience daily is entangled with knowledge treated taboo, all-the-while they are regurgitated a false narrative that strongly suggests to them to just be more White or more like Whites? Students' supported ability to know and apply what they learn through the curriculum, adds to how they understand and make informed decisions throughout the various intersections of their lived realities. To discard the tools beneficial to their daily living is at the least humanly deceptive. It appears another plaintiff is taking the stand to testify about the impact of CIC and ways it has functioned in her life:

... But owe how we had been deceived!!! We were being manipulated out of our Black Cultural respect, out of energy that could be spent building up the communities, homes, and people in our lives. We were manipulated out of access and resource, right-into some plot to make Domination feel more dominating. Come to find out our friends could not get "Good" jobs because Domination was behind that, too. Is only the White Culture of people allowed to have unchallenged basic humanizing respect? During this manipulation, our time could have been spent on building our confidence, encouraging ourselves and members in our lived cultural realities to practice what we know, and to follow our curiosity to learn more and address what we need. Instead.... Domination (behind the scenes) was using CIC to manipulate and control us for the furthered maintenance and production of White Cultural Hegemony. CIC ... slowly omitting what we knew through our Black Culture labeled it wrong at almost every turn. The labeling was a tactic to reinforce our supposed need for CIC's peddler knowledge packaged by the Meritocracy Brand. While we were committed to CIC and CIC's principals, CIC was committed to Domination. We also found out Domination is in a polygamous marriage with CIC, Politics, Socialization, Capitalism ... and some other spouses I cannot even recall. You see Your Honor, Domination used everything and was pimping us through CIC's pedagogy. What—kind—of—sick—game!!!

Why must it be Domination's insistence that all White Cultural Norms drive the curriculum or nothing? Is humanity as a whole not already damaged by racializing it? Is basic human regard not being extracted by this racialized practice of CIC? It is not like any culture is on this Earth alone. Can we all not work together for our collective well-being? In some way, shape, or form we impact the condition of others (how we care for the environment, the usefulness of water supplies, how we impede or contribute to the access someone has to health care that could make the difference between spreading highly contagious communicable diseases, and so forth). With all that Domination is in possession of, cannot the curriculum we are administered be extracted from Racialization? CAN IT NOT BE STOPPED, this Cultural Restriction by this Institutionalized Manipulation of Ethos?

CIC as a Racialized Text

To understand the implications of racialization on Black Students administered the hegemonic CIC, we should first understand that race is not a biological construct (Pinar, Reynolds, Slattery, & Taubman, 2006). Race was conceptualized as a way to organize power structures by separating populations into cultural divisions based on skin tone and nationality (i.e., Africa, Europe, Asia, or India). This practice started with "a racialized conception of property implemented by force and ratified by law" (Harris, 1993, p. 1715). Racialization meant that the different appearances of skin by color would be assigned a value. These values were aligned to cultures of which particular tones of skin appeared to derive. CIC is a part of the continuum of this color based and culturally aligned conceptualization. CIC is historically connected to issues of race and cultures. However, CIC as a racialized text is not about merely pointing out its connection to the historical marginality of people based on race. It is about understanding how CIC's function works in the same manners, perpetuating inhumanity of certain groups through a practice of separatism that can be easily marked by culture and race. We know the practice of separatism via "racial classification" (Pinar et al., 2006, p. 316) was validated through an idea of "racial logic" (according to Pinar et al., 2006, p. 316). CIC is a residue of racial logic. Though biologically insignificant, race is institutionalized and is attached to separatism, marginalizing some populations and advantaging others.

The institutionalization made race and the cultures in which people's races are deemed attached, a necessary point of general consciousness. There should be no exception for the existence of this general consciousness when making decisions about curriculum. This means race and cultural consciousness intersecting with what should be curriculum in schooling environments should manifest a universal responsibility to support the humane and equitable education of all students. The alternative—curriculum as a product of racial logic, persists in our present through the historically grounded discourses that have fueled the United States with an unnatural existence – supports and helps to sustain the structure and function of racism. According to Peter McLaren and Michael Dantley (1990) as cited by Pinar et al. (2006),

> Racism must be seen as a set of structured social practices which reproduce themselves through individuals who are imprisoned by historically conditioned regimes of discourse, by market-logic interests, and by interests of dominant groups. Racism, therefore must be described as structured (through historically and ideologically loaded discourses, social practices, relations of production, gender and social class) and as structuring (through the individual's active, yet often contradictory, participation in these discourses, relations, and practices) while it often is simultaneously destructured (through both formal and informal resistance to these discourse, relations, and practices. (pp. 318-319)

Race is not something we can just ignore. Since it has been institutionalized, it now must be critically addressed and policed. Race and its attachment to culture cannot ethically be ignored in a curriculum being administered to a diverse racial and ethnic culture of learners sharing a society in which systemic racism exists. As explained by Derrick Bell (as cited by Ladson-Billings (1994), acknowledging racism is important

> Not [... to ...] legitimate the racism of the oppressor. On the contrary, we can only delegitimate it if we can accurately pinpoint it. And racism lies at the center, not at the periphery; in the permanent, not in the fleeting; in the real lives of black and white people, not in the sentimental caverns of the mind. (p. 130)

In short, in order to change something it has to be acknowledged and pinpointed first. Remember, standards have been put in place ultimately leading to what drives the notion of normal. The failure to interrupt a set, socialized normal cultivates the space for the ideas around the socialized normal to be institutionalized. So the failure to counter notions of hegemonic norms, will not by default lead to change. Change must be intentional, but more so it must be paired with relevance.

The next Plaintiff has just been called to the stand to testify about how the curriculum was decided for them and the impact it had ...

Plaintiff's Testimony on CIC, Dominations, and the Standard Curriculum

... Once we knew about CIC's and Domination's marriage, things started to clic. We could read their behaviors clearer. Domination was always trying to harm one

of us. Domination was determined not to remove White Cultural Hegemony in the Curriculum. And as far as Domination was concerned, that was the entire reason for Domination being in a relationship with CIC. One day we were so hungry, but Domination controlled all the curriculum pedagogy meals in our school's district. Domination's children, The State Departments of Education, spent their money on maintaining a steady supply for Domination. Domination subjected us, through CIC, to one school reform after the next. These CIC ordered meals were BAD!!! They were often always undercooked and indigestible, never making it onto culturally relevant teaching plates before being administered to us. It's sad the Federal Department of Education never shut it down. All it did was make the State Departments of Education stock different meals. As if changing the meals would cause CIC to do a better job cooking and seasoning. CIC just used the same cooking and seasoning process applied to a different meal. The Federal Department of Education chronically failed to understand CIC was not trained to work/function differently. One day we realized FDE did not do anything because it too was linked to Domination. Domination funded FDE's entire existence. Domination gave our school district access to only one place to consume knowledge, the "Standard Curriculum." CIC's cousin Colorblind runs it. Colorblind refused to disclose ingredients in the meals at the "Standard Curriculum," as if not informing people would somehow make what they are highly allergic to go away. Sometimes CIC would order us a little Black, an artificial side, and a house special.

We were given just enough Black to ease our confusion. It was not a stretch considering it was the month of February. Before consuming it, our cultural blood sugar (Ethos-glycemia) had dipped very low. We were headed towards HYPO-ETHOS-GLYCEMIA. It seemed as though we were departing from our bodies. At that time our ability to function was being impaired. I remember it well, because when given the pieces they were not enough to get us fully oriented but enough to make us restless. We barely even broke the surface of becoming oriented—and down CIC shoves an artificial side—Whiteness. CIC was on the phone with Domination at the time who apparently gave the order to shove it. We overheard Domination say our restlessness was a sign we were heading towards getting out of line. To wheel us back in, Domination told CIC to make us consume an artificial side of Whiteness. Your Honor, it NOT only tasted toxic, but it was also disorienting, immediately attacking our dignity, ability to self-determine, and construct acts to support the uplift of people who exist in our same culture. Domination wanted us to consume the side of Whiteness so that we had no existing frame of reference to focus on what was best for us. CIC declared through the forced consuming of Whiteness that we remember what the system determines value. The last thing we consumed was the house special, a standardization test called Assimilationist Acculturation. If this test was clear on nothing else, it clearly communicated that the system declares the extraction of regard and respect for our culture and reality so we function, think, and believe we need to possess what Whiteness embodies. BUT we should not ever think through our consumption of Whiteness that we can be equally treated or become better than any person that is White. Our consumption of Whiteness is for the main purpose of sustaining its existence, to know what we are not in order to go to our "rightful" place. For this is how we help maintain society, that is what Domination needed us to fall in line with.

*BUT Your Honor and People of the Court, we do not want this position!!!! We have our own lives and families to secure and protect. Is there not enough knowledge, work options in the present or projected future, or basic human needs that can be serviced for us all to receive a basic respect of our different cultures? There is no one person in this United States that can ever be in possession of every dollar, every bit of food, every plot of land, every service to meet people's needs, or every bit of knowledge to address every possible instance upon which something known can be applied. So, why must it be made such a drastic ordeal for us to share and respect these possessions collectively, without the manipulation of certain realities that whether acknowledged or not still exist? Why not stop **C**ultures from being **R**estricted by the **I**nstitutionalized **M**anipulation of their **E**thos??? This standard curriculum is beyond simply not okay ...*

... Standardized curriculum that seemingly denies students opportunities to evolve their knowledge through a practice of school to life functionality is not okay (Ladson-Billings, 1994). As the curriculum is becoming more standardized, it can fail to measure students on what they actually know. One Culturally Relevant Teacher in Ladson-Billings study expressed

> frustration at the limits of standardized testing in measuring student knowledge accurately.... Nobody ever really measures what the children really know. They have knowledge and skills that don't show up on standardized tests—important knowledge and skills, the kind of stuff that can mean the difference between life and death. (p. 88)

The court is now on recess. People attending the trial are talking. Let us listen in on those on the side of the defense ...

RECESS

The Court of Public Opinions

...I am not surprised Black people make everything an issue of Race and Racism. HELLOOOO—STANDARDIZED TEST!!! There is not a WHITE test and BLACK Test—this means everyone is required to take the SAME test. We are not in the period of Slavery anymore ... so they ought to get over it. This America is Post-Racial, Barack is President—even though he is doing a Hrrible Jobm probably because he is not a real American and does not really care!!! He lied about everything he said he was going to do—RIDICULOUS!!! Anywaym they need to learn how to get over things and live in the present reality ...

The thought of a Standardized test serving as a sort of gateway between life and death or racism is not an acknowledgment shared among everyone. To some, the pros and cons in individuals' lives are not impacted by the relevant inclusion of culture in curriculum—CRC. Therefore, CIC is also not considered an appropriate concept from which to understand disparate realities between Black and White students administered the same curriculum content. Rather, such individuals may believe that the disparate realities of people, even if largely between Black people and White people, are better explained by individuals' behavior, willingness, and beliefs— NOT a system—and surely not one in which universal curriculum acts to aid racial and cultural problems. Such perspectives can be understood through the concepts of meritocracy and social contracts.

Meritocracy is the belief that those individuals who do not believe they have a meaningful education to secure their fair space in American Society, have not worked hard enough to accomplish that which is free for them to obtain (Delgado & Stefancic, 2012). Jeremy Waldron (1989) in *John Locke: Social Contract versus Political Anthropology* explains: Social Contracts, are based on the context of "free will" (Rousseau, 1997, p. 388; & Waldron, 1989, p. 17) or "natural rights" (Waldron, 1989, p. 17) to mean the unrestrained existence or rather an existence "created without manifest subordination" (Waldron, 1989, p. 17). The positions which people occupy are realities to which they have given their consent. Those who choose not to give their consent but behave or align within the social structure are still responsible. Waldron explains that those arguing the unconsented expression of will or natural rights are merely "dominated by the warning that the gravity of the consequences of rebellion places heavy and inescapable responsibility on those who make these judgments" (p. 18).

... Furthermore, how is racism even relevant when we give their Black kids the same curriculum our White kids get? They try to argue biology is not a fact, but if they are still struggling even with the same material, the help of welfare, affirmative action and who knows what else, then maybe someone needs to re-research intelligence between Black and Whites AGAIN. Someone also needs to make it clear to them that laziness is a real contribution to why they do and do not have things. THAT is not WHITE PEOPLE'S FAULT.... Trying to reason with them is EXHAUSTING ... and as a matter of fact...we should not have, too!!! After all, we were not around to put them in Slavery, and none of them living today ever been in Slavery, it was their Ancestors! GESHHH! I could only imagine what my White Ancestors went through following the Emancipation of Slavery!!!

In so many ways these comments embody the characteristics of Whiteness, which the Plaintiffs articulate as being at the center of the problem. Leonardo (2002) as cited by Gillborn (2009), discusses "some of the defining characteristics of whiteness" (p. 32):

- *"An unwillingness to name the contours of racism"*: inequity (in employment, education, wealth, etc.) is explained by reference to any number of alternative factors rather than being attributable to the actions of Whites.
- *"The avoidance of identifying with a racial experience or group"*: Whiteness draws much of its power from "Othering" the very idea of ethnicity. A central characteristic of Whiteness is a process of "naturalization," such that white becomes the norm from which other "races" stand apart and in relation to which they are defined. When white-identified groups *do* make a claim for a white ethnic identity alongside other officially recognized ethnic groups (e.g., as has been tried by the Ku Klux Klan in the Unied States and the British National Party in England), it is the very exceptionality of such claims that points to the commonsense naturalization of Whiteness at the heart of contemporary political discourse (see Swain & Nieli, 2003; Ratcliffe, 2004, pp. 115–117).
- *"The minimization of racist legacy"*: seeking to "draw a line" under past atrocities as if that would negate their continued importance as historic, economic and cultural factors. (Gillborn, 2009, p. 32)

Furthermore, Leonardo (2002, as cited by Gillborn, 2009), explains that the Whiteness characterization should not be equated as a description of White people. "Whiteness' is a racial discourse, whereas the category 'white people' represents a socially constructed identity, usually based on skin color" (p. 31).

In summary, what you are reading in this section of Public Opinions, is a familiar conversational and rationalizing pattern of displacing the issues and concerns. CIC is being justified through these patterns of displacement and the characterizations of Whiteness as mentioned above. CIC itself is not analyzed because its existences is attached to a system that is socially-vetted on a large societal scale. The system is able to take over the focus of individuals' consciousness, helping them to think and respond uncritically. In other words, the system (an existence of cultural hegemony) surfaces, operating the lens by which sight is and is not clear with regard to the ways in which the functions of CIC and CRC are deemed to operate.

... Court attendees on the side of the Plaintiffs are talking, too. Let's listen in on what they are saying ...

Who's Consuming the Curriculum?

... What the Plaintiffs are saying makes sense. It seems like there is a challenge for some people to hear explicitly the question: Who is consuming the curriculum?

Whose property is the curriculum and what does ownership of this property mean? It's like they cannot understand how the current state of curriculum is being divided by partakers of the curriculum and the owners of the curriculum. I find it unsettling that there are extensive records on students: names, dates of birth, race, grade level, grades, test data, and so forth. YET, less recognized, practically ignored, is the need to include their culture as a mode to support the knowledge they acquire through the curriculum. It is not that standard curriculum does not sound sensible in theory; it is that the exclusive and main focus is on external matters (career readiness, sustaining the economy, global competitiveness, etc.), FIRST. These focuses are not based on external matters present in all communities and cultures. While this is the focus, internal matters of the learner (the community, individual needs, personal connections to curriculum and the learning process, exploration of talents and skills), are practically ignored. Such a curriculum ignores how individuals produce from within—outward. It allows us to reorient or orient what we know with what we are trying to know. I am not suggesting that concerns with external matters (career readiness, sustaining the economy, global) ultimately unaddressed will go ignored if we negate our internal. However, I am saying there is a cost of doing so and it is our responsibility to understand and humanely respond to what is known. We must honestly answer the question: Are these potential implications on diverse racial and cultural groups worth it? And it would not hurt to ask the question how might this impact those not of color in the long-term.

Ladson-Billings' (1994) CRC study demonstrates the ability to have a curriculum that focuses on both internal and external matter, that is a curriculum that is essentially shared property. However, attempts at acknowledging multiple cultural realities, truths, and therefore knowledge, are subverted from the general and daily curriculum to be regarded in specific spaces. For example, it is redirected to particular days or months upon which specific culture will be acknowledged and not necessarily engaged deeply. This form of creating the appearance of CRC highlights the starving nature of multiple cultures and cultural relevance in schools. The false appearance of a CRC means education if we can call it that, in many instances is simply futile, and that there are important pieces that can go missing/remain unknown. Ladson-Billings highlights how this can occur and should be combatted. One teacher in her study led students through an extensive lesson on Egypt, where the curriculum arrangement failed to pursue depth in understanding Egypt. In other words, Egypt in so many ways was presented like an acknowledgment. The students of the lesson, questioned the culture of Egypt: what race are the people? It was a question the teacher skillfully responded to, and by default created cultural relevance for the students. Instead of a direct answer to the question of race, the teacher directed students towards researching Egypt. Directing students to research meant they would ultimately find-out the answer to their question, and in so doing find out much more about Egypt. It was content that students related to their existences, noting comparisons and contrasts with their cultures and others, by discussing their research findings upon returning to class.

Let us transition … court is back in session. It appears they are calling the last plaintiff to testify on the stand about the impact of CIC on their lives …

TRIAL RESUMED

Plaintiff's Testimony about an Educational Coma

… Your Honor, we have been fighting to delegitimize the chronic inhumane disregard of our cultural difference carried out by CIC. Do we not deserve to be helped out of infidel curriculum learning prisons? We came to school as our authentic selves, showed up unmasked. However, CIC not so much. CIC was marketed through a false narrative of democracy, as education as some great equalizer. We were committed in our efforts to being good students, but despite our commitment, our relationship with CIC was toxic, and one built on infidelity. We committed to CIC and CIC was committed to Domination. Simply stated, CIC was committed to us being dominated and cared not about what we needed. We faithfully complied to CIC, and CIC manipulated our humanity, our respect, and disregarded our basic need to be acknowledged and more knowledgeable in the context in which we lived our lives. Our capital "B" Black Identity is more than its connection to the once illegal right to be educated, the separatism anchored through Jim Crow, school desegregation with no equity, and now sophisticated forms of segregationist racism that we are in now!!! NO, it is not as explicit visually as it was during such periods as Slavery and Jim Crow…but it is no less present.

We are tired!!! We must be allowed CRC. Though it is not an ultimate fix, it is one among many that needs to be established in the effort towards humanizing historically dehumanized cultures and identities. Yes, we are Black, AND we have given the story to you through our experiences. BUT we also represent people from other non-white cultures fighting for their equity and respect for knowledge through CRC. Like us, they, too, are currently being starved into educational comas, cheated on by an infidel curriculum, mistreated through the justification of racialization, and overlooked by perpetual displacement of conscious attention to their realities.

CLOSING ARGUMENT

The Plaintiff's counsel has included a final statement for the Jury to take into account before deliberating.

Plaintiff Council's Final Statement

*It is time for Domination and CIC to pay restitution for the disregard they have toxically shoved upon my Black Clients and Others of non-White Culture. My clients have been subject to a Curriculum most Relevant to Whites, and even then it is distorting the realities in which White Students live. Domination by way of CIC should be held responsible for creating CRIME (**C**ultures being **R**esisted by the **I**nstitutionalized **M**anipulation of their **E**thos). In other words, institutionalization is a tool that has been used by Domination to manipulate people on the basis of things they cannot control, like their culture of normativity. Because Domination accepts certain realities as important and other realities as flawed (in need of Domination's interventions), certain cultures are resisted by the hegemonic system. In particular, the resistance is an act of making into a problem, culture's distinct Characteristics (ethos), their guiding beliefs ideas and practices.*

It is our belief that a just verdict would extract CIC and use CRC as a basic ingredient in the way knowledge is acquired by students through school. It would help to rehabilitate and empower a diversely ethnic and racial culture of students. This is one way to hold Domination and CIC responsible for criminal acts they have committed against students, teaching them through false notions in generalizing ways. Students who have been frustrated out of school. Students who find unreturned to them more humanizing living conditions after executing CIC acquired knowledge. There are many people of color who have sustained identity murders or lie unresponsive in educational comas at this very moment.

Your Honor, Ladson-Billings (1994) informs us that CRC is not just a Black thing, it is a people thing. It is invested in people acquiring knowledge that works in their lives as they are and where they decided they would like to go, PERIOD. It does not negate the acquisition of knowledge that allows people of different cultural ethos to live or work with and among each other. CRC should be permanently taken into account when thinking about Educational Reforms, Standardization, and articulations of accountability through Curriculum and Pedagogy. Your Honor, Men and Women of the Jury, it is time for Domination and CIC to step down from their hegemonic positions. These are positions where certain Cultures get Resisted, by Institutionalized Manipulations of their individuality—to be labeled what is and what is not relevant ethos. I am not suggesting that we move to a curriculum that has no standards, as some standards are necessary just for the safety and well-being of individuals in PARTICULAR INSTANCES. All need to know that a red stop light in America means stop, or that some form of currency is typically used in the exchange of goods. So it is clear we need to have a shared breadth of knowledge. But it is not necessary to omit individual's cultures knowledge to do this.

THEREFORE, the curriculum should:

- *Not be Assimilationist,*
- *Not reproduce ways of existing through a standard of cultural hegemony,*

- *Not create HYPO-ETHOS-GLYCEMIA,*
- *Not construct relationships of curriculum infidelity,*
- *Not construct Learning Prisons,*
- *Not encourage new faces acting out the same disgraces,*
- *Not help dislodge students' cultures,*
- *Not act as a racialized text,*
- *Not ignore what history has taught us about humanizing and dehumanizing practices towards people,*
- *Not induce educational comas,*
- *Not contextualize a culture as deficient to justify the facilitation of new knowledge,*
- *Not aid in hegemonic system tweaks,*
- *Not encourage skill/drill/kill approaches to teaching,*
- *Not be built on rationalized racialization,*
- *Acknowledge the way the sociopolitical attachments placed upon certain identities like Blacks has a functional presence that is counter-productive to their ability to have equity,*
- *Encourage Educational Connosourship, allowing students to develope habits of perceptual exploration they follow to understanding and responding to phenomena—therefore, triggering more and more refined thinking and application,*
- *Aid the existence of a Universal Human Ethic,*
- *Evolve out of an intersectional understanding/thinking of history and possibility that critically engages known, predictable, and potential contexts (Critical Conscious Reflecting),*
- *Clarify codes and prepare students for different structures of authority,*
- *Provide a platform of translation,*
- *Aid in understanding what students know to help them acquire more knowledge, and*
- *Integrate cultural difference throughout school as normal.*

Though this list is not exhaustive, it is a necessary part of the comprehensive thinking that should go into the decisions made about what serves as appropriate schooling curriculum for students of different cultural ethos.

Charging the Jury

As the Jury prepares to deliberate to reach a just verdict, they need to ask the following questions to inform the verdict:

1. Should curriculum support assimilation, cultural relevance, or something else?
2. Who should make these decisions and how does that intersect with whose being decided for?
3. Are the potential impacts on those lives that will be impacted by deciding curriculum in this way more equitably humanized by this decision or less humanized, meaning with greater or lesser ability to have what they need when they need it?
4. What will create greater functionality in the curriculum that best prepares racially and ethnically diverse populations of students in the short and long-term?
5. What will allow students to possess knowledge that can be used throughout the different realities in which they currently live their lives or may desire to go?

Deliberation

It is now time for the Jury to deliberate. In the case of this chapter, I allocate the deliberation time for justice to you. As you are making your decision about what is just, allow me to leave you with one more thought. The trial symbolically used in this chapter embodies the existence of a power struggle. Trials traditionally give a lot of attention to identifying if there is legal evidence to prove there is a victimizer, to validate if a victim exists. Though I believe we can understand the necessity in this, at some points and in some cases this process can spend more time focused on manipulating the boundaries of the system than seeking real justice. A humanely just response should not become marred in a battle of wittiness, manipulation, and a culture's traditional way of considering, upon which the verdict will then be rendered. A just response should surface through a universal human ethic, and respect for a kind of individual freedom that reproduces itself in the life of the individual spilling into a larger existence of which others live, too.

CONCLUSION

In this chapter, I interwove the trial and Ladson-Billings' text to communicate realities, pros, and cons with regard to how the pedagogical handling of curriculum impacts students' lives. My interweaving acknowledges the past as a way to think about the present and future function desired from curriculum and pedagogy. Through CCR guided by the four questions, a **curriculum window** opened: What must we understand about our past and Ladson-Billings research to cultivate potential for a better today and tomorrow? More than one culture lives and and has knowledge that works in this collective space called the United States of America. This America does not simply take place in schools or on a job, but it takes place in homes and communities as well.

Gloria Ladson-Billings' (1994) text *Dreamkeepers* focuses on cultural relevance. Cultural relevance can be deemed biologically akin to Cultural Pluralism despite the fact her study focused on a Black population to explain this concept. Cultural relevance fights against students as victim-inmates needing to be exonerated. Students' cultures matter in their education and should not be negated in their educational process. This type of education allows students to reinvest in their development by following their knowledge downs paths of inquiry and reframing their schema to log additional knowledge. Helping students to reinvest in their development in this manner is a reality we must embrace if we intend to provide nourishing education to students cross-culturally. Do we want to help students obtain the kind of nourishing education that helps them today and prepares them for the future? We cannot justifiably continue to educate students "as usual" while also understanding the process has acted and in many ways is criminal.

Ladson-Billings (1994) essentially placed a charge to anchor cultural pluralism in schooling curriculum and teaching practices. She highlighted the power of knowledge that comes when working with students to co-construct their dignity, conflate their individual realities in which they live their lives, and still acknowledge their differences as truth and not a threat to democracy. This work will include a change in behavior by Communities, School Boards, Departments of Education, Parents, Teachers, and Teacher Training Institutions. It is a call that we are committed to understanding the problems of our tried and tested practices to really move FORWARD, Not for White America, not for Black America, Not for any other cultural group in American, but collectively for us ALL.

REFERENCES

Bell, D. A. (1995). Who's afraid of critical race theory. *U. Ill. L. Rev.*, 893.
Delgado, R., & Stefancic, J. (2012). *Critical race theory: An introduction*. New York, NY: New York University Press.
DuBois, W. E. B., & Lester, J. (1971). *The seventh son: The thought and writings of W.E.B. DuBois*. New York, NY: Random House.
Eisner, E. (1979). *The educational imagination* (Vol. 103). New York, NY: Macmillan.
Freire, P. (1998). *Pedagogy of freedom: Ethics, democracy, and civic courage*. Lanham, MD: Rowman & Littlefield.

Gillborn, D. (2005). Education policy as an act of white supremacy: Whiteness, critical race theory and education reform. *Journal of Education Policy*, *20*(4), 485–505.

Harris, C. I. (1993). Whiteness as property. *Harvard Law Review*, 1707–1791.

Ladson-Billings, G. (1994). *The dreamkeepers: Successful teachers of African American children*. Hoboken, NJ: Jossey-Bass.

Leonardo, Z. (2002). The souls of white folk: Critical pedagogy, whiteness studies, and globalization discourse. *Race Ethnicity & Education, 5*(1), 29–50.

Pinar, W., Reynolds, W., Slattery, P., & Taubman, P. (2006). *Understanding curriculum: An introduction to the study of historical and contemporary curriculum discourses* (5th ed.). New York, NY: Peter Lang.

Ratcliffe, P. (2004). *"Race," ethnicity and difference: imagining the inclusive society*. Maidenhead, UK: Open University Press.

Rousseau, J. J. (1997). The Social Contract, 1763. *The Spirit of Laws; On the Origin of Inequality; On Political Economy; The Social Contract*, 387–439.

Stovall, D. (2015). The radical imaginary: Personal collection of (David Stovall), Chicago, IL: University of Illinois at Chicago.

Swain, C. M., & Nieli, R. (Eds.). (2003) *Contemporary voices of white nationalism in America*. Cambridge, UK: Cambridge University Press.

Waldron, J. (1989). John Locke: social contract versus political anthropology. *The Review of politics, 51*(01), 3–28.

CHAPTER 13

SUBTRACTIVE SCHOOLING

Mexican Youth and the Politics of Caring

Priscilla Tamankag

You gotta be smart to go to college. I wish I had what it takes.

(Student at Seguin High School quoted in Valenzuela, 1999, p. 150)

I am a devoted teacher. I work hard. I am at school every day. I have my lessons planned. I even stay after school to help. I can't understand why these students don't get it!

—A public school teacher

One cold Tuesday evening in February 2015, Dr. Poetter, our EDL 765 professor, asked us to pick from a list of curriculum books of the 1990s he presented to students. He asked us to write a chapter about our chosen books, relating it to our experiences as educators. I scrawled down the list and Valenzuela's (1999) text titled *Subtractive Schooling: U.S.-Mexican Youth and the Politics of Caring* caught my attention. I found the title fascinating. As an educator, I wondered what the author meant by "subtractive schooling." I selected the book, and could not have made a better choice. The book brought back numerous memories and made me think of my childhood

Curriculum Windows: What Curriculum Theorists of the 1990s Can Teach Us About Schools and Society Today, pp. 199–216
Copyright © 2017 by Information Age Publishing
All rights of reproduction in any form reserved.

days as a student. It also made me reflect on my life as a teacher in Africa and of my experiences as an African woman teaching in an American urban school.

As I read, my mind drifted back to my own education in Africa. I thought of my teachers and questioned how much of my schooling was subtractive and how much of it was additive? I recall that we lived in abject poverty, and my parents continually reminded me that school was the gateway out of poverty. As a student, I went to school each day hoping that one day I would finish school and become rich. I did not know how, but I knew if I went to school and worked hard that I would eventually become success-ful. Our classrooms were overcrowded. We sat on old benches, sometimes four students to a bench. Despite our modest facilities, we enjoyed school immensely! I don't remember much of what was taught, but I recall the fun we had playing outside during break (i.e., recess in America). I looked forward to going to school every morning, because I wanted to meet my friends and play. Back then I saw nothing subtractive in what we did at school.

Fast forward today. I look at the struggles at Seguin that Valenzuela (1999) chronicled, and think how lucky I was to have made it through primary, secondary, and then university education. Here I am today, a teacher! Maybe by a stroke of luck or hard work, or even both, I don't know. I think of my friends who for one reason or another did not make it. While at school, we learned using the most rudimentary methods, following a curriculum that was put in place in a bygone era by our colonial masters. This curriculum had undergone little or no changes since the official abolition of colonialism decades ago. We learned math, English, English literature, history, geography, the usual subject areas. I knew more about the British and American histories than I knew about my own country. I could recite more poems by Shakespeare, William Butler Yeats, T. S. Eliot Edgar, and Allan Poe than I could recite poems in my own dialect. Our parents never insisted we learn the dialect. They were bent on making us learn the "Whiteman's book." They told us it did not matter if we knew our local poems, because we may never need them to succeed. In order to "make it" in the world, our parents insisted that we acquire the Whiteman's knowledge. Without any formal education, our parents already understood the importance of learning the dominant curriculum as a means of secur-ing competitive employment. They envisioned that one day we would be able to work in a Whiteman's office somewhere, and the only way to get there was through school. The Whiteman's office to them was equated to a white-collar high paying job. Our school system required us to learn using a curriculum that had little or no incorporation of our heritage and culture, but that did not matter to our parents. As I read *Subtractive Schooling*, I wondered if our curriculum robbed us of our identities. Maybe. The one thing I am certain about is that education helped me get out of the slum I was born in. It sculpted the person I am today. My teachers and my community played an important role in securing that outcome. They provided a loving and caring environment that was both formative and instrumental in my development as a person.

I knew nothing about colonialism back then and simply did what my parents asked me to do to succeed. I cherished school, partly because of what our parents told me about school and partly because of the fun of being with friends. Of course, no child wants to go to bed hungry or live in poverty; so I believed my parents when they told me education would be my ticket to freedom from poverty. We were taught to respect everyone in our community and so we revered our teachers. They represented our parents at school, and were seen as authority figures commanding a tremendous deal of respect. Our teachers knew our parents, and so we had little room for misbehavior. If we did anything wrong at school, we were corrected by our teachers, who had no fear of getting in trouble with the law or our parents. Teachers had permission to beat us if it came to that. I know this might sound outrageous to most Americans, but for us it was seen as simply tough love. This discipline and care is part of the reason I am able to write this chapter today! In Africa, it truly took a village to raise the child.

Midway through Valenzuela's (1999) book, I wondered if I would have succeeded had things been different. I was an average student who struggled like everyone else to get through school. Would I have succeeded in an American system? Maybe not. Like many children, there were times when I would get into trouble. I got in the same kinds of trouble that gets students suspended or kicked out of school every day in America. I recall a day when, as kids, my brother and I skipped school to go steal fruit from a nearby farm. Of course, that's outrageous and wrong. But as children, we simply didn't know any better. We had no money for snacks or little treats at lunch. So we thought it was a good idea to steal from a nearby farm. The owner caught us and took us back to school and alerted the school authorities. We received beatings and punishment from the headmaster of the school. Then a teacher accompanied us home to our parents to explain what we had done wrong. We received more beatings from our parents. We were not suspended or dismissed. At my current school in the United States, I see my students get suspended or dismissed for similar offenses. The system has zero tolerance for misbehavior. Children can no longer be children. There's no room for error or mistakes. At times, U.S. schools can be impersonal and individualistic to the point that the well-being of those who make up its community can be damaged.

In Valenzuela's (1999) text, she recounts that story of a girl named Elvia who suffered as a result of the impersonal nature of the public school system. Elvia routinely skipped school and was eventually recommended for expulsion. Although Elvia was frequently truant, her mother was never informed by any school authority. Elvia stumbled onto her daughter's dismissal by accident when she came to school for another reason. After reading her story, I began to question how a school could be so devoid of human compassion. Her story was a clear reminder of how lucky I was to have been a student in Africa. My community looked out for me and gave me hope. Elvia saw no hope in her community or school and subsequently rebelled: "If the school doesn't care about my learning, why should I care?" (p. 88). Elvia's story stirred up some question in my mind: what are our roles as teachers and administrators in helping students like Elvia? What role does the system play in helping students such as Elvia? Where is the community's involvement in Elvia's education?

As a collective group, we as educators and as a community fail students like Elvia. Her mother was too busy working, and the school was only concerned with test scores and teaching curriculum standards. The system sees Elvia as a problem, and so she gets ejected from her school and her community. She is viewed as liability that will lower the school's test scores. Schools call for teacher accountability, but who is accountable for students like Elvia? Do we not simply create failure for students when we expel them from school? These are the many questions I struggle with as a teacher every day.

Valenzuela (1999) addresses this problem as the politics of care, which is a characteristic that is often conspicuously missing from teachers and administrators. We fail our students in our responsibility to protect and guide them. We place the blame everywhere but on ourselves. We blame students' cultures, students' languages, students' upbringings, but refuse to take a look at the school system as the culprit. Dismissing Elvia does not solve a problem, but instead it creates one. As administrators, we are putting her on the streets where she becomes vulnerable through exposure to violence, drugs, and unplanned pregnancies as well as a host of other potential tragic outcomes. Dismissing students should be a last resort after accessing and attempting numerous community resources.

In American schools, children are kicked out for offenses that the school is supposed to protect them against. In Elvia's case, her mother trusted in the schools to educate her child. In the Mexican and African context, education is the collective responsibility of the school and the community, and discipline is not accomplished through student expulsion. Looking at the United States' policies, I wonder at times if the system creates teachers or monsters. The United States' school laws and policies focus on standards. The system forces teachers to teach to tests to get the most students to graduate, regardless of whether these students are prepared to succeed in today's tough and competitive world. The United States system of education is an anti-social, capitalist and individualistic system that makes teachers vulnerable, because school laws and policies do not protect them. Teachers have a fine line to walk between being their students' caretakers, maintaining discipline, and raising test scores, without fear of losing their jobs. As a teacher, I am constantly on the lookout for anything that will jeopardize my license and profession. When parents blame me for not being American enough in teaching their children, I have to be careful as to how I respond. Parents' threats, coupled with school sanctions and accountability make it very difficult for teachers to do the job of educating children.

As I read *Subtractive Schooling*, I reflected on my relationship with my students while in Africa and my relationship with my students in America. I notice as a teacher, that I relate to students in different ways in both systems of education. In the African system of education, there exists an unwritten law/policy that protects teachers and gives them authority over every student in their care during school hours. African teachers are generally their brother's keepers at school. In the African and the Mexican context, everyone in the community has the duty of raising the child. The community looks out for you as a student and redirects you at school and in the streets. The U.S. system of education, on the other hand, is invested in a culture of individualism and testing. Its laws and policies are written based on individualistic business/capitalist principles of education that are geared toward standardized tests and catering to an idealized version of a student. It has a powerful and dominant culture that perpetuates a neoliberal and authoritarian culture in schools and elsewhere.

When I compare my education and upbringing in Africa to that of the students at Seguin, though both systems have elements of poverty, our miseries are different. As previously colonized countries we experienced aspects of subtractive schooling. However, our values as Africans kept us from becoming educationally derailed in contrast to the students at Seguin. African students experienced subtractive schooling through a colonial curriculum that imposes colonial languages as dominant languages. This privileging of the colonizer's culture not only assailed our own languages and dialects, but subtracted it through creating a hybrid culture.

So far I have situated you in the African educational system, we will take a more nuanced look at Valenzuela's (1999) curricular work on the politics of caring. This next section will give an overview of the book as well as a vignette into the problems of subtractive schooling and suggestion on how to make schooling additive.

SUBTRACTIVE SCHOOLING: U.S-MEXICAN YOUTH AND THE POLITICS OF CARING

Subtractive Schooling: U.S-Mexican Youth and the Politics of Caring by A. Valenzuela (1999) is a three-year ethnographical study about immigrant-Mexican and Mexican-American students' attitudes toward schooling and a review of their academic achievements. The study was carried out at Seguin High School and outlines immigrant-Mexican and Mexican-American students' educational struggles in the United States public schooling system. There are three main themes in the book: (1) The United States public schools are agents of subtractive schooling; (2) there are differences between immigrant students' achievement and U.S.-born students' underachievement in American schools; and (3) emphasizes the need for teacher-student relationships and the politics of caring. Below is a description of what Valenzuela's scholarship does to illuminate these three themes.

The United States Public Schools as Agents of Subtractive Schooling

Valenzuela (1999) portrays Seguin High School and by extension most U.S. public schools, as places of "subtractive schooling" with adverse effects on students with low income/underprivileged backgrounds, especially African American, immigrant students, and U.S.-born children of immigrants. U.S. schools diminish the languages and cultures of immigrant students, coining terms such as "limited language proficiency" as a way of subtracting their values and diminishing their worth. Students' "accents" and languages other than what is perceived as standardized English are viewed as barriers that hinder their learning of the English language, hence the term "limited language proficiency." Immigrant languages are therefore seen as negative rather than positive identification markers. Frustrations from being labeled "limited" create students who reject schooling and look for counter reactions that make them acceptable or "cool" enough for American society (Valenzuela, 1999). Ironically, the "cool" society is that society that exposes these students' "failure." It is therefore fair to say U.S. public schools, instead of preparing these students for progress, prepare them for stagnation, regression and/or failure, thus the title "subtractive schooling" (Valenzuela, 1999). Schools prepare students toward a culture of subtractive schooling that is manifested in the:

> subtle negative messages that undermine the worth of their unique culture and history…, [T]he structure of the curriculum is designed to divest youth of their … identities and to impede the prospects for fully vested bilingualism and biculturalism…. [S]tudents' cultural identities are systematically derogated and diminished. (Valenzuela, 1999, pp. 172–173)

The U.S. system places immigrant students in a crossfire. They are generally caught between two languages, sometimes identifying with neither, thus creating what the author identifies as cross-generational divisions. The author uses examples of students caught in arguments, each side trying to prove themselves as being more American than the other. The concept of undermining other languages and placing the English language as the dominant language puts immigrant and U.S.-born students of immigrants into conflict frequently, conflicts which sometimes become aggressive. The cross-generational division at Seguin is a reflection of the division among many immigrant students and their U.S.-born counterparts.

As an urban schoolteacher, it is commonplace to find cross-generational arguments between my students whether they are from Africa, Asia, Latin American countries, or elsewhere. These cross-generational arguments lead to voices being suppressed and some students being considered as the "other" in their schools. These othered students often associate school in light of these negative interactions. When U.S.-born children of immigrants join their American counterparts and label immigrant students as speaking with an "accent," the immigrant students feel doubly rejected because those they consider their own brothers/sisters also reject them, thus creating a greater level of subtractive schooling.

Valenzuela (1999) therefore views language as the root of subtractive schooling. Language is an instrument that is used by the White curriculum to diminish others. She describes language as a powerful human resource needed to maintain a sense of self-identify and self-fulfillment (Trueba, 1993, as cited by Valenzuela, 1999, p. 169). Most immigrant students view their languages as second-rate in American schools, the same way African American students may consider themselves as second-class citizens in their own country. Class segregation is an important aspect of subtractive schooling. Most poor school districts are located in urban areas away from the suburbs that are predominantly inhabited by White middle-class families. Urban schools are often left with limited resources, inexperienced teachers, and a dearth of community resources which in turn leads to a further propensity toward subtractive schooling.

Immigrant Achievement and U.S.-Born Underachievement in U.S. Schools

The book outlines the achievement gap between immigrant and U.S.-born students in America. Seguin High School is an inner-city school and is described by Valenzuela (1999) as "nearly all-Mexican" (p. 33). The school is a reflection of the problem that exists in urban schools across America. Valenzuela's study shows that there is a generational gap between immigrant Mexican and U.S.-born Mexican students in American schools, which plays a significant role in the respective students' schooling experiences as first, second, and later-generation students. These first generation students are more academically adept as compared to subsequent generations (Valenzuela, 1999).

In her comparison between U.S. born students' achievement levels and their immigrant peers, Valenzuela (1999) observes that U.S.-born Mexicans perform lower than their immigrant counterparts. This achievement difference is one of the reasons behind the cross-generational divide between both groups. She attributes the achievement gap between the two groups to the fact that immigrant-Mexicans come to the U.S. with "strong aspirations connected to their prior schooling experiences in Mexico ... which prepared them well for schooling in the United States" (pp. 11–12). On the contrary, the U.S.-born Mexican students, especially second, third generations and beyond, lack these aspirations and see their immigrant counterparts as "acting White" (p. 17). Immigrant-Mexican students, on the other hand, see their Mexican American peers as "wannabe" Americans (p. 19). The gap between these two groups of students could account for the "social decapitalization" (p. 225), where there is limited or adverse joint-social engagement between immigrant and U.S.-born students. The network between these two groups of students is often that of tension and misunderstandings. Many immigrant-Mexican students before moving to the U.S. had been "socialized toward the ideal of [schooling and of] someday attending college, [even if they were] insufficiently socialized into an understanding of their need to reach such a goal" (p. 151). Their Mexican-American peers often see little or no interest in schooling. When I look back to my education in Africa, I could not agree more with the author. I was able to succeed because of the values of my African culture. As a public school teacher, I often observe adaptive cultural and community values to be missing from students like Elvia, because students are left to themselves to develop these social and communal assets.

Teacher-Student Relationships and the Politics of Caring

Valenzuela (1999) condemns the misdirected care shown by teachers in American schools, as compared to care from Mexican schools. She presents Mexican schools as more engaged in the ethic of care as described by Noddings (2003). As someone from Africa, I view the ethic of care through my African context. My experiences narrated above are instances where care pushed me through school. In the African context of education, the community is responsible for every student's well-being. I was able to make it through school because my community stood up for and believed in me. The typical American teacher's notion of care is a commitment to schooling as seen through the White curriculum, that is, a teacher instructs students in order to get them to pass a standardized assessment.

Valenzuela (1999) narrated the story of Mr. Chilcoate, an example a teacher who comes into the teaching field with the misguided notion that caring about students is teaching them how to read and write without understanding what the students are feeling or experiencing. His first attempts to educate students were unsuccessful, causing him to reflect on other methods. Once he understood his students and empowered them, the students' attitudes towards him and his lessons changed. He portrayed the concept of authentic caring and the students considered him a great teacher from then on. He was able to create a nurturing atmosphere with made room for students' intellectual growth.

Valenzuela (1999) views the White education and the White notion of success in school as compliant to cultural ridicule and de-identification. She argues that teacher-student relationships in Mexican schools portray "caring" at a stronger level than do teacher-student relationships in American schools. She presents the Mexican curriculum as more inclusive of national values, with higher expectations for students. Contrast this to the American subtractive curriculum that takes away from its "students' cultural identities [and] systematically derogated and diminishes" (p. 173) them as second-class humans beings.

The teacher-student demography at Seguin High School is a reflection of the imbalanced teacher-students cultural ratios in most urban schools across America. Valenzuela's (1999) observation of the teacher-student composition shows that Seguin was comprised of predominantly White teachers teaching a predominantly Chicano/a and Latino/a student population. These teachers knew little or nothing about the students they taught. Through their cultural ignorance, they perceived students as nonchalant and indifferent about school. Valenzuela asserts that the politics of care was missing component in Seguin High School and also in U.S. urban schools. Teachers' perception of care is based on a colorblind notion that all students are homogenous and should learn at the same rate. The students, on the contrary, have a different perception of caring. They view caring as representative of home affection. Students ask the question, "If my teachers do not portray care, then why should I care about school?"

Teachers are often disconnected from their students' personal lives and well-being. They but they expect students to be fully receptive of schooling regardless of whether they connect with lessons or not. The outcome is resistance from students, which is often manifested in different ways such as skipping classes, class disruptions, violence, and passiveness towards their learning to name a few examples. Conversely, students do not perceive their school environment as colorblind; rather they perceive their teachers' actions as uncaring, and the result is an uneasy or estranged marriage between teachers and students.

The politics of care following the White curriculum pertains to the notion of a colorblind, equality-driven, English-only education. Teachers often misdirect care in the teaching-learning process, and unconsciously mistake schooling to mean caring. According to Valenzuela (1999), in the Latino/a community "educación" is caring in the Mexican sense. "Educación" is the process of developing and teaching the child as a whole being. Educación is a complete education that involves life lessons and should include teaching loving and caring relationships alongside building social capital. "Educación" develops the well-being of the child as a complete person and justifies the child's being, not only in academic achievement but also in society. Compare this to my African upbringing; I succeeded because my community exhibited love and care for me and connected that love and care to school. School had value for me and I could relate to my teachers culturally and linguistically. The Seguin teachers' conception of caring was the elimination of the cultures and languages of its students. Their curriculum and school practices required students with previous identities to value the Western identity over and against their own. Students were intelligent enough to sense the disconnection, and their responses ricocheted between responses of resilience or rebellion.

At Seguin, the teachers perceived that they cared for their students if the children were able to perform well on the state or national standardized tests. Valenzuela (1999) refers to this type of caring as "aesthetic caring," which subtracts, devalues and replaced the students' cultural and linguistic resources with academic achievement. When teachers view caring relationships with students as the act of simply presenting information and behave in an administrative and colorblind manner towards students, the students disconnect from school and consider education as irrelevant (Pimentel, 2011). This disconnection makes it difficult for even the best teachers with the greatest of intentions to succeed as educators. When students view their teachers as not caring, they become "progressively vulnerable to academic failure" (Valenzuela, 1999, p. 3).

As a public school teacher, I have often questioned my attitude towards students and wondered how much I impact them in my lessons and behavior. After reading Valenzuela (1999) I questioned my ability as a good teacher even more. Do I understand my students well enough to teach and treat them as whole beings with the care as described by Noddings' (2003)? Do I view my students as capable of success, but needy of love and compassion? These are questions that every teacher should ask on a daily basis before beginning any lesson. I suppose many teachers like myself have experienced a degree of guilt after reading *Subtractive Schooling*. I believe this guilt in rooted in not only how we have failed to care for students, but also treated them as robots in the name of schooling. I think of their stories and how much I have subtracted from them. A few of their stories stood out to me; the stories of John (pseudonym) and Brianna (pseudonym), two African American students; and Seydou (pseudonym) an African immigrant student. These were students in my first year of teaching in an American urban school when I did not understand the distinction between schooling and educating. I will use their stories to open a window on my current perception of education.

Student 1: John. John was a 16 year old African American student in my high school, who came to school two or three times a week and was always late. He was inattentive, seldom spoke to anyone in class, and didn't seem to care about anything. He was often in trouble, and I gave him my share of punishments because I thought he was very lazy. John got an "F" and had to take summer school. He didn't show up for summer school and eventually had to repeat the class. The following year I did not see John for an entire quarter. I enquired of him, calling home frequently only to connect to voicemail. One day I heard students talking about a shooting that occurred in their neighborhood. Shootings are commonplace in the neighborhood so I did not find that strange. One of the students came up to me and asked if I remembered John. She said he was involved in the shooting and that there was a possibility he would spend some time in jail. She tried to explain what happened, but I was more focused on my thoughts and what must have gone wrong for a student I taught to be involved in a shooting.

Student 2: Seydou. Seydou was one of my student from Africa. He had been in the U.S. only about a year. He was 15 and attended classes every day, though he struggled in many of his classes. He was an English language learner (ELL). He achieved "Cs" and "Ds" and struggled to understand his teachers. Frustrated one day, Seydou told he was not planning to attend college. He said he would never be able to speak the English language well enough to make it through an even more rigorous academic setting. He was often frustrated because his friend laughed at him when he tried to speak English and felt he would be an object of ridicule if he went to college. Seydou lived with his father and siblings. His father worked two jobs to sustain the family. He had an older sister whom he told me essentially the parent of the house, since his father was always gone. His mother was still in Africa, and he did not know if and when she would join them.

Student 3: Brianna. Brianna 16, was very intelligent and attended school every day. When she worked, she excelled. However, she did very little in class, and only when she wanted to. She achieved good grades for the work she did, but overall had "Ds" or "Fs." That frustrated me a lot as a teacher. I tried to encourage Brianna to come after school for help. She never showed up so I called her mother several times to complain. I never got through to her mother and left several messages. I wondered why such an intelligent student would refuse to do the work. I asked fellow colleagues and almost every teacher labeled her as lazy. Like John, Brianna was scheduled to repeat my class the following year. She never showed up. About one month into the beginning of the school year, I called and left another message for her mother and never received a response. One day I asked the students if they knew Brianna's whereabouts. One student said she was very sick and Brianna did not have long to live. When the student left I closed my eyes and fought back tears. I resented myself for not asking questions about her before now. Brianna never came back to school and her name was eventually taken off the roster. To this day, I think about her and wonder what might have happened to her.

THE THEORY OF CARE AND EDUCATION IN U.S. PUBLIC HIGH SCHOOLS

"Miss, I feel scared about my future, I really don't like to talk about these things."

(Student at Seguin High School, Houston, Texas, quoted in Valenzuela, 1999, p. 150)

John, Seydou, and Brianna were all students placed in my care during my first year of teaching. I was new to the school district and full of energy. I was devoted and gave it my all. I eventually grew more and more disillusioned and eventually hit a brick wall. By the end of that year, I was deflated and worn out. Many students had failed and very few students showed any interest in my classes the following year. I was even more heartbroken when many told me they were not interested in education beyond high school. Like Mr. Chilcoate, I had the wrong connection with many students during my first few years of teaching. Like thousands of teachers in urban schools across America, I had a misguided principle of education and care. I did not understand why even the simplest concepts of a lesson were so hard for my students to grasp. There was no doubt in my mind that I was a devoted teacher. But, I spent my energy teaching the wrong way. I directed my focus solely on my lessons and instruction without engaging my students and connecting with them on a personal level. I realized in many ways I was wrong in my approach.

When John was my student, I requested he come in after school for help. When he did not show up, my conclusion was that he was not interested in improving his life. I gave him "Fs" thinking that low grades would frighten him into coming to class. I was wrong. He ended up in jail. A few years down the road I had another student who, like John, did not come to school. With him and many others like him, I tried another approach. I told him I will give him a "C" simply for attendance. He showed up regularly for a quarter and got a "C" grade. Then one day he came up to me during lunch to say he was hungry. When I asked why he did not go to lunch, he said he could not afford lunch. We had additional conversation, but I could get no further clarification on his situation. He came to me regularly for lunch. I gave him a dollar or two here and there for food. Down the road he trusted me enough to confide in me and explained why he did not qualify for free lunch. He lived with his aunt and she had never signed the forms that would permit him to get free launch. She received custody of him because his father was in jail and his mother was on drugs. I wished I would have been able to develop the same type of relationship with John and been able to speak into his life.

Thereafter, I made it a point to ask my students personal questions. I brought snacks to class for hungry students. It wasn't much but it changed the atmosphere in my classroom. I realized my principles as a teacher had been wrong, and that I should do more to understand and relate with students. I lament the fact that as a pawn in an uncaring system of education, I failed John. I failed him partly from my own doing and partly because of an educational system that restrains me. In America today, following the political and racial events in the country: the shooting of Michael Brown (August 2014) in Ferguson Missouri and the death of Freddie Gray (April 2015) in Baltimore, there has been an outcry for an improvement of the conditions of lives of impoverished minorities in schools and in the community as a whole. I realize as a teacher that my role in the improvement process is to help students like John not fall between the cracks or become victims of our educational system.

Noddings (2003) argues that care is a basic necessity to human life and that every human being wants to be cared for and feel validated. As teachers, we ignore students' distress signals while at school and blindly think we can school them without educating ourselves about these students and their backgrounds. As a teacher, I did not look beyond John's behavior to find out if other problems hindered him from attending classes. I did not show compassion for him because, like the teachers at Seguin, I had been brought up in a postcolonial system where care meant teaching the content. John and every student of color want to be cared for, yet the system is reluctant to change direction and create a curriculum that appreciates their cultural backgrounds. John was born in America and speaks English, but like the students at Seguin, he does not feel validated as a person and rebels against schooling by being absent or refusing to participate in class. To validate my students today, I ask them more personal questions and try to relate to them. I discipline students less for absences and tardiness and encourage them in ways that validate their being. I have failed a teacher evaluation for being too lenient with students that many consider trouble makers at my school. However, I more than welcome the failure if my care for students give them value as human beings.

Noddings (2003) gives an outline of how educators can use the care theory to develop alternative approaches to education and teaching. These approaches focus more on students as individuals, with moral attributes and skills that can breathe life into communities. The ethic of care is a fundamental element to relationships (Noddings, 2003). Noddings' (2003) ethic of care requires relationships to be dealt with in a context that promotes the well-being of caregivers (teachers in this case) as well as care-receivers (students) in a network of social relations (the school). It involves meeting and maintaining our needs and the needs of others. Students in public schools are vulnerable and have needs; they want to feel loved and cared for by those in charge (teachers and administrators). They, however, do not feel the love from the latter and so develop resistance to schooling. When students feel uncared for, perhaps it's natural to expect students to rebel and become disengaged. Perhaps, "some students act that way to get at the teachers" (Valenzuela, 1999, p. 104). Despite how teachers struggle to care, it's certainly to be expected with today's high stakes testing milieu. Teachers feel immense pressure due to issues of accountability and test scores. With that at the back of their minds, they too are vulnerable to the high demands of their administrators and a system that constantly accuses them of failing students.

Student Update

I ran into Seydou last year in an African store not far from where he went to school. He worked as a salesperson at the store and recognized me as soon as I walked in. Seydou told me he never went to college, but said maybe one day he will take a chance. He said he had worked at a few places but preferred working at the store because he could understand and relate to the people who came there. I never got any news about Brianna and John.

ADDITIVE SCHOOLING: WINDOW INTO 2015 AND BEYOND

Law makers and school authorities generally blame minority students for their failures, painting minority cultures as negative, primitive, and lesser cultures than the White culture. Most public school teachers are White, middle-class, and monolingual English, teaching in schools predominantly comprised of students of color with whom the teachers cannot identify with. Most of these teachers have no notion of what it means to be of color, poor, and underappreciated. They do not understand the cultural differences that exist between them and their students, partly because the American preservice teacher training does not lay enough groundwork on the importance of teaching culturally and linguistically diverse curriculum; and partly because their own Whiteness stands in the way of true understanding.

John Dewey's definitions of education uphold the notion that all students are intelligent and can succeed if properly educated. Education from Dewey's perspective does not simply refer to schooling. Rather, education is the combination of schooling and the recognition of the child as an individual with rights and claims of his or her own. These rights include the right to have a language and culture other than the White culture. These rights give value to the students, and give them a cultural identity.

Minority students' failures in American schools come from an educational system that fails them. Studies such as the Raza Studies program in Arizona is an example today that disproves most White teachers' notions that Chicana/o and Latino/a, and by extension minority students are uneducable. In reality, when students are validated through their cultures and identities, they are more likely to experience positive educational outcomes (Cammarota & Romero, 2014). When students are treated with dignity and taught to understand their roots, using culturally relevant pedagogy, they feel empowered and able to the challenge the status quo. They "acquire advanced skills in reading, writing, and analysis, [and] they also learn to address the social, educational, and economic problems that hold people in oppressive and subordinated conditions and spaces" (Cammarota & Romero, 2014, p. 4).

Like the African and Educación examples I described earlier, the Raza studies program demonstrates that when students understand the importance and value of school and can relate to it, they become more engaged and are more likely to succeed (Valenzuela, 1999). As students in Africa, we were taught the value of education through our teachers and communities. Those teachers were concerned about standardized tests and wanted students to make it. Standardized tests were a priority but they did not blind them to our feelings as humans and the issues we faced at home. It was commonplace for teachers to bring cooked food to school and share it with students. Teaching content was their priority, but not their sole priority. They still validated our existence as humans and encouraged us with tough love to make it through. They went out of their way to go to students' homes to make sure the students' parents knew what was going on at school. When my brother and I got into trouble, our teacher took us home. Our parents welcomed her and together they worked to instill a value in us. Teachers were not held accountable in the American sense, nor were they punished for our failures. They were responsible for our well-being, but did not feel threatened when teaching and handling students' affairs.

The American educational system is set up such that teachers are held responsible for students' failures, but no one is held accountable for the mistreatment and dehumanization of the immigrant and/or impoverished students' cultures. As a teacher in the United States, I sometimes feel the need to intervene and advocate for students, but I am also hindered by boundaries imposed by the system. Teacher accountability and the privacy laws in America make it difficult for teachers to fully get involved in their students' personal lives. In conversations with my colleagues, there is the constant fear of not wanting to get involved due to the potential for lawsuits from parents, or of losing their positions because they have gone against district directives. In my first year of teaching my fear of getting involved in the personal lives of my students like John and Brianna, created a disconnection between us that affected their learning as students and disengaged them from the classroom experiences. The teaching-learning process is about upholding the community and improving the home-school relationships. However, politics have often pushed teachers away for fear of getting reprimanded. For meaningful learning to occur in America, the nation has to evolve in its notion of what schooling consists of and make teaching more human and relational, and less political.

Valenzuela (1999) condemns this system and calls for students' unique cultural voices to be heard. She condemns the fact that immigrant and U.S.-born students of immigrants have to choose between their cultures and the American culture in school. She condemns subtractive schooling. In her epilogue, she calls for additive schooling where students will not have to choose between being Mexican and/or American, but where they can be both. The Raza studies program in Arizona also validates the fact that involving students' cultures and histories into the learning process validates the students' existence and gets them more engaged in the learning process. The program proved that Latino/a and Chicano/a students' scores improved during the program. Unfortunately, the program was ultimately banned for fear it would take away students' patriotism and create rebellious attitudes toward America.

Education should be about authentic caring as portrayed by Mr. Chilcoate (Valenzuela, 1999). Authentic caring can occur despite a subtractive schooling system as Mr. Chilcoate demonstrated. In a school environment where the students' languages and cultures are diminished, Mr. Chilcoate embraced and validated his students by listening to their personal stories and empowering them as humans. The result was productive and additive. After my first year of teaching and my struggles with understanding my students, I finally realized as a teacher that the more I got involved in my students personal lives, the more they became engaged in the learning process. Asking students how they feel or what they will like to do, and engaging them in conversations that involve their personal problems brings the students closer to their teachers. By my third year of teaching, I had some degree of understanding of many of my students. Now I start my year by asking students to tell me any special things they will like me to know about them. They generally do not open up easily but as time goes by and they understand I truly care about them, they do begin to open up and share their lives.

School rules are generally rigid and require firm classroom rules. I have learned to balance my lessons in response to my students' personal lives. My experiences with John taught me to come to school prepared for students that might not have had a meal all day. Students are allowed to take a bite at whatever food they have to eat or pick a snack from a jar in the front of the class without fear of reprimand. I assign students to encourage and organize their peers so that I don't have to worry about them becoming unruly. They are their brothers' keepers in my classroom, which is an important lesson in of itself. I try to relate my lessons to their lives and give them a platform for their voices to be heard. My relationship with my students is still a work in progress but has come a long way from what I experienced in my first year as a teacher in an American public school. I had gotten in trouble with administration a few times for transgressing school rules such as allowing students to eat in class. I must agree it is a difficult line to walk for teachers. However, we need to balance care and standards to make our students succeed.

CONCLUSION

As someone who has had the privilege of being in both the U.S. and African educational systems, I view subtractive schooling with a double lens. From a purely African perspective, subtractive schooling can be defended as a necessary evil that prepares students for global readiness and the global market. As a student while in Africa, I understood the only way I could get out of my situation was to learn the only form of schooling that was available to me then: the White curriculum. Had I not been given a chance to read and write in the Whiteman's language I would never have had the opportunity I have today to live and teach in the U.S. Did I lose the value of my culture and language? Maybe, though not in the same way as the children often do in U.S. schools through a lack of care.

ABOUT THE AUTHOR ANGELA VALENZUELA

Angela Valenzuela is a seasoned professor, a renowned author and blogger. She is the author of the best-selling book, Subtractive *Schooling: U.S. Mexican Youth and the Politics of Caring*, as well as *Leaving Children Behind: How "Texas-style" Accountability Fails Latino Youth*. Her blog: Educational Equity, Politics, and Policy in Texas, is a newsworthy corner for critical discussions on hot topics in education. Valenzuela's research and teaching interests are in the sociology of education, minority youth in schools, educational policy, and urban education reforms. She looks at urban education from a sociological and multicultural perspective and focuses on minority youth and their struggles in U.S. schools.

In personal conversations I had over the phone with Dr. Valenzuela, she expressed her frustration at the current plight of migrant students in America. As a third generation, U.S.-born Mexican American, subtractive school has fueled her current and enduring research interests. She considers her research to be personal because she can identify with the "loss," or more correctly stated, "subtraction" of children's cultural, linguistic, and ethnic identities. She views this subtractive schooling is part of a larger narrative of dispossession embodied in policies that promote family separation and deportation. She condemns policies that separate families, erases identities, and represses the voices of the voiceless. She grew up in a Christian community and is against a dominant culture that rejects and devalues other cultures, languages, and ways of knowing and being in the world. "Rather than subtractive schooling, we need to promote additive schooling, an approach that honors and respects the humanity, diversity and unique contributions of all groups to society" (Valenzuela, personal communication, March 25, 2015).

REFERENCES

Cammarota, J., & Romero, A. (2014). Introduction: Paulo Freire in Raza Studies. In J. Cammarota & A. Romero (Eds.), *Raza studies: The public option for educational revolution*. Tucson, AZ: The University of Arizona Press.

Noddings, N. (2003). *Caring: A feminine approach to caring and moral education* (2nd ed.). Berkeley, CA: University of California Press.

Pimentel, C. (2011). The politics of caring in a bilingual classroom: A case study on the (im)possibilities of critical care in an assimilationist school context. *Journal of Praxis in Multicultural Education, 6*(1), 49–60. doi:10.9741/2161-2978

Valenzuela, A. (1999). *Subtractive schooling: U.S.-Mexican youth and the politics of caring*. New York, NY: State University of New York Press.

CHAPTER 14

INTEGRATED CURRICULUM

A Catalyst for Contextualized Learning

Jennifer Ellerbe

It's just not enough for them and for those exercising surveillance over teachers and our classrooms if students find an experience meaningful and valuable in myriad ways or if an activity teaches without being tied to some set of learning outcomes or objectives.

(Poetter, 2006, p. 319)

Four years ago, I was hired to begin an alternative program in a rural district with another teacher. I anticipated a natural, streamlined, and gratifying process because of my educational background in psychology and education, and my coteacher's 6 years of teaching experience. I felt prepared and expected to walk in, change lives daily, and feel fulfilled and accomplished at the end of every day. I was naive and believed teaching at-risk students was going to play out like a movie in which I would somehow reach all of the unreachable students. As the first quarter of school came to a close, I realized that I could not have been more wrong. I clearly had no idea what I was doing. By Christmas, I felt like a failure to myself and my students. I was not sure if I was cut out to teach such challenging students in any way,

Curriculum Windows: What Curriculum Theorists of the 1990s Can Teach Us About Schools and Society Today, pp. 217–233
Copyright © 2017 by Information Age Publishing
All rights of reproduction in any form reserved.

217

shape, or form. I could not imagine how anyone could handle the stress of teaching students who seemed to have no chance in life.

In reflection, although my first year had been exhausting and was not the easy process I had predicted, I was right about one thing. I felt accomplished and fulfilled with a strong determination to make myself and my program better to serve my students. Over the summer and the next year, my coteacher and I strategized together, visited other alternative schools, and sought advice from experienced alternative teachers and administrators to change our program and ourselves, both with our students and for our students. My students had changed me and inspired me. They not only made me want to be a better teacher, they made me a better person.

THE SEARCH FOR AN ALTERNATIVE TO ALTERNATIVE

In my first year of teaching at the alternative school, the program was assigned an exclusively online curriculum that allowed for minimal adaptability and less academic opportunity than the already rigid and over standardized state curriculum. The factory-made content for the apparent robots the state assumes children to be could never meet the needs, address the issues, or even begin to help the children in my class reach their full potential. Online curriculums are barebones, standardized, and rudimentary curriculums that I believe only hinder growth and opportunity for student learning. As such, I began to research options to add flesh to the curriculum that was being forced upon my already academically, socially, and economically impoverished students.

Since then, the alternative school has become a place within my district that integrates students' lives into their school curriculum. The alternative school allows the most at-risk students to have learning and instruction catered to their learning style and ability, to have a mentor that visits once a week, to participate in group therapy, to have a schedule that allows the opportunity to work and go to school, to work flexibly at their own pace, and to receive the education everyone deserves. Most important of all, the relationships that I foster in the school between myself and students and amongst students provides the social consistency they need in their lives and in the curriculum.

I feel that at-risk students are often just misunderstood. It is essential that schools provide more curriculum options and supports to allow them to grow and be successful at school and in the future. Many at-risk students greatly benefit from a curriculum that integrates the social and intellectual world. They need to see, touch, and feel how knowledge is interconnected, utilized in daily life, and instrumental toward their goals. The alternative school is a place that integrates the problems and challenges students face outside of school into the curriculum to meet their needs. Each student knows that we are in this together, for better or for worse.

Living in poverty and being labeled as at-risk are not isolated consequences of individual choice, but rather the result of an inability to provide equal opportunities to individuals and families. Often there is a deep sense of marginalization and oppression that youth face when they come from at-risk family environments. However, living in at-risk environments is very much interwoven with many social issues including: health, family characteristics, income, geographic planning, and employment. As a country, we:

> face many very difficult issues: sharp divisiveness among interest groups, huge disparities in the distribution of wealth, erosion of environmental protection, continuing injustice toward minority groups and more. The fate of the nation largely rests on whether issues such as these can be resolved for the benefit of common good. Moreover, they will need to be resolved by people, including young people, for they will not simply go away by any other means. (Beane, 1997, p. 93)

Only when all of these factors are acknowledged can we begin to effectively change the issue of being at-risk and turn academic failure and school avoidance into achievement and success.

Yet instead of acknowledging the factors that Beane (1997) mentions, we are giving "larger doses of fragmented information and skills divided into separate subject categories that are remote from compelling issues in the larger world" (p. 93). We need contextualized curriculum to address these issues and create meaningful learning, purpose, and the utility of knowledge that allows children to apply and use what they learn to exit the cycle and life of poverty.

END THE CYCLE

There was one moment in particular when I knew I had enough of standardized curriculum and tests and that has replayed in my mind over the years. It was during my second semester of teaching during Ohio Graduation Test (OGT) week. The OGT is a standardized test administered to sophomore students that all students must pass in order to graduate, even if they have earned all of their high school credits. During the administration of the exam, a boy in my class, who in my opinion would have otherwise been labeled gifted if it had not been for the path that led him to the alternative school, had an outburst of anger and began to cry as he took his OGT.

Afterwards, I asked him about the incident. He looked me straight in the eyes and said, "You know, I'm just not lucky enough to get out of here."

I asked him what he meant and he said, "I don't even know if I am smart enough to pass that test, but does it even really matter? Because I know that I am not lucky enough to be able to do anything because I always barely pass. None of this stuff has anything to do with real life or what I need to know to make some money." I thought about what he said for a long time. I had not helped him to see value in what he was learning, and he merely attributed the rest of his life's worth to a score on a test. He saw everything he had learned over the last 10 years as not applicable to himself or his life. And it wasn't just me that had failed, it was everyone before me, and everyone that taught me about teaching who never tried to change the way things are.

No one should ever feel like that about themselves. My student had seen all of his past years in school as pointless. He saw an education system that labeled him as a failure and others as successful, all because of the perceived importance of scores and grades. I could not imagine how it had gotten to the point that this young person, and so many young people like him, relied on test scores to judge their education in school as a big failure, or their ticket to college and a better life. How has learning become so decontextualized from the immediate? Shouldn't all learning be seen as applicable and meaningful to the context of a learner's life, issues, and interests - instead of something to be used at a future time, or in the opinion of some, not at all?

James A. Beane (1997) offers an alternative to amend decontextualized and standardized learning in his presentation of curriculum integration in *Curriculum Integration: Designing the Core of Democratic Education*. Beane presents education and learning as a context for unifying knowledge and life. Beane rejects the boundaries we have created between life and education. Instead, teaching and learning are centered around significant problems or issues that contextualize knowledge and connect it to the real world. Knowledge is organized and applied. "So, organized, the curriculum and the knowledge it engages are more accessible and meaningful for young people and thus, more likely to help them expand their understanding of themselves and their world" (p. 2).

Integrated curriculum encourages students to create their own meaning, contextualizes learning to allow for deeper understanding, and shows knowledge as something to be utilized in the present; rather than something that is being learned and stored for future use. "Curriculum is organized around personal and social issues, collaboratively planned and carried out by teachers and students together, and committed to the integration of knowledge" (Beane, 1997, p. 6). The curriculum promotes social integration, togetherness, social responsibility, and accountability leading to a more democratic learning environment.

The standardization of curriculum into separate subject areas has taken away the power that knowledge has to offer in providing clear solutions to everyday issues. An integrated curriculum uses knowledge as a dynamic instrument to attack issues in life (Beane, 1997). Knowledge becomes powerful and is no longer seen in bits and pieces used to solve decontextualized problems, but as something that gives students control over their lives. The knowledge and skills they gain in school become contextualized and unhindered by boundaries. Learning becomes more than scores and grades; it becomes something students create and discover themselves. Learning becomes something that can be used to solve the issues and problems of today for a better tomorrow.

STANDARDIZATION AND ANTI-INTELLECTUALISM

As industrialization devoured our world, the imagination that flowed through the veins of society was overrun by the seemingly harmless innovations towards standardization and efficiency. An integral part of industrialization was the development of assembly lines with their guaranteed standardization of each product and the efficiency of production. Each item produced is as identical as possible, and accountability for each assembled piece is easily identified because each product is seen as pieces. As the benefits of assembly lines, standardization, and accountability were utilized in industry, the concepts bled into education. However, as the emphasis in education shifted to standardization, efficiency, and accountability through measurement of people as if they were homogeneous products, the depth and substance of education that truly makes individuals unique was being lost. Creating a standardized path for all learners to follow step-by-step is unreasonable and sets many students up for failure before they even begin school. It is anti-intellectual and dehumanizing.

Teachers are given a map with the exact path to be taken. And by following that path, creativity and imagination dwindle for both teachers and students out of fear of deviating from the path and suffering the consequences of poor performance. The teacher is no longer seen as an intellectual, guiding children through the contours of the terrain to be travelled, but as a transmitter of predetermined information in a linear and mechanical fashion. The impression given to children is that the improvement of society through learning and growth of knowledge by fostering creativity, curiosity, and imagination is no longer the goal of or even an option in education. For our children, the goal of education has been diminished to learning isolated rote skills that are applicable to tests. If we continue with the standardization of curriculum, if we function like manufacturing plants, if we no longer foster a love of learning, and if we continue to develop students who believe their worth can be attributed to a score, then I fear our humanity and the artfulness of our being will be lost.

The current curriculum is systematic and mind numbing. We as teachers, leaders, and citizens no longer openly question the current curriculum, its values, and consequences or the imprint left on the views our children hold about learning. We must release ourselves from the belief that a child and his or her intellect is something quantifiable. Once free, we can create an environment that contributes to the betterment of society instead of its maintenance and, thus, release the damper on our potential to flourish.

James A. Beane (1997) suggests that the current system can be thrown out and forgotten. Time after time we continue to try to make small changes to the curriculum and hope that they will have the desired effect of improvement; but time and time again we are left with little improvement, or worse. We only change how we do things in small increments, leaving what we do in place, or why we do it unquestioned. Beane acknowledges that accountability and standardization seem to promote equality in education, but in reality, children are being forced to fit a mold that may not allow their strengths to be discovered or their issues to be addressed. They are left feeling detached from knowledge and not seeing its use or potential. Standardizing and producing children like products contributes to the maintenance of society, not its improvement.

NEW INTELLECTUAL TERRAIN

Teachers ought to be valued as intellectuals whose purpose is to guide children and who, together with students, create an environment that places learning as meaningful and applicable to the reality that children face. Knowledge should be valued as applicable to the world around us and transformative toward a more democratic and just education for all, not just those that have the ability or desire to follow the highlighted path. Education needs to value the dignity of all children, not just those with the qualities of the status quo, and "take their ideas, hopes, aspirations, and lives seriously" (Beane, 1997, p. 68). These beliefs extend democratic values and rights to our children and permit the social issues that consume children's lives to organize work in the classroom (Beane, 1997). Beane (1997) argues that standardization has taken away social components that provide meaningful shared experiences and promote a sense of the common good or values. Diversity should be used to spark curiosity and intellectual discourse and seen as a source of strength as opposed to a weakness (Beane, 1997).

Instead, the most prominent social component is the maintenance of the current knowledge and maintenance of the current society. We have come to see knowledge as a collection of independent components separated by subject areas, and its uses and power are confined by those boundaries (Beane, 1997). The separate subject areas have not only become the means by which we educate, but also the ends of education (Beane, 1997). Learning and the curriculum should be centered around the self, and social issues and knowledge should be drawn upon collectively without boundaries to solve those issues (Beane, 1997).

Beane (1997) believes that the knowledge that is included in the current curriculum reflects the interests of high social cultural and academic elites. Education is seen as a commodity, and those in power have placed a monopoly on success by defining *what* and *whose* knowledge is of most value (Beane, 1997). This is a reflection of a capitalist society; education and learning are regarded as capital to be gained to achieve high test scores or a certain status in society. The question has become not what knowledge is applicable and beneficial, but whose knowledge and which application is of most worth (Beane, 1997). Education, now more than ever, has become a process used to maintain society as it is and to manufacture children to maintain the status quo.

Beane (1997) urges us to create a new world that deviates from the path of maintenance of the current curriculum and removes us from the world of standardization in this time of accountability and high stakes testing. We can deviate to a place where curiosity is sparked, the knowledge of the status quo is no longer of utmost importance, and subsequently, the concerns of real life take the stage. Personal and social concerns are quite literally the stuff of life and are likely to be the organizing schemes young people already use for knowledge and experience (Beane, 1997). And this should be our starting place for curriculum development and learning.

CURRICULUM INTEGRATION

According to Beane (1997),

> the idea of curriculum integration emerged earlier in the century in relation to ideals of social integration, democratic classrooms, holistic learning, and the integration of knowledge. Its late twentieth century version reduced it to the matter of correlating content and skill from various subject areas around some theme. (p. x)

Beane argues that the late 20th century definition is totally wrong and a misinterpretation of what curriculum integration is. The essence and the possibilities that lie within true curriculum integration are concealed by this definition. Beane defines curriculum integration involving four dimensions: the integration of experiences, social integration, the integration of knowledge, and integration as a curriculum design.

Integration of Experiences

Our experiences construct dynamic and fluid meanings, beliefs, and ideals into schemes that we use to approach issues (Beane, 1997). These schemes are shaped by our

> perceptions, beliefs, values, and so on—this kind of learning involves having constructive, reflective experiences that not only broaden and deepen our present understandings of ourselves and our world but that also are "learned" in such a way that they may be carried forward and put to use in new situations. (Dressel, 1958, as cited in Beane, 1997, p. 4)

This type of learning, in short, becomes unforgettable and, quite literally, a part of our identity (Beane, 1997). It integrates new experiences into our schemes of meaning, and we integrate our past experiences to help us solve new situations we are presented with (Beane, 1997). Experiential integration is crucial to providing a more meaningful experience that allows knowledge to be more accessible, readily understood, learned, and remembered (Beane, 1997). Too often, the notion of learning and knowledge is dispensed as something for future use.

> Almost everyone has had occasion to look back upon his school days and wonder what has become of the knowledge he was supposed to have amassed during his years of schooling, ... but it was so segregated when it was acquired and hence is so disconnected from the rest of experience that it is not available under the actual conditions of life. (Dewey, 1938, as cited in Beane, 1997, p. 5)

Integration of the Social

To encourage a democratic learning environment and society, an imperative purpose of schools is that of providing common or shared educational experiences for children with diverse characteristics and backgrounds (Beane, 1997). These shared experiences promote a sense of common values and common good (Beane, 1997). The purpose of this in education, that many refer to as general education, is to provide a place that is meant for all learners regardless of background or aspirations (Beane, 1997). Advocates of curriculum integration believe that any good curriculum should be organized around "personal and social issues, collaboratively planned, and carried out by teachers and students together, and committed to the integration of knowledge" (Beane, 1997, p. 6).

A democratic environment and curriculum require collaborative work on common problems aligning with the "democratic concept of participatory, collaborative governance, and decision making" (Beane, 1997, p. 6). Knowledge should be used as an instrument for intelligent problem solving through the "inclusion of personal issues alongside social problems that creates the democratic possibility of integrating self and social interest" (Beane, 1997, p. 6). These arrangements not only make knowledge more accessible, but also create democratic practices with the classroom as the context for social integration (Beane, 1997). Social integration and democratic practices have largely eluded the curriculum of the public schools (Beane, 1997). This departure, and the creation of what is now the traditional curriculum, is also sadly one of the most "persistent sources of inequality and 'disintegration' found across the whole society" (Beane, 1997, p. 6).

Integration of Knowledge

When we are confronted with an issue or a problem we do not stop and think about which part of the problem is history, or mathematics, or art or any of the other separate subject areas (Beane, 1997). "Instead we take on the problem or situation using whatever knowledge is appropriate or pertinent without regard for subject area lines" (Beane, 1997, p. 7). We do not see knowledge boundaries when problems and issues arise in our lives. We see the knowledge used to solve our issues as seamless. "In this way, we come to understand and use knowledge not in terms of the differentiated compartments by which it is labeled in school, but rather as it is 'integrated' in the context of the real problems and issues" (Beane, 1997, p. 7). Children should be encouraged to break the boundaries of knowledge to define problems as broadly as they are in real life and use a wide range of knowledge to address them (Beane, 1997).

When we confine knowledge to the boundaries and treat it as an accumulation of capital for future use, two things happen: (1) children believe knowledge that is considered important is irrelevant to their lives; and (2) they are robbed of the opportunity to learn to organize the knowledge they have in a way that is most accessible and applicable to their lives (Beane, 1997). The integration of knowledge allows for learning to take on deeper meanings and make meaningful connections within the context of children's lives. "This aspect of the democratic way of life involves the right, obligation, and power of people to seek intelligent solutions to problems that face them, individually and collectively" (Beane, 1997, p. 8).

Integration as a Curriculum Design

A crucial aspect of providing a democratic education is the participation of students in their own learning and the design of their curriculum. If integrative learning is a serious intention, and the promotion of democratic values is of importance, student participation in planning their own experiences is necessary. Their participation and stake in their education is the last and final distinguishing factor. Along with the students' participation, three ideals are crucial to the implementation of an integrated curriculum:

> First, the curriculum is organized around problems and issues that are of personal and social significance in the real world. Second, learning experiences in relation to the organizing center are planned so as to integrate pertinent knowledge in the context of organizing centers. And third, knowledge is developed and used to address the organizing center currently under study rather than to prepare for some later test or grade level. (Beane, 1997, p. 9)

These items, in tandem, allow children to truly contextualize knowledge and learning to "experience the democratic process of problem solving" (Beane, 1997, p. 9).

LET'S DO SOMETHING DIFFERENT

Curriculum integration is not just about doing a few things differently, but about rethinking the connections between everything. Curriculum integration is not about rearranging content from several subjects around themes (Beane, 1997). Curriculum integration is a collaboratively planned, high pedagogy that takes place in an integrative learning community. Curriculum integration begins with the idea that sources of curriculum should come from problems, issues, and concerns posed by life itself. Since life knows no boundaries, then the knowledge and learning used to address the curriculum should seek connections that know no boundaries.

> Of course, all curriculum designs claim to create connections of some kind or another-with the past, with the community, across subjects, and so on. But here is a curriculum design that seeks connections in all directions,

and because of that special kind of unity, it is given the name *curriculum integration*. (Beane, 1997, p. 2)

Beane's (1997 definition creates meaningful and contextualized curriculum. Students become invested in their learning, and in collaboration with teachers, students decide what is worthwhile and make their own meaning from the information and problems that they encounter.

There is a long history of central authority and bureaucratic control on what goes on in classrooms. Beane's (1997) notion of integrated curriculum defies bureaucratic beliefs by utilizing a bottom-up planning structure. "Planning begins with a central theme and proceeds outward through identification of big ideas or concepts ... without regard for subject area lines" (p. 10). This strategy frees teachers and students from many obstacles created by the curriculum being tied to classic disciplines and by efforts to maintain economic interests and the status quo through the dissemination of the knowledge and skills.

CLASSROOM EXPERIENCE

Curriculum integration allows students to use and practice the skills necessary to lead a more democratic way of life. Students are grouped in a more heterogeneous way, which promotes collaborative planning and the development of tolerance and understanding. Students attack problems that are of concern to their lives and community, giving them experience in democratic problem solving. Students incorporate knowledge, experience, and popular culture providing them with a stake in their learning and curriculum. Students are expected to take on and search for solutions to issues of everyday life. The curriculum is dedicated to the tensions and problems children face, and in turn, students are more dedicated and committed to their own learning.

> I am not saying that no other teachers care about such tensions or the problems young people face, but those who have made an explicit commitment to focus the curriculum on self and social meaning must face those issues squarely and with no other "curriculum" to hide behind ... their classrooms are filled with a disproportionate number of students whom other teachers in the building cannot or will not work with ... those responsible for dealing with office referrals and student placements may come to love curriculum integration without knowing or understanding anything about it. All they know is that there seem to be fewer referrals out of those rooms. (Beane, 1997, pp. 72–73)

There are a variety of reasons that many teachers are reluctant to use curriculum integration in their classrooms. Curriculum integration is not protected by the foundation and history of the core subject areas. "Teachers who use a separate-subject area approach can hide behind the symbolic walls that surround each subject and claim immunity from pedagogical discussions on the basis of each subject's 'uniqueness'" (Beane, 1997, p. 75). Many are afraid of the vulnerability this creates. Often, teachers are just unsure of how to proceed or are devoted to their subject area and the units they have designed, or they simply are mistaken about what curriculum integration truly involves. Many critics believe if we depart from the current subject areas "it will destroy the integrity of the disciplines of knowledge" (Beane, 1997, p. 46). Beane (1997) is:

> puzzled by this ... what possible integrity could there be for any kind of knowledge apart from how it connects to other forms to help us investigate and understand the problems, concerns, and issues that confront us in the real world? (pp. 46–47)

Beane questions the integrity of the criticism by asking:

> what kind of integrity is it that the disciplines of knowledge now have in the minds of young people? Or is it the case that "integrity" is really code for "subject boundaries" and "dominant-culture knowledge?" (p. 47)

These critics lack the understanding that a discipline of knowledge is simply a "lens through which to view the world—a specialized set of techniques or processes by which to interpret or explain various phenomena" (p. 39), and a subject area is a subset of that. But those who believe in curriculum integration do not believe in these boundaries and "know that discipline boundaries are fluid and often connected" (p. 39).

Subject areas are institutionally-based, bounded representations of knowledge from the known disciplines and contain the compartments of knowledge that the status quo has deemed as "worth knowing" (Beane, 1997 p. 39). Currently, learning transpires in separated pieces that a puzzle that children must manipulate without ever seeing all of the pieces collectively. Alternatively, learning should be viewed as a whole, not in individual pieces that they must connect on their own and hope to fit together. The disciplines should be seen as "resources from which to draw in context of the theme and related issues and activities" (Beane, 1997, p. 44), not as individually subjugated pieces.

Integrated curriculum provides contextualized learning; uncovering the interconnectedness of knowledge gives it purpose and meaning. Children learn much more in a meaningful context. It is very possible to contextualize geometry, history, English, and science along with developing a sense of community and togetherness from building something as simple as a school garden or providing food for a homeless shelter. To build a garden, children must make a plan, assign jobs, work together, consider what foods will be most healthy, learn to make the frame for the garden, learn how to cut the angles of the boards, learn about and study the contours of the terrain it will be placed on, examine weather patterns to know how often to water and account for soil erosion, learn about the plants that will best grow, and so on. In this type of project centered learning, children apply knowledge without boundaries and seek answers by attacking the issue or problem as a whole. In this type of learning, young people are "engaged in an enormous range of knowledge, from information to values, and include[e] content and skills from several disciplines of knowledge" (Beane, 1997, p. 2). In this example, knowledge is not categorized. Instead, knowledge is integrated into the context of the project and immediately takes on purpose and importance; knowledge is not for some future event, but something to be applied to what needs to be done now (Beane, 1997).

In the current accountability era, "How will student participants perform on standardized tests?" is a frequently asked in response to proposing an integrated curriculum approach. That question alone should raise a red flag about the current state of affairs in education today for every single person who cares about children and their futures. According to Beane (1997), many studies have shown that students participating in integrated curriculums do at least as well or better on measurement based assessments, and it seems particularly helpful for students who traditionally have trouble in school. Just because the way things are now seems set in stone, it doesn't make it right or mean that a just and meaningful education is being provided for all. If, when approached with an idea that has so much potential, such as an integrated curriculum, we worry about "How will we test them?" I think that it is we who need to reevaluate what education and learning should be about and, more importantly, what the values and ideals about knowledge, education, learning, and growth are that we are instilling in our children.

BREAKING THE WINDOW

As a teacher, I can't imagine anything more despicable than allowing our children to see themselves, their success, and their failures as a reflection of filling in bubbles and writing five point essays just as the boy in my class had done. Learning is so much more than that. It is the result of curiosity, imagination, and discovery. It is what unravels the mystery of the universe and fills our souls with purpose. We are allowing one of our most attractive, unique, and precious activities as people and citizens to be presented as a mere score on a piece of paper. Our children are being denied the privilege of experiencing learning as meaningful and meeting their potential. We have allowed their dehumanization through rigid standards and teaching methods that advocate learning that is compartmentalized and decontextualized from daily life.

Standardization ignores the link between "personal and social issues that promote the integration of self and social interest, a marker of social responsibility in a democratic society" (Beane, 1997, p. 50), and hinders democratic practices that have the capability to contextualize learning and provide equality and equity in education. Standardized testing and grades rank children and their worth in society based on their performance of rudimentary skills or a one size fits all assessment.

Curriculum integration does not rank students based on performance, instead students present, demonstrate, and exhibit their work for the group. The expectations of completion are no longer placed on the individuals to collect and accumulate knowledge for themselves. But now we expect students to put knowledge to use to further the understanding of the problem or issue for the entire group, creating expectations of social responsibility to and for each other (Beane, 1997). As Beane (1997) says, "the departure from the current expectations tend to make some people nervous" (p. 78). But departure should be seen as necessary considering what is being lost and what is being imposed upon our young learners. "There is surely something compelling about having your work count for something bigger than a grade at unit's end" (p. 62).

The current curriculum that has been socially constructed and historically constituted by the status quo as the "the best way" or "the only way" ought to be left behind. Schools must no longer manufacture students like products; instead, they should provide a space for a democratic educational discourse in an unrestrained, contextualized, and meaningful way. Teachers who feel disempowered by the compliance measures aimed at maintaining the current reforms that support standardization in education are not doing students a service towards a meaningful and relevant education. The façade of the way things ought to be conceals the truth and prevents any conversations about the oppression created by educational standards. The facade upholds the ideology of the current curriculum and presents it as unquestioned truth. This unquestioned truth has invaded not only the school curriculum, but the social curriculum that governs the way students are allowed to exist, learn, and succeed in educational environments.

The dominant ideology of the current curriculum is recreated through educational practices, as well as justified and reinforced by labeling testing as "accountability." The dominant ideology of the current curriculum is trapped in a technocratic rationale, obscuring the emancipatory possibilities of a social democratic learning environment with the capacity to contextualize learning and educate morally upstanding intellectuals.

The goal of education should no longer be to force students to fit a mold and follow the highlighted path; "instead, the primary purpose should be (is) to stimulate their passions, imaginations, as intellects so that they will be moved to challenge the social, political, and economic forces that weigh so heavily upon their lives" (Giroux, 2001, p. 201). The only way to create this purpose is to socialize and contextualize learning to issues that are relevant to students, their lives, and the world around them. This purpose creates the foundation for a democratic environment that is free from the dominating constraints of oppression, and all students gain the opportunity to flourish through more meaningful and contextualized learning.

Children will flourish in a contextualized curriculum that does not enhance the constraints already present from the circumstances of life, poverty, and culture by centering learning on "life itself rather than on the mastery of fragmented information within the boundaries of subject areas" (Beane, 1997, p. 18). Students' worth as people will no longer be attributed to test scores, and no longer will they be confined by "those who want a rigid, predetermined curriculum that satisfies the adult craving to push their own interests and desires onto children" (Beane, 1997, p. 102). Children will determine their own place in education and as intellectuals by participating in a curriculum that "encourages them as young people to use their minds to think critically about the world and construct their own meanings" (Beane, 1997, p. 102), that is, "rather than merely assuming the validity of others' meanings" (Beane, 1997, p. 18).

In this environment, democratic ideals spring into life and create opportunity to fulfill children's right and "capacity to act on their environment" (Beane, 1997, p. 26). These are the fundamental ideals that bring democracy alive in education and society.

> Those of us who advocate for curriculum integration believe that young people have a right to be intelligent, to be well informed, to search for meaning in their world, to be engaged with significant issues, to do authentic work, to learn the whole story, to think critically, to form values, to make judgements, and to be respected. (Beane, 1997, p. 103)

Those of us who believe that curriculum reform is necessary believe that there is a better future, and children are necessary participants. Children paint the future, and we are thwarting its beauty by forcing them to follow the color-by-numbers path.

By filtering our children down the same path and reprimanding those that fail or deviate from the expectations of the status quo, we are creating oppression. If we continue down this path of marginalization and oppression by allowing the status quo to define the knowledge that is important, we might as well chain all of our children to the same room and ignore the beauty outside. We can ignore it all we want, but our children can see through the window; they don't know what's out there, but as teachers, we can feel their curiosity and yearning for our guidance in its discovery. They are trapped in a room with technocratic educational values and unchallenged practices and content, and just beyond the glass shines the warmth of emancipation and democratic learning that are currently restrained by our misplaced value on the standardization of performance and the rote knowledge of the status quo.

We are dehumanizing and manufacturing children like products, oppressing their natural curiosity, imagination, and creativity, all the while restraining the stunning uniqueness that lies within each of them and us. By doing this, we pose a threat of destroying endless possibilities in the future for many children. We must break the glass window to allow our children to discover the "outside" they are yearning for. When we break the glass, we break the boundaries of learning and knowledge, our possibilities of where we can go, what we can imagine, and what we can change for the better are endless.

Not every child will make the same choices about how they want to live, but the opportunity to choose should not be limited by standardized curriculum and poor teaching methods that continue to oppress many children. Advocates of curriculum integration believe "that all young people can learn, though not always the same things or at the same level" (Beane, 1997, p. 69). But it is up to teachers to provide the opportunities and the environment that allow children the opportunity to reach their full potential. The choice of defining his full potential was taken away from my student during OGT week my first year of teaching. The system had failed him. It had caused him to see knowledge as useless and disconnected from his life. No child should ever feel disconnected and out of place in the context of a learning environment.

Children should be given the choice to navigate the world in different ways. The one size fits all path limits opportunities to those who know the "rules" of the status quo, and it neglects the real issues in life. My student was forced into an environment that saw the consequences of life outside of school as irrelevant to life inside school. Advocates of curriculum integration "believe that life inside and outside the schools should be integrated" (Beane, 1997, p. 69). They believe in a curriculum that is not simply a "farm system for the next grade, or for the next school level, or for college or work, or for 'later in life'" (Beane, 1997, p. 70).

As Elliot Eisner (2002) says, "standardized teaching, from an educational perspective, is an oxymoron" (p. 7). By leaving the current practices unquestioned and in place, we are allowing circumstances that "hide what young people can do" (Beane, 1997 p. 64). Education should "open the way for them" (Beane, 1997, p. 64) and not be bound to content areas teaching the simple skills in each, or about rearranging content from several subjects around some theme; instead, it should truly integrate the "stuff" of life into the school. Mere coverage of material does not equate to learning (Beane, 1997). Children are not robots; we need to stop manufacturing them and hold children socially accountable to each other, for their own learning, and the creation of a better tomorrow. In the case of learning and for the sake of our hope for a better, more democratic tomorrow, we must always remember that it is the "whole" context that gives knowledge its meaning and accessibility (Iran-Nejad et al., 1990, as cited in Beane, 1997, p. 47), not just the pieces the status quo wants us to see.

REFERENCES

Beane, J. A. (1997). *Curriculum integration: Designing the core of democratic education.* New York, NY: Teachers College Press.

Eisner, E. W. (2002). *The educational imagination: On the design and evaluation of school programs* (3rd ed.). Upper Saddle, NJ: Prentice Hall.

Giroux, H. A. (2001). *Theory and resistance in education: Towards a pedagogy for the opposition.* Westport, CT: Bergin & Garvey.

Poetter, T.S. (2006). The zoo trip: objecting to objectives. *Phi Delta Kappan, 88*(4), 319–323.

ABOUT THE
EDITORS/AUTHORS

ABOUT THE EDITORS

Thomas S. Poetter is Professor of Curriculum Studies in the Department of Educational Leadership at Miami University in Oxford, Ohio. Since 1994, Poetter has been engaging students in inquiries into theory and practice in curriculum and teaching. His first book, *Voices of Inquiry in Teacher Education* (1997, Lawrence Erlbaum) challenged teachers to view inquiry as a key orientation for a lifetime of professional practice in schools. Since then, his students have authored and coauthored many books and articles as a result of coursework taken with him at Miami University including book-length works such as *Critical Perspectives on the Curriculum of Teacher Education* (2004, UPA), *No Child Left Behind and the Illusion of Reform* (2006, UPA), and *10 Great Curricula: Lived Conversations of Progressive, Democratic Curricula in School and Society* (2012, IAP), and the first three volumes in a four volume series entitled *Curriculum Windows: What Curriculum Theorists of the 1960s Can Teach Us about Schools and Society Today* (IAP, 2013), *Curriculum Windows: What Curriculum Theorists of the 1970s Can Teach Us about Schools and Society Today* (IAP, 2015), and *Curriculum Windows: What Curriculum Theorists of the 1980s Can Teach Us about Schools and Society Today* (IAP, 2016). Recently, Poetter outlined his curricular and pedagogical approaches with students in "Taking the leap, mentoring doctoral students as scholars" (*The Journal of Natural Inquiry & Reflective Practice, 24*(1), pp. 22–29) and penned two memoirs, *50 Christmases* (Sourced Media Books, 2014) and *Losing to Boehner, Winning America* (2016). A longtime public school advocate and school partner, Poetter continues to write and teach with remarkably talented, focused students at Miami in the areas of curriculum, teaching, and public education renewal. This volume on Curriculum Theorists and their books from the 1990s will be followed by the future volumes in the series on the 1950s and 2000s in 2017/2018.

Kelly Waldrop graduated from Miami University's PhD program in Educational Leadership in August of 2014. She has two degrees (BA and MA) in English literature and composition from the University of Tennessee, Knoxville, and spent 5 years teaching English composition, literature, and business and technical writing at the college and university level before leaving academia to work at the executive level in the private sphere for an international manufacturing company. After moving with her family to Cincinnati, she worked for a year in a market research firm and then found her home in Miami University's Farmer School of Business as a business writing instructor, where she taught full-time for 5 years. In this capacity, she redesigned the curriculum for an introductory business writing class from a case-based course to a pragmatic, experiential course, and this work became the source material for her doctoral dissertation. The 1990s volume of Curriculum Windows marks her fourth appearance in the series, which include a feminist treatment of Philip Jackson's (1968) *Life in Classrooms*, a critical review of Tanner and Tanner's (1975) *Curriculum Development*, a and a critique of Alan Bloom's *The Closing of the American Mind* (1989), in addition to coediting the 70s, 80s, and 90s volumes. She now owns and manages The Publish House, an academic editing and document preparation company, where she helps professors, graduate students, and academic authors of all sorts polish their writing. Her areas of study include educational philosophy, curriculum theory, performativity theory, experiential education, business education, and writing.

Tasneem Amatullah is a doctoral student in the Department of Educational Leadership at Miami University. She has over 8 years of teaching experience in K–12 settings in International Schools in the Middle Eastern Countries. Her research interests include women and leadership, Islamic leadership, feminism, curriculum and instruction, educational reforms, Rasch psychometric analysis, and policy analysis. In addition to these, she also researches textiles and fashion designing, an interest that stems from her other graduate degree earned before entering the teaching career. Amatullah currently teaches a course on the sociocultural foundations of education.

Jody Googins is a doctoral student in the Department of Educational Leadership at Miami University. Her research interests include curriculum theory, teacher professionalization, social class, and educational equity. Jody currently teaches in an area high school's Teaching Professions Academy, a program for high school students interested in becoming educators. Jody has been a high school teacher for 15 years, teaching English previously to her current position.

Cleighton Weiland is a doctoral student in the Department of Educational Leadership at Miami University. His research interests include educational policy, critical theory, progressive education, and disability studies. During the past 10 years, Cleighton has worked passionately on the behalf of students as a school psychologist in Cincinnati area schools. One day, Cleighton hopes to bring scholarship through the doors of public schools as both a leader and administrator.

Vanessa Winn is a doctoral student in the Department of Educational Leadership at Miami University. As a former early childhood educator, Winn enjoys working with early childhood preservice teachers on concepts of leadership that promote social justice and culturally responsive practices in her teaching assistantship at Miami University. In addition to working with preservice teachers, Winn also pursues research on play and young children.

ABOUT THE AUTHORS

Jennifer Ellerbe is a doctoral student in the Department of Educational Leadership at Miami University. She has several years of teaching experience in the field of alternative education and has recently accepted a new position in special education. Jennifer currently teaches a course on adolescent development in diverse families at Miami University. Her research interests include alternative education, social class, and social justice.

Richelle Frabotta is Director of Education Services for SO SECS, Southern Ohio Sexuality Education and Consultation Services, and a full-time doctoral student in the Educational Leadership department at Miami University. Her two-plus decade experiences in community-based education informs her research. Richelle's scholarship challenges contemporary sex ed curriculum standards, including preparedness for pre-service and professional educators dealing with sexuality in the classroom. She has been an active volunteer member for AASECT and serves on the Board of Directors as the Public Relations, Media, and Advocacy Chair. Teaching about Human Sexuality is Richelle's passion.

Ryan Graham is a doctoral student in the Department of Educational Leadership at Miami University.

Shaobing Li is a doctoral student in the Department of Educational Leadership at Miami University. His research interests include character education, multicultural education, and Deweyan philosophy of education. Shaobing currently works as a teaching assistant for a quantitative research class and also a research assistant for relational mentoring studies. He will begin teaching sociocultural foundations of education in the fall of 2016.

Kurtz K. Miller is a fourth year doctoral student in Miami University's PhD program in Educational Leadership. He has over a decade of experience teaching earth science, geology, physical science, physics, and teacher education at the secondary and university levels. His areas of research interest include STEM education, STEM school administration, Geographic Information Systems (GIS), school-business partnerships, preservice teacher education, and near-surface geophysics.

Loveness Ngorosha is a doctoral student in Miami University's Department of Educational Leadership. She has over a decade of teaching experience as a primary school educator in Zimbabwe. Loveness currently works with pre-service teachers and teaches a teacher leadership course at Miami University. She collaborates with rural communities in Zimbabwe to promote opportunities for early childhood education. Ngorosha's research interests are in the areas of teacher professional development, educational technology, culturally responsive teaching, and relational pedagogy.

Thao Nguyen-Horowitz is a recent masters graduate from the Department of Educational Leadership at Miami University. She arrived to study with already a decade of teaching and counseling experience. Her research interests include multiculturalism, developmental psychology, school leadership, and family-school-community partnerships. Thao currently participates in a Reggio Emilia style school with her 4 year old son. She and her family currently reside in the San Francisco Bay Area.

Crystal Phillips is a doctoral student in the Department of Educational Leadership at Miami University. Crystal has 20 years of experience in urban education as a teacher, student services advisor, ninth grade transition coordinator, and currently, a high school principal. Her research interests include urban school reform, critical race theory, Black male academic achievement, and autoethnography.

Genesis Ross is a Doctoral Student in the Department of Educational Leadership at Miami University. Her research interests include the de/humanizing functions of educational policy, pedagogy and praxis, employing non-traditional approaches to help facilitate meaningful education, and rethinking education to help enrich the social practices within and between communities. With over 10 years of professional, voluntary, formal, and informal educational experiences, she has worked with diverse student populations from preschool students to active and retired military personnel. She has also worked with students of various cultures, socioeconomic strata, dis/ability groups, races, and religious affiliations.

Priscilla Tamankag is currently a doctoral student in the Department of Educational Leadership at Miami University. She is an immigrant teacher of color working with Cincinnati Public Schools. Her research interests include education and immigrants in the diaspora in general, with special interest in the immigrant teacher of color.